Intimate Companions

Also by David Leddick

Intimate Companions

A TRIOGRAPHY OF
George Platt Lynes, Paul Cadmus,
Lincoln Kirstein, and Their Circle

DAVID LEDDICK

St. Martin's Press ❧ New York

The author is grateful for permission to reprint extracts from:

Writing by Lincoln Kirstein, copyright 1935, 1966, 1984, 1991, 1994, 2000 by the New York Public Library (Astor, Lenox and Tilden Foundations).

The unpublished biography of George Platt Lynes by his brother, Russell Lynes; reprinted by permission of Mr. and Mrs. George Platt Lynes II.

Laurie Douglas's conversations with Russell Lynes; reprinted by permission of Laurie Douglas and Mr. and Mrs. George Platt Lynes II.

Design by James Sinclair

Library of Congress Cataloging-in-Publication Data

Leddick, David.
Intimate companions : a triography of George Platt Lynes, Paul Cadmus, Lincoln Kirstein, and their circle / David Leddick. —1st U.S. ed.
p.   cm.
Includes bibliographical references.
ISBN 0-312-20898-7
1. Arts, American. 2. Arts, Modern—20th century—United States.   3. Lynes, George Platt, 1907–1955. 4. Cadmus, Paul, 1904–1999. 5. Kirstein, Lincoln, 1907–1996. 6. Photographers—United States Biography. 7. Artists—United States Biography. 8. Authors, American—20th century Biography. 9. Gay men—United States Biography.   I. Title.
NX504.L44   2000
700'.92'273—dc21
[B]   99-34004
                    CIP

First Edition: April 2000

10   9   8   7   6   5   4   3   2   1

For my true and beautiful friend
Catherine O'Brien Blondes

Contents

Acknowledgments

I would like to thank very much:

Paul Cadmus and Jon Andersson, always warm and generous and unstinting of their time and treasures. Paul was kind enough to read the proofs of this book shortly before his death and was happy with the way I've told his story.

Bernard Perlin, handsome and witty, whose mind is crammed with memories.

George Platt Lynes II and Jane Cady Lynes, his wonderful wife, who have so thoroughly endorsed and abetted this project.

Elizabeth Lynes Kaestle, who loved her uncle very much.

Mrs. Russell Lynes, the formidable Akin, now gone, brave and droll and the donor of many marvelous photographs.

Jensen Yow, the handsome and winning "Pooza," who remembered so much and contributed many important photographs.

George Tooker, mild and mysterious, who tells it like it is.

Donald Windham, a great writer and a wise remembrancer.

Will Chandlee III, the great charmer who was there and told me all.

Anatole Pohorilenko, the dashing contributor of memories and memorabilia.

John Connolly and Ivan Ashby, who shared a great collection of photos.

Edward DeLuca and *Heidi Lang* of the D.C. Moore Gallery, who have been so very helpful and supportive of my many projects.

Keith Kahla, my editor, so good-looking and so patient and so excellent, who has brought a real book into being here.

Alan and Kathie Nengel, who made their way backward and forward many times through this text until it was recorded on paper, neatly and in order.

Robert Cloud, whose editing amazes me and makes me look so good.

Michael Storrings, for yet again a cover design that suits the book and me so well.

James Sinclair, whose book design is so beautifully clean, concise, and communicative.

And to many, many others who shared their memories and their mementos with affection and enthusiasm. All in all, this has been a remarkable group of people to know.

Foreword

by Bernard Perlin

George Platt Lynes

George Platt Lynes was the prototypical established gay man of the thirties, forties, and fifties. He personified everything most homosexual men strove for: to be extraordinarily handsome, successful in his work with universal recognition and status, living a princely life in excellent style, having a prodigious sex life plus love affairs that were serious and meaningful. He was the role model for us. He was the epitome of a stylish life, also an artist's life, successful and admired. He brought his aesthetic home and used it to create a superbly elegant and luxurious life. He *was* style. He was elegance, without the pissy connotations. He was the aristocracy of the New York homosexual world. He was so princely that he would have been quite at home in the eighteenth century.

If George had any snobbism, it was for attractive and bright people: his ballet boys and talented friends. He was the center of a gay cabal that included Monroe Wheeler, his lover of many years, and Glenway Wescott, the third member of a triumvirate that typified civilized male culture in New York society. Lincoln Kirstein, Paul Cadmus, Jared French, Allen Porter, and visitors like Cecil Beaton, Christopher Isherwood, as well as dozens of happy, beautiful youths, were in this group also, all of whom were quite reconciled to, and happy to be in, the carefree gay life of the forties and fifties in New York.

As for style, George Platt Lynes personified it. Even when he was broke after the Hollywood mess, his tenement walk-up flat in New York was beautiful. The actual paintings in his collection (Picasso, Tanguy, Tchelitchev, Cadmus, French, Hartley) having gone to his brother and elsewhere as collateral, photostatted copies were framed in wallpaper borders and pasted onto the walls. His dinners then were reduced to inexpensive entrées (such as beef liver instead of calves' liver, but cooked in milk and served with masses of sour cream), dollar conscious but deluxe.

In good times or bad, as a good host George kept a record of each dinner party, listing the guests and the menu so he would not bore the guests with a repeat meal. Somehow he managed to cook the meal, serve it, and remain the host without being fussy. He kept the drinks filled, the party atmosphere happy and fun. Whatever sex games that may have happened after dinner—depending on the company, of course—were easy, joyous, and opulent on Jared French–designed needlepoint pillows and cushions under a marvelous Tchelitchev nude, *The Golden Leaf*, a transparent portrait of Jonathan Tichenor's back. A real log fire would be blazing in the fireplace, the room would be alive with enormous houseplants, the walls covered with grass-cloth wallpaper and those great pictures (later absent), and the great sofas covered with quilted silk damask and loaded with even more needlepoint pillows executed by George and designed by his artist friends.

One might have imagined oneself in the Petit Trianon (sans etiquette). George Platt Lynes was a sexpot sensualist who wanted to enjoy himself while giving his guests pleasure. He was liberal and permissive. For example, after one cozy, memorable dinner, one of the guests, Mike Miksche, a sexual braggart and extrovert sexual athlete, took another guest, a married lady, to George's bedroom for a postprandial lay. Soon the other guests were trying to ignore the sounds of bodies bouncing off beds and walls. Mr. Miksche was putting on quite a performance. George allowed it to continue on and on, presuming that if his guests were enjoying themselves, he was happy to provide the place for them to do so. There were no snide comments, no jokes, no worry about the other guests. His hospitality and generosity was lordly, never condescending. Perhaps, in this case, he was glad to rid his living room of the boisterous Miksche. Monroe Wheeler once remarked that Mike had the same displacement in a room as the *Queen Mary*.

George was spoiled in the way physically beautiful people simply take for granted that everything is their due because everything has always been theirs for the asking and taking. When he couldn't "marry" George Tichenor, his photo assistant who, despite some years of sex play now and then with his boss, was basically straight, Lynes wooed and won Jonathan Tichenor, George T.'s younger brother, who appeared one summer to work on Lloyd Wescott's farm. George Platt Lynes remarked, "If I can't have the Tichenor I want, I'll take the Tichenor I can get." And he did. He created a magnificently decorated apartment for Jonathan and himself just across Park Avenue from the flat occupied by Monroe Wheeler and Glenway Wescott. This scandalized Glenway, because up until then Monroe Wheeler and he had presumed that their sexuality was unknown to their grand society friends. Now, when Lynes was so socially incorrect as to set up a lavish home with a very handsome, much younger man, who rapidly transformed from a naïve farmhand into a remarkably soigné homosexual with superb cufflinks and an arch manner, the game was up. There could be no mystery about the new setup. Wescott felt compelled by the "scandal" to leave New York for distant New Jersey permanently. Stone-blossom, which had been the weekend retreat for the three friends on the New Jersey farm of Glenway's brother for some years, now was to be Westcott's home. Before the big breakup, Lynes had been lavishly generous to Wescott by supplying the money for the construction of a two-story wing to the house for his use and work, consisting of a writing room, a bedroom above, and a bath. Indeed, it removed him from propinquity with George and Monroe's bedroom, which had been right across the hall from his own. George also spent a good hunk of money on what he called the "wild acre," which was planted with a thousand or so daffodils. When he had many accounts and portrait commissions, which he often did in the thirties and into the forties, he was characteristically and aristocratically grand and generous. But when he was poor in the 1950s, he "borrowed" money from his friends and even the longtime pal who did his retouching, Bob Bishop.

His alienation from Lincoln Kirstein during this period of straightened circumstances remains a mystery. Perhaps Lincoln was rankled because George had tried to borrow yet another time against the cost of photographing the super new *Nutcracker* ballet. It was 1954 and George was looking forward to memorializing and ennobling the new Balanchine-Kirstein masterpiece. He had been the official photographer of the New York City Ballet from its earliest days as the American Ballet through Ballet Caravan to Ballet Society, arriving at glorious long last as New York's very own ballet company. His photographs are simply the best pictures ever made of ballet. However, Lincoln suddenly put George on his whimsical shit list after some twenty years of good personal and professional relations. Kirstein spitefully hired Fred Melton, a man who amused Lincoln somehow and who ran a silkscreen company called Pippin Press, taking the name from Melton's lover, Wilbur Pippin. This company was originally going to make collectible prints of ballet designs, Tchelitchev drawings, and other art subjects, and wound up making silkscreen wallpaper—all under Kirstein's patronage. It was Melton who photographed *The Nutcracker* and Kirstein got his money's worth: The pictures were forgettable and are forgotten. The insult to George when he was on his downward slide to ruin and death from lung cancer within the year probably hastened his unhappy end. It certainly made him utterly unhappy and furious.

But even in his misery ("I feel like an elephant is sitting on my chest"), he continued his happy-making lifestyle. He continued to give great all-boy parties (liquor was frequently paid for by François Reichenbach, a rich, rather fey Frenchman, nephew of Jacques Guérin, a quite talented documentary movie maker and heir to a French fragrance fortune; François was quite possibly the only unattractive person George tolerated).

George Platt Lynes remained supremely attractive throughout his final days, and continued his fun-and-games sex romps, often threesies. One of his ballet kids reported S&M games. To my knowledge this is false. George would be a ringmaster, calling the shots, directing the players, but never did he suggest the unseemly or disagreeable or impossible. Many of his loving friends were lovingly faithful to him forever (the model Laurie Douglas, for example), even when he was suffering and demanding. Still, he protected those loving friends from the anguish of having to reveal the truth about his disease to him by pretending ignorance also. He would sunbathe while reclining at the stern of a rowboat rowed for hours around a lovely lake in western Massachusetts, recovering from his exploratory surgery. "What's wrong with me? What did those fucking surgeons do to me, anyway?" he would say. At the same time he informed Mike Miksche, whom he didn't like, that he had cancer. Another example of his kindness to his beloveds and his harshness to the "unwashed."

It is difficult to portray George's generosity, his sense of fun, his sharp wit and warmth, because he was so aristocratic, so without affectation, so elegant. These qualities can be fearsome. He didn't take any shit from anyone, simply. He was honest and he was courageous. And generous. When he had success and wealth, he spent lavishly—when he was in need, he borrowed to maintain the beautiful milieu in which he lived and so went on to the next party and the one after that until the end.

After his death I seemed to have become possessed by him in that I began hosting very large all-male parties where there was joyous dancing, drinking, and conviviality. I had learned how to live it up, to have fun by supplying the place and space for fun. There was at least one party where a large group of young men was lined up, soup-kitchen style, in the street-level entrance foyer of my building, a foyer that led to the basement. It was a blow-job line. I didn't know and still don't know who was providing the services in the basement, but I did see Lincoln Kirstein meekly waiting his turn, towering over everyone, trying to be unnoticed. George would have been happy with the fun-loving party upstairs, and possibly amused by the basement action. But anonymous sex was not his style, and style was his byword.

One more thing: George was a superb letter writer. He would sit at his typewriter, clacking away, giggling wickedly at his devilishness and rocking back and forth with pleasure. One of his axioms was, "I may forget, but I never forgive." Some of his letters were very unforgiving. Bless him—of all the dearly departed, George is the most missed.

Paul Cadmus

I was young and cheeky when I had my first encounter with Paul Cadmus. It was in Times Square on the evening of the first reelection of Franklin Delano Roosevelt. I was sketching unusual-looking people in the mob there and happened to draw Paul and also Jerry French, whom I didn't know at the time. I showed the sketchbook to a fellow Art Students League student who knew Paul and recognized my sketch of him. He suggested that I show it to him when he came to drawing class at the League on Saturday. I did so, and although Paul was very polite, I don't think he was amused. Years later, when we had become friends, I reminded him of this first meeting; he didn't remember—also very politely.

Paul Cadmus was a paradox, in fact. He was the gentlest of gentlemen. He had a sweetness of nature and a delicacy of manners and a politeness that seemed to be from another culture and century. All genuine. The other side of Paul could be seen in his art, which could be ruthlessly wicked and wildly funny and outrageously vulgar. In his marvelous big pictures *Bar Italia* and *Subway Symphony*, he managed to insult and offend almost every ethnic, cultural, or anti-cultural group. But then he also glorified the human creature, mostly young men, but also some fortunate women who posed for him. For me, his drawings are right up there with Michelangelo, Raphael, Ingres—only Cadmus's nudes are more frankly sensuous and alive.

Sometimes Paul Cadmus displayed a surprising crassness, an inside-jokery, as though the idea for the picture was conceived on a few seconds' whim and painted diligently for months, to dignify the whimsical joke. Note the wood veneer in the headboard of the bed in which lies the pearl-skinned sleeper of *The Nap* or the bicycle seat in *Finistère*. Or the exaggeratedly campy *David and Goliath*. These rare flukes are indeed rare. Who else could—or would—achieve the marvelous iridescence of Reynaldo Hahn's kissing sprite in *Le Ruban Dénoué*? Cadmus's generosity was in full display when he gave us amazing beauty of painting sometimes even canceling or refuting the clunkiness of a subject like *Goliath*. Indeed, it was his generosity that was remarkable. He gave us mankind in his best skin. Even the satirical *Subway Symphony* was given as an encyclopedia of ourselves at our funniest worst.

Away from the studio (which was seldom) Paul Cadmus was the most cultivated man. He introduced me to Schubert lieder and to E. M. Forster and to the *Tale of Genji* and Henry James and Luca Signorelli and Piero della Francesca, as well as the contemporary English painter Michael Leonard. Cadmus and his muse and life-companion Jon Andersson played and sang Fauré duets. Easily.

Once many years ago when I had a mural job to do and no studio, Paul loaned me his studio at 5 St. Luke's Place in which to work. He simply gave me the keys with no restrictions. What a generous gesture! How sweet-natured—how unselfish! He was really a dear man.

His courage must be noted, too. He never denied his sexuality—never pretended to be anyone other than the man he was. He was never in a closet. He was honest about himself and his life and his relationships, which were very, very few. He was an atypical unpromiscuous homosexual. For good reason he was loved and revered by all his contemporaries. For very good reason.

For me his greatest picture is *The Bath*. It is a treasure chest of 100 percent gorgeous painting. Nobody else paints flesh so exquisitely. He nudges Rubens, Titian, Lautrec. He was our own Old Master—but never old—always vital and fresh.

Lincoln Kirstein

Lincoln Kirstein was the Impresario Extraordinaire. He is universally known as the cofounder of the New York City Ballet and its predecessors: Ballet Society, Ballet Caravan, and the earliest, the American Ballet. What is not known as well is his passion for the visual arts. He disdained the New York School and all "modern" painting. Bonnard, even. He had passion for classical sculpture also. But he loved recognizable, program art. That is, subject matter as relating to the human—namely Cadmus, French, Tchelitchev, Tooker, Koch, and for a while, me.

Lincoln Kirstein was probably the single most influential person in my career. I don't recall how or where we met, probably through Cadmus or the Lynes-Wheeler-Wescott milieu—but soon he introduced me to a tough Marine colonel in Washington, D.C. (we were already in the war), who wanted a gung-ho magazine cover. I lost out on that job, but it led eventually to a position with the domestic Office of War Information, and subsequently to a job with *Life* and *Fortune* magazines as a war correspondent/artist, which became a superb adventure for me. At the same time, Lincoln, as a mere private in the U.S. Army, was in Europe liberating art stolen by the Germans.

After the war we became reacquainted, and he liked my post-war painting. Soon he stage-managed my first one-man show at M. Knoedler, the brown velvet Old Master gallery. Lincoln used his considerable clout to bring the gallery into the present with "his" kind of painters: realists, magic realists, etc., although the major artists Tchelitchev and Cadmus were already tied to Durlacher and Midtown, respectively. Jared French didn't have a gallery at that time.

Lincoln proved his interest in my work by purchasing two pictures from the 1948 show at Knoedler. One was donated to MoMA and is in its permanent collection, proudly stored in its underground racks. The second picture was offered to the Tate Gallery in London at the time of the phenomenal success of the New York City Ballet in London in 1951. Concurrently he had arranged an exhibition of again "his" American Art at the ICA gallery, which was also as successful critically as "his" ballet company was in London. My picture *Orthodox Boys* was in the show, which included Andrew Wyeth, Cadmus, French, and Tooker. I happened to be in London at the time, and Kirstein commissioned me to make portrait drawings of the New York City Ballet stars—including Mr. Balanchine, who was quite skittish, alas, and couldn't be bothered. I lost out to Lucian Freud, who got the job. He made a portrait of Lincoln that admirably depicts his manic side. Lincoln was intensely overstimulated in London and became somewhat crazy. I've been told that it developed into straitjacket crazy, but I don't know for sure.

Lincoln had bought an early silverpoint portrait of mine, and later commissioned me to do a portrait drawing of a young man for whom he had a hot enthusiasm. However, my drawing didn't jibe with Lincoln's vision. Like a Medici, he made me do a second portrait which was less "editorialized," which he accepted. Both the drawings and the young man have vanished.

It isn't clear just when Lincoln became disenchanted with me and/or my art. There has always been a suspicion at the back of my mind that our longtime personal association was a big factor in his patronage. He liked me, he liked the life I led, and he liked hearing about it. When I divulged the information that my lover of some years and I no longer made physical love but still loved each other firmly nonetheless, it may have dimmed his enthusiasm for me. Or perhaps when I abandoned tempera painting with its precision and delicacy for looser, richer oil paint with its fuzziness and imprecision, his interest may have become less precise also.

Soon the dinners, the invitations to the ballet (free house seats!) stopped, and when we happened to encounter each other on the street, Lincoln would cross the street to avoid our meeting. Odd when one has been *persona grata* for years and suddenly becomes very much *non*. When one got on Lincoln's shit list, that was THAT.

Lincoln Kirstein was much larger than the ordinary man. His aspect was that of a huge raptor: a condor. I have an image of him, which is Goya's *Saturn Devouring His Children*. Except for Paul Cadmus and Fidelma, Lincoln's wife and Paul's sister, and Jensen Yow, I can't think of any past favorites of Lincoln who weren't devoured by him. He was a listener voyeur. He adored wild, raffish sexy stories told factually by Pete Martinez and a longtime live-in friend, Danny Maloney. The experiences he had vicariously were virtual reality for him, perhaps. He delighted in our shocking stories, which we poured out for his delectation and delight. He worshiped beautiful people—mainly his ballet boys. His enormous clout and power in that world afforded him access to any one—or all—of them, but I suspect that he was too proud to use his power in this way, and thought himself unattractive and therefore noncompetitive. However, he enjoyed the vicarious experiences of others. But this is all speculation. I think that actual sex for him wasn't that important. But I don't know, simply.

Lincoln would have been a natural for Shakespeare. A complicated man blessed with his universal knowledge, privilege, and power—and enjoying a vast range of enthusiasms. His first love was ballet, but he adored painting, sculpture, classic architecture—classic everything. He rediscovered Elie Nadelman, personally finding the ancient Mrs. Nadelman in Riverdale, living in the dusty litter of the late sculptor's studio. He relished Grandville's anthropomorphic illustrations for La Fontaine's fables. He initiated the use of Bibiena's architectural drawings as an elegant backdrop for Balanchine's *Concerto Barocco*. He actively suggested colors (watermelon pink) to be used in Lew Christensen's ballet *Blackface*, now the Ruthanna Boris ballet *Cakewalk*.

But any of Lincoln's ideas were worth considering. He conceived and backed *Dance Index* magazine, the Pippin Press, Ballet Society. His mind was a constant fountain of exciting ideas. He either loved a project, a work of art, a book, a person passionately or loathed it equally passionately—and this included new friends and old friends. I doubt that he could be indifferent to anything. But he could be clever and devious, too. In his late memoirs *Mosaic* and *By With To & From* he publishes a story about his youthful love for a man, Carl Carlsen, who had known Hart Crane. Both books feature a photograph by George Platt Lynes, purporting to be Carlsen in 1932. Actually the model was a Hollywood gym owner George Platt Lynes photographed in Hollywood in 1947 or '48. Harvey Easton was quite a hunk, who might have been Kirstein's sex dreamboy, as he obviously was for many homophiles. So why did he lie about this man? Is the whole Carlsen story a fabrication, too? My take is that the publication was his method of "coming out." But why the elaborate subterfuge? Everyone knew of his homosexuality—everyone knew of everybody's homosexuality—so what? He was admired, exalted, honored. His long service to the world, his originality, his genius was appreciated, in short. Did anyone of importance question his sexuality—or care? Did he make love to his ever-enduring and sometimes daft wife, the dear Fidelma? Who knows? Who cares? Who actually slept with whom when Pete Martinez lived with them on East 74th Street? Everyone was happy in that ménage. Fidelma had an interesting life, plus security. Pete had a comfortable place to dwell and a live, appreciative audience in Lincoln, who had cozy domesticity and a male Scheherazade. This arrangement continued on East 19th Street with Dan Maloney and Jensen Yow, each in turn.

One knew that when Lincoln whispered baby talk to you, you were IN. Fidelma and he called each other "Goosie." Yet the image of him that remains is that of the gleeful malice with which he listened to outrageous, preferably negative gossip about whomever (Ed Hewitt, the gallery owner, was a favorite target). His eyes would shut tight and his mouth compress into a gleeful grimace. He really adored the absolute worst. As he listened, he went from condor to snapping turtle.

Yet he remains the primary force in my life. He opened ways to whatever success I have had. And despite his later dislike of me, I am indebted to him for my happy and exciting life. He enriched my life, and for that I thank him forever.

—◈—

Introduction

This book came about with a certain inevitability because of a previous book, *Naked Men*. Originally *Naked Men* was planned as a collection of photographs, art, and drawings of men who had posed nude between 1935 and 1955—sometimes for artists, sometimes for experimentation, sometimes for artistic erotica. My own modest collection of male nude photographs prompted me to wonder who the models were. With the art of the nude there is a tendency to idealize, so that the subject becomes godlike, unreal. This is particularly true in painting and sculpture but often in photography as well, and it is true whether the subject is male or female.

There seems to be an additional homosexual trait of placing beautiful men, figuratively, on a pedestal. To dream about but in actuality to think, "They are not for me." All of this, of course, fits into a structure of shame about being homosexual, of internalizing society's homophobia, and closeting homosexual feelings out of shame or fear. Often, in the past, interest in the naked male body was veiled and expressed cautiously as an interest in art or sport or psychology. If *Naked Men* had any mission at all, it was to give these nude models names and identities and histories—to make naked men real and strip their images of any sense of shame or "badness."

The introduction of *Naked Men* recounts how, upon looking through a book of photographs by Paul Cadmus and Jared and Margaret French (artists who called their collaborative photo work PaJaMa, an acronym of the first letters of their first names created by Cadmus in 1978), I recognized a friend from the 1960s, Joe Santoro. I knew him as a prominent fashion photographer but had no idea he had been in the circle of good-looking young men who surrounded Cadmus and the Frenches in the late 1940s.

Destiny played its part when a Miami Beach friend called several days after I had seen the book to tell me Joe Santoro was visiting her. Thirty years had passed since we'd last seen each other, but Joe remained as good-looking and vital as ever; a striking and attractive evolution from his photographs in the late 1940s. I immediately wanted to know where the other good-looking men in the PaJaMa book were and what they looked like now. Soon after, I met Paul Cadmus, still handsome and intense in his nineties, at a gallery opening of his work, and this meeting led me to suggest that a book about the nude models might be interesting. He said he would certainly be happy to be in it and knew the whereabouts of many of the men in the PaJaMa photographs.

Finding these men meant finding art and photographs, too. As I discovered the men, I also discovered many George Platt Lynes photographs, as he had played a major role in the group that included Paul Cadmus. He had photographed Cadmus and French, often together, and had shared many of the models used by the painters. And in many cases the models were his discoveries.

At first I conceived of a "then and now" book, solely about the models. But I soon realized that the book demanded more than this, as most of the models knew each other and their lives were interwoven. Often they were artists themselves, posing for friends, who then posed for them in exchange. Their stories needed to be told.

Tracking down the models and identifying them was fun. Anyone who would like to have been at the opening of the tomb of Tutankhamen can understand the thrill of showing an unidentified photograph to someone who says, "Oh, that's Randy Jack. He lives in Bahrain." And then calling Bahrain information (you actually can) and getting Randy Jack's phone number. And seconds later speaking to Randy Jack. It was pretty exciting stuff.

Calling information in Phoenix or Puget Sound or the island of Saba in the Caribbean turned up other men, who in turn had to be visited, interviewed, and photographed to show the world what they look like today. Only a few were reluctant and only one man declined.

Armed with the excellent book/catalog done for the Kinsey Institute exhibition at the Grey Gallery in New York in 1993, the beautiful Twelvetrees Press books done by Jack Woody on George Platt Lynes, and a German edition of Platt Lynes photos edited by Peter Weiermair, I visited model after model, got more and more identifications and addresses, made rendezvous for interviews and photographs, and the circle of subjects grew ever larger.

Perhaps it was their ages or perhaps they had always been open and communicative, but all the men I saw seemed happy to talk about themselves and the period in which they had posed nude.

Only one George Platt Lynes model declined to be in the book. A studio assistant in the late 1930s, he seemed cooperative when I first tracked him down in an obscure town in California. He said of his posing, "I never thought when I got in front of the camera, I'd wind up with all my clothes off." The photographs, including a famous one called *The Sleeper*, suggest that he was actually quite at ease with his clothes off. He evidently discussed my project with his wife and, after receiving my explanatory letter about the planned book, wrote back a tense note requesting that he be omitted "for reasons of privacy." But he was the exception. Everyone else seemed to be pleased, even excited, that their beauty was to be remembered.

What slowly became clear as I traveled from the Caribbean to Puget Sound to Vermont and on to Paris was that what was being revealed was a world. A world of artists of all kinds and the subjects they had painted, drawn, sculpted, and photographed. A world where artists posed for each other; where lovers posed, friends posed, and family posed. And not only for nude studies—there were also many portraits, many figures in landscapes, figure studies that were not nudes, and a rich interlinkage between all the various aspects of these works. This was a world of art that was later to be called Magic Realism. The artists and models involved perhaps did not call it that, perhaps did not see the shape of the art they were creating well enough to give it a name. Art critics had to create categories in order to write about them, and so were born Surrealism, Neo-Romanticism, Magic Realism, and others.

Charles Henri Ford, the longtime lover and companion of the painter Pavel Tchelitchev, defines the categories this way:

Surrealists: Salvador Dalí, René Magritte, Paul Delvaux.
Neo-Romantics: Pavel Tchelitchev, Eugene Berman, Leonid
Berman, Christian Bérard.
Magic Realists: Paul Cadmus, Jared French, George Tooker,
Bernard Perlin.

Art categories do not break down this simply, of course. Where to place
the photographer George Platt Lynes? A close friend of the Magic Realists, he also knew Pavel Tchelitchev well, and they clearly exchanged
influences. And many of Platt Lynes's photographs are obviously inspired by the work of the Surrealists.

Defining where these artists fit into categories is the work of art critics. But for me, describing and reviving their world became more and
more interesting. *Naked Men* includes a brief history of this period,
which revolved primarily around Lincoln Kirstein, George Platt Lynes,
and Paul Cadmus. But many of the other figures in their circle deserved
fuller attention.

Kirstein used his family fortune to bring ballet to the United States in
the person and choreography of George Balanchine, created the School
of American Ballet, aided and promoted many artists he found interesting, and later created an American Shakespeare company. With great
enthusiasm, he used his not-enormous family money to do more for art
in this century than perhaps anyone else. How did his marriage and his
continuing interest in good-looking, creative young men affect his life?
And why did he become reclusive toward its end?

Platt Lynes photographed everybody, knew everybody, and slept with
everybody. Like many beautiful people, he felt the gift of his beauty was
not something to be stingy about. Living in a ménage à trois with the
Museum of Modern Art exhibitions director, Monroe Wheeler, and the
writer Glenway Wescott, he was famous in New York for his photography, particularly his portraits, which played a major role in presenting
the famous of his period to the public. In addition, he captured the male
beauties of the time in privately distributed photographs. But what
about the effect of this ménage on the careers of these three men? And
how and why was it so well accepted in the "don't ask, don't tell" atmosphere of the 1930s and later?

Paul Cadmus, whose sister, Fidelma, married Lincoln Kirstein,
moved through this world in a gracious and charming manner, unaf-
fected by trends and the tides of events that swirled around him. His focus on his work seemed greater than many of his contemporaries'.

Indeed, he set an example for some of the younger ones as to what focus meant. Seeing himself in a clear line of descent from the artists of the Renaissance and early nineteenth century, he did no questioning about what his art should be: precise, beautiful, finely drawn. And yet many of his paintings reveal a biting criticism of human beings. He saw them as ugly, stupid, uninsightful, and ignorant of the beauty of the world. To many, these are his greatest paintings. How does this combination of clear artistic vision and social criticism relate to Cadmus, who was calm and smiling and even in his nineties still possessed great vitality and charm? Did his work in some way relate to his lover Jared French's decision to marry a woman of some fortune in the late 1930s? And why in his later work did the classicism become ever stronger and the criticism only flash through incisively from time to time?

These are interesting questions. These were and are interesting people. This is a period that was until recently almost completely neglected by the art world. Yet by themselves the artists who lived and worked there make reexamining it worthwhile.

Submerged rapidly by the interest in Abstract Expressionism that exploded in the mid-1950s, this period in art history is now long enough past to afford a clearer look. Obviously the artists of this period saw themselves as responsible for carrying on the classic tradition of art making, but interpreted through the events of this century. The advances of psychology had made clear that beneath the surface of life there are great emotional tides that dictate life's patterns. But how to understand and express this? All of these artists, however one may choose to categorize them, used reality as a base for their work, making it dreamlike or unreal or beyond real to communicate what they sensed was the nature of the human condition.

The Abstract Expressionists had none of this interest in the nature of humans. Their interest was only in the nature of painting. As the Impressionists were fascinated with optics and the effect of light upon color, the Abstract Expressionists were interested only in how paint went on canvas.

This was true of all the arts at midcentury. Composers were only interested in how different music could sound, not how it expressed what people felt. Balanchine himself became interested only in what steps and shapes the dancer's body could make. Art became "abstracted" from its historic interpretive role. The emotionality of the Surrealists, Neo-Romantics, and Magic Realists became embarrassing to an art world that only felt comfortable handling the materials of its trade. The world had become difficult to interpret. Perhaps it was better to make no attempt. There was, of course, a great falling off of public interest in this kind of new art, which had nothing to do with people's lives and feelings. Art became for the most part a world only interesting to its practitioners and the millionaires who bought artworks as a kind of banking. Or gambling.

Now an interest in the art world that preceded the Abstract Expressionists is reviving. Many figures from this time survive and still paint. George Tooker and Bernard Perlin never abandoned their ideas of what art is about and continue to practice them.

The work of the photographer George Platt Lynes, and especially the largely underground part of it that involved male nudes, went on to greatly influence later photographers. Robert Mapplethorpe, Dianora Niccolini, Bruce Weber, Herb Ritts, and many others carried on the tradition of images of male beauty first created in the 1930s. A perfected, idealized kind of male beauty that was erotic without carnality. Many younger photographers who are inspired by this second generation have no idea that their debt goes back to Platt Lynes.

In addition, Lincoln Kirstein's role in the promotion, stimulation, and creation of art in this century lies largely unexplored. His own two biographical works, *Mosaic* and *By With To & From*, owe too much to the Magical-Realist tradition. Like Diana Vreeland, when he writes of his own life, there is much magical and fantastical overlay, and the great motivational subjects of sex and money are largely omitted.

So this book will attempt to bring to life this period through the interwoven lives of George Platt Lynes, Paul Cadmus, and Lincoln Kirstein. There are surely other ways to breathe life into this time. But these three lives offer a fascinating framework for exploring not just the art that was created but the personalities who created it and the public and private lives they led. Beyond doubt their personal lives were of the greatest interest to themselves. As with all of us, they were trying to find fulfillment and self-expression in the arms of other people as surely as they were interested in the art their lovers were creating. And if they were as human as we are, we can guess they were even more interested in their private lives than their public ones.

This is what will be explored. Not only what they did, but also why they did it. As well as facts, there will be divination and interpretation, and an assumption that we know more about human motivations at the start of this new century than was known then—or at least we are more willing to talk about them.

In his review of my book *Naked Men* in *The Advocate* magazine, Peter Galvin wrote, "Author David Leddick's text ultimately focuses more on the titillating sexual shenanigans that helped bring about some of these pictures than the social context in which they were taken." Actually, right or wrong, the shenanigans were my point. I believe the social context *was* sexual. I believe that sexuality or the lack of it dominates and directs almost all of life's proceedings, be it a man's desire to be president or a basketball star. Or a woman's wish to head her law firm or make it big in Hollywood. Mr. Galvin will be disappointed to find that I concentrate on sexuality in this book also. A lot. That is why my book about these artists and friends is called *Intimate Companions*.

In many ways, my subjects were pioneers in the expression of emotion for the decades that have followed. Theirs is a fascinating story. This book is just the beginning of the telling of it.

In the Beginning

Paul Cadmus was born in 1904, and Lincoln Kirstein in 1907, shortly after George Platt Lynes, who was also born in 1907. Close in age, their lives had some differences and some similarities when they were very young. Lincoln Kirstein was born into wealth, Platt Lynes into gentility, and Cadmus into art.

Lincoln Kirstein and George Lynes, as he was then known, were to meet relatively young. They were both at a boarding school that specialized in boys who did not assimilate easily in schools preparatory to Ivy League colleges. In other words, they both did poorly in school. They were not particularly good friends then. Kirstein resented the fact that their friendship was often considered to date back to that period and said, "I didn't like him at all. He got all the good-looking football players."

They were to become working compatriots later when Platt Lynes photographed the dancers of the budding ballet companies that Kirstein was developing. It was in this period, in the 1930s, that Paul Cadmus entered their circle. His art fascinated Lincoln Kirstein, who encouraged him and married his sister. Kirstein first saw beautiful Fidelma Cadmus at a party given by George Lynes (as he was still known). Turning to Paul Cadmus, Kirstein said, "I'm going to marry your sister." Paul replied, "But, Lincoln, she's nothing at all like me."

However that may have been, Fidelma Cadmus Kirstein seems to have gotten along well with her husband during a marriage of almost fifty years.

But before their intertwined lives can be explored, some examination needs to be made of the early years before they met.

George Platt Lynes

There's not an unpretentious bone in my body.

—*George Platt Lynes*

When you are beautiful, life is a different experience from what it is for others who are plain. George Platt Lynes was to find this out, and he never voiced any regret about it. He used the power of his beauty to achieve his goals, and he delighted in doing so. It was his good fortune to be endowed with talent as well as looks.

George Platt Lynes was the first child of two good-looking parents. His father, Joseph Russell Lynes, had been a handsome blond child and grew up to be a handsome blond man. His mother, Adelaide Sparkman, had less regular features, but she was also considered a beauty—perhaps more for her "ship under full sail" style of high Gibson Girl coiffure and prominent profile. A New Yorker with a Southern family background, she graduated from Hunter College in New York and was married to Joe Lynes in 1904. George Platt Lynes's father was a young lawyer when he married, and was still practicing when George was born on April 15, 1907.

Good looks went back on both sides of the family, as well as autocratic behavior and a sense of entitlement that did not match family income. Among the family's memorabilia is a photograph of a young man with a hat tipped over one eye and a fancy tie who has exactly the same hand-

George Platt, the great-grandfather of George Platt Lynes, circa 1855. (Courtesy of Anatole Pohorilenko. Reprinted by permission)

Joseph Russell Lynes, the father of George Platt Lynes, circa 1915. (Courtesy of Mrs. Russell Lynes. Reprinted by permission)

some face George was to have later. The clothes suggest the mid-nineteenth century; the face suggests George's father's side of the family, as his father had much the same features. It is identified by the family as George Platt, the photographer's great-grandfather. George Platt Lynes's physical beauty was not a fluke, and his family should have been used to it. But they never became so. His niece, Elizabeth Lynes Kaestle, when asked about her uncle, whom she knew as a man in his thirties and forties, said, "The first thing you must know, he was breathtakingly handsome." So the family, as well as the rest of the world, was always a bit overwhelmed by his physical presence.

George was named for his handsome ancestor, his grandmother Lynes's father, George Platt. George Platt had been born in London in 1812, and if not the most illustrious ancestor of the Lynes family (a Russell ancestor on the same side of the family had been a judge of probate and a treasurer of the province in Connecticut in the seventeenth century), he was certainly the most colorful. He came to New York in his midtwenties and set up as a "blinds" maker, but quickly began to call himself an "interior decorator." This was some eighty years before the term came into general use to describe someone who decorated other people's houses—which was what he did. The first George Platt had a furniture factory, some of whose wares were to accompany George Platt Lynes throughout his life in a series of homes. Much of the neo-Victorian style he often used in decoration was the result of integrating a small inlaid, oval table, a black Empire bookcase with brass beading around its glass doors, a Gothic side chair, and several other small pieces into a personal and modern decor. Some of this furniture would later turn up as props in his photographs, notably in his portrait of Dr. Alfred Kinsey in George Platt's Gothic chair.

The original George Platt died in 1873 and was buried in Woodlawn Cemetery under a large and impressive tombstone, which reads "George Platt of London"—chic to the end. This man's taste, tenacity, and ability to deal with difficult clients seems to have been inherited by George Platt Lynes.

Shortly after George Platt Lynes's birth, his father decided he wanted to join the ministry. Joe Lynes enrolled in the Union Theological Seminary in the Chelsea section of New York City. The family was living in East Orange, New Jersey, and included both the young couple's mothers and his mother's divorced sister, with her six-year-old child. Where the money came from to support both this very extended household and Joe's studies is unknown. George's father worked evenings in the box office at the Metropolitan Opera to augment his income, a somewhat unusual part-time job for an aspiring clergyman. It was a long commute home every night to East Orange, but the additional income must have been welcome to the struggling, good-looking young student of religion, with a lot of relatives at home to support and a sickly baby.

In 1910, Joseph Lynes finished his schooling and became the rector of St. James Episcopal Church in Great Barrington, Massachusetts. And in December of that year George's brother, Russell, was born.

George had not been a healthy baby, almost dying of convulsions when he was tiny. From that time on, he was greatly coddled, and little effort was made to discipline him. Russell was a very healthy baby, and was to grow up to prove to his parents that they were capable of having a trouble-free child who could accomplish goals and live life in a way they could understand.

From the start, George was quite the opposite. Leaving the child in a Great Barrington barbershop, his father returned to find his son with his

George Platt Lynes dressed for a costume party, circa 1915. (Courtesy of Mrs. Russell Lynes. Reprinted by permission)

hair cut and claiming that he was not in fact the reverend's son, but a Russian prince who had somehow gone astray. If he *had* been a Russian prince gone astray, his behavior would have been a lot more comprehensible.

As a small child he returned from a walk with his nursemaid to find his mother entertaining a church sewing group. Straightaway, George entered the room and declared to one lady, "I certainly don't like you." Crossing the room to address another lady, he said, "But I do like you." The congregation never ignored him after that, and this was very much a hallmark of his later manner. He knew exactly what he liked and what he didn't like, and was not loath to say so.

In his memoir about his brother, Russell Lynes recalls the idyllic childhood world of Great Barrington before World War I, with its band shell, soda fountains, and innocence. He remembers going with his brother to take cookies down to the local jail to hand through the bars to the few inmates who had been locked away after imbibing too much on a Saturday night. This has the ring of reality to it, echoing George's later lack of concern for the proprieties and what other people might think.

George was never a good student. His preschool teacher, who long outlived him, remembered him in her later years as "a handful who knew his own mind . . . quick but dreamy." His quick but dreamy mind led his parents to send him to a private school, Fessenden, in West Newton, a Boston suburb. This must have been an extraordinary expense for the parson, but the family obviously believed it was necessary. The only Fessenden records left indicate that George was then in the eighth grade and that he did not graduate with his class. One can imagine him returning to Great Barrington quite unabashed after having screwed up at Fessenden.

A letter to his mother from the school's summer camp reads "the misquoties are tabiliril [*sic*]," which would suggest that the school was not making much headway in teaching him to spell. And his slow start makes it all the more surprising that in later years he would type all his letters with impeccable spelling, not to mention witty and charming self-expression.

Another letter from the school in 1919 asks his father to take him to the postwar victory parade in Boston. Airplanes were to fly overhead, which would have been an unusual sight in those days.

When his father accepted a new parish in Jersey City, New Jersey, George left Fessenden and was sent to the Newark Country Day School.

This evidently was a no-go, and in 1920 he was packed off to the Berkshire School in Sheffield, Massachusetts, which was not much of a success either. The school, based on its English boarding-school counterparts, had a lot of sports, a lot of Christianity, and a focus on English literature that did not include any modern writers. One wonders to whom this school appealed—probably to parents desperate to send their children *somewhere*.

George was the best in his class in literary appreciation and could even do well in mathematics and physics when he chose. One of his teachers wrote in a report, "He will do well what he likes and will make little attempt to do at all what he does not like." Another wrote, "Works in streaks and only when the spirit moves him . . . plenty of ability to do as well as he wants at any given time."

George was more overtly effeminate then than in later years, and his life was made difficult by what the head of the school referred to as the "red-blooded elements." Yet the boys who were teasing and roughhousing with him for being girlish were also sleeping with him. His nickname Tess, which friends used for years afterward, came from Titless Tessie, as he was known at Berkshire.

George reminisced to his friend the artist Bernard Perlin in a letter in the 1950s, "'They' almost always hated themselves in the morning; but almost always they came back for more. I wasn't 'older' in those days, though; if anything younger. Still I know the tone, the expression; the greediness—bless their horrid hearts."

The positive side of his being so unaccepted at the school was that he was drawn into fantasizing about the arts and his relationship to them. He wrote for the literary magazine, *The Dome*, and his English master cannot be called wrong for describing his work as having an "utterly weird element." Certainly, reading T. S. Eliot and the exotic French writer Joris-Karl Huysmans must only have made him feel more out of place than ever in his rowdy, windy Massachusetts school.

George Lynes was in the Camera Club at the Berkshire School, as a yearbook picture shows, but only when he first arrived. He is the only boy in the picture holding a Brownie camera; all the other boys have more expensive equipment. In subsequent yearbooks he is no longer in the club, probably because he couldn't afford a competitive camera.

The school offered no art classes, which was not uncommon in schools of the period. All that George could have learned of painting and sculpture would have been through conversations with fellow students, of whom a few were interested in the arts. Among them must have been Lincoln Kirstein, who was also at the Berkshire School at the time.

Upon George's graduation from the Berkshire School in 1925 at the age of eighteen, he lacked the required credits in Latin and history to enter Yale, the college he had chosen. His parents were torn between his cramming to fulfill these requirements or his accepting an invitation to visit his mother's cousin in Paris. George made the decision for them and departed to visit Aunt Kate in France as soon as he had graduated.

As he was setting sail for France, George wrote his parents: "My darlings—Adlai has just left me. In a few minutes we sail. There is not very much I can say. My ears are burning; the pen shakes in my hand. I am hoping with all my heart for many things—a double reward. Someday there will be satisfaction for us all—but now, this is the last frightening moment and the iron-ore water is of the same stuff as my mind, I am drugged, I cannot think. I wish I knew so many things. Tomorrow I will write again.

"Always, always your true, devoted George."

This is amazingly affected writing for an eighteen-year-old in the United States in the 1920s communicating with his parents. George's self-image seems based on flappers such as Zelda Fitzgerald and Caresse Crosby—dashing, "wild" young women abroad.

F. Scott Fitzgerald wrote at that same time, "Joan Crawford is doubtless the best example of the flapper, the girl you see in smart nightclubs, gowned to the apex of sophistication, toying iced glasses with a remote, faintly bitter expression, dancing deliciously, laughing a great deal, with wide, hurt eyes. Young things with a talent for living." What better role model for a young male homosexual in 1925?

In Paris, George Lynes (the Platt was to be formalized later) came into his own. Instead of hearty schoolmates making him feel inferior and unworthy, he had Gertrude Stein and her circle idolizing him. During this first trip abroad he sprang full-blown into the adult persona he was to maintain all his life.

He lived near his older cousins Mr. and Mrs. Hardy in Paris and studied physics and history at the Auteuil Day School and French at the Institut du Panthéon. But his major coup occurred when he was taken by his cousins to visit Gertrude Stein and he captured the attention of Miss Stein and her companion, Alice B. Toklas. Gertrude named him Baby George, which is how he signed his letters to her.

While still at the Berkshire School, George and a friend, Adlai Harbeck, had published a pamphlet with a story by a classmate, Paxton

George Platt Lynes, circa 1927. (Courtesy of Mrs. Russell Lynes. Reprinted by permission)

George Platt Lynes dressed as a flapper, circa 1927. (Courtesy of Mrs. Russell Lynes. Reprinted by permission)

Howard. They planned a series of these pamphlets, and in Paris, George decided that the second one should be the essay "Descriptions of Literature" by Gertrude Stein, from whom they had lifted a phrase for the name of their series: The As Stable Publications.

The cover was to be decorated with a drawing by the young Russian artist Pavel Tchelitchev, whose work Gertrude espoused. She said of him, in *The Autobiography of Alice B. Toklas*, referring to the young artists of her circle, that he was "the most vigorous of the group, the most mature and the most interesting." Thus we know that George Lynes and Pavel Tchelitchev were acquaintances at this early date.

Of George himself, Miss Stein says in the Toklas autobiography, "During the next two or three years all the men were twenty-six years old. It was the right age for the time and place. There were one or two under twenty, for example George Lynes, but they did not count as Gertrude Stein explained to them."

What did count was that George Lynes was beautiful and amusing, and when he set out to please, few could resist him. It was probably his fantasizing about what it would be like to mingle with the famous in exotic locales that had prepared him for this sudden ascent into the literary and artistic world of Paris in the 1920s. He had already imagined it and knew how to behave when he got there.

Although the critic Edmund Wilson described Gertrude Stein as a "great iceberg of megalomania . . . on which . . . conversations and personal relations might easily crash and wreck," she must have been a warm iceberg, as Russell Lynes points out in his unpublished biography of his brother. She was genuinely interested in helping George develop a career in the arts, critiqued his sporadic efforts at poetry, and was enthusiastic about his publication of her work. His early photographs of her, in which she cooperated willingly, also gave him prestige and seriousness when he began his career as a photographer.

Although busy with his studies and his socializing with the Stein circle, George Lynes also found time to have an affair with the French writer and *enfant terrible* René Crevel. At eighteen George must already have been something of a practiced heartbreaker. Crevel wrote him many love notes and continued to do so into 1929.

Much later George wrote to a friend about a Crevel biographer who had contacted him, "How can he write a biography of René, who did write a half a dozen unreadable Surrealist-sort-novels but whose life was all charm charm charm and LOVE LOVE LOVE and T.B. and drugs and calamity in general, ending in suicide? Not material to be handled with 'tact'; mealy-mouthed would be so dull . . . he suggested for example that Alice B. Toklas was 'in love' with René; first I heard of it and I saw plenty of them together. Do I disabuse the dear man, set him straight?"

Even at eighteen, George seemed quite capable of seeing through the romantic stratagems of a René Crevel. George slept with him and went his own way. Quite unusual for someone who was in fact still very young.

George returned to the United States at the end of 1925. He had only been in Paris about eight months, but he had used his time well. He had qualified to enter Yale and had been accepted for the term beginning in the autumn of 1926; he had salvaged his self-esteem by being accepted and even admired and pursued in the major-league world of Paris expatriates, and he had made valuable contacts that would serve him well for years to come. Little wonder that he was bored and unhappy living with his parents in Englewood, New Jersey, where his father was now rector of the Episcopal church. Affluent Englewood, not far from New York, was a definite step up for his father, but it was nevertheless a dull, conventional suburban town.

He devoted his time to producing the Gertrude Stein essay and soliciting subscriptions to it. He also planned and produced subsequent pamphlets on René Crevel (that connection proved to be useful) and Ernest Hemingway, with a cover design by Jean Cocteau, the French poet/artist. He was to come to know Cocteau well in a few years. Only after publication did he discover that Hemingway heartily disliked Cocteau.

George annoyed his parents by changing his mind repeatedly as to whether he would go to Yale or not. He worked briefly at Brentano's Bookstore in Manhattan. The amazing degree to which he felt at ease communicating with the famous is evident in a letter to Gertrude Stein about this job: "I am working at Brentano's as the personal whatduck (I have been there a week and really have not yet discovered what I am supposed to do) of Mr. Brentano Sr.; I BROWSE all day among ancient tomes of Petronius, Voltaire, etc. and peruse many volumes on Magic, Witchcraft, cooking, sporting, costuming. I am in the OLD and RARE Dept. Of course I do all the dusting but that does not really matter. . . . "

His personal and literary style was very much of the "bright young things" led by Cecil Beaton in London, though he could only have read about them. There were certainly many androgynous American "bright young things" about, but one has to remember that George Lynes had not yet even attended college.

George also spent time at the summer house his father had rented in Norfolk, Connecticut, not far from Great Barrington, where George had friends. His father had bought him a secondhand black Dodge, on whose hood he painted "Whatduck" in large white letters. When asked what that meant, he said, "Nothing." Whizzing about the dusty roads of rural Connecticut and Massachusetts, he must have made quite an impression. He often visited the wealthy Mrs. Blanc and referred to her in a letter to Gertrude Stein as "one grand person." That she had bought $25 worth of his As Stable pamphlets probably had some effect on his opinion of the lady.

Writing to Gertrude Stein in the summer of 1926, he gave this description of himself: "Picture me being oh-so-pastoral this summer in the meadows of Connecticut. Here I am completely rural. Sunshine is giving me that well-reputed tan. Surrounded by extraordinarily shaped near-mountains, coveted EARLY AMERICAN furniture, red and white mooley cows, and every known variety of stupidity, I am becoming muscular and disgustingly healthy." Perhaps the masculine Stein enjoyed this kind of society-girl letter. Somehow one doubts it.

He entered Yale in the fall, and it was not at all a success. Obviously he was far past being impressed and excited at being in college. His letters to Stein are the best reflection of how he felt. In one he wrote, "This afternoon I had expounded to me the only way that one might be eccentric and live. By insinuating oneself quietly into 'the group,' by writing and publishing a few 'charming' lines in the *Lit.* (a supposedly literary monthly which avowedly refuses to be alive). . . . Having been quite accepted one is to a small extent able to be amusing. No other way is possible." Later in the letter he says in capital letters, "I CANNOT DO IT." And he was right. By Christmas he was back with his family in New Jersey. They seemed to accept this patiently. George moved upstairs to their attic, where he made a small apartment for himself and returned to his publishing activities. He was only nineteen years old.

He had big plans for working with Gertrude Stein, with which she firmly refused to cooperate. She wrote, ". . . let me be the judge of the weather when it is my weather." Their correspondence was not only interrupted by her intransigence but also by a severe illness of George's. There seems to be no information about this illness, but George told his doctor he did not think he would live to see twenty. Certainly this illness of a talented and beautiful young person who couldn't find a satisfactory role in life had some psychosomatic aspects. By the summer he was well and enrolled at Columbia in a program to learn about "retail book selling." Stein felt he should return to college and wrote, ". . . not learning anything for four years systematically is not bad as an education." She added, ". . . hanging around New York is not good for little boys."

It wasn't bad for that particular little boy, for George soon inserted himself into the artistic circle surrounding Muriel Draper. Miss Draper was a kind of hostess in New York who dominated Upper Bohemia. Lincoln Kirstein was also in the group of young people who attended her salon, and perhaps George met her through his Berkshire classmate. The composer Virgil Thomson and Buckminster Fuller, the architect, were also in her circle.

The writer Max Ewing moved in the same artistic milieu. He had the amusing habit of photographing all his friends in his apartment in front of a window shade painted with a view of Venice. In the George Platt Lynes photo albums is a series of these pictures taken at a costume party. Everyone is tanned, the women smartly made up, some men in Tyrolean shorts showing off their legs, some men actually nude. In a glance, the entire zippy and fun ambience of New York in the 1920s comes to life. The world in which George Lynes wanted to live was appearing before his eyes, and he was helping to make it happen. At twenty, he must have been appreciably younger than most of his pals, but he seems to have had no trouble fitting in. Again, his beauty and charm had to have played their part.

In the same building with Muriel Draper lived art dealer Kirk Askew and his wife, Constance. They, too, conducted a salon, but one that was much more oriented toward advancing the careers of the artists of all kinds who frequented it. George was to enter their world a few years later, much to his advantage.

But for now, he was studying how to sell books at Columbia in a summer course and gadding around New York with his new friends in the evenings, undoubtedly going home to New Jersey on a ferry and riding a trolley through the night to the Englewood rectory.

Early in 1927 he dropped in at the Hotel Lafayette to meet Glenway Wescott and Monroe Wheeler at the suggestion of a Parisian acquaintance, Bernadine Szold. Wescott and Wheeler were in New York briefly on their way back to France, where they had been living for several years.

Glenway Wescott and Monroe Wheeler were a homosexual couple who had first met in Chicago as students. The talented Wescott found early fame as a novelist. Wheeler decided they could never be comfortable as lovers in the United States, and they first traveled to Europe in 1922. Both good-looking and socially adept, they were soon moving upward in expatriate circles. They moved to France in 1925. With a young American heiress, Barbara Harrison, Wheeler began a business of publishing fine editions, called Harrison of Paris. Glenway Wescott's judgment undoubtedly aided them in their decisions about material to publish. The beautiful Barbara Harrison was the daughter of a former ambassador to the Philippines and a wealthy mother whose money came from the Californian Crocker fortune. She was interested in the arts as well as in the handsome Monroe Wheeler. (Her interest in Wheeler was unrequited, though it lingered for a number of years until her marriage to Glenway's brother.)

For now these two energetic, attractive young men were finding their fortunes in Paris and finding them quite well. They had come to New York in December of 1926 for literary reasons. Wescott was seeing his publisher. His new book, *The Grandmothers*, was published the next year and won the Harper's Prize novel contest.

When George Lynes dropped by their hotel, only Glenway was at home. George almost immediately saw a photograph of Monroe

Glenway Wescott, circa 1920. (Courtesy of Mrs. Russell Lynes. Reprinted by permission)

Glenway Wescott *by Jean Cocteau, circa 1926 (ink on paper, 9¹/₂" x 7³/₄"). (Courtesy of Mr. and Mrs. George Platt Lynes II. Reprinted by permission)*

Wheeler taken at Villefranche and said, "That's the man for me." One wonders if the photograph was of Monroe in striped bathing trunks (unusual for that time when men wore one-piecers with shoulder straps that covered their entire torsos). Monroe had a strong, muscular body, despite the impression he gave of slightness, and a handsome, almost Valentino-like face.

When they met the next day for cocktails, George accompanied Wheeler on the subway to his dinner engagement and made it quite clear how he felt. Monroe Wheeler said later, "He just took it for granted that I was to be his."

Glenway Wescott seems to have had no objection to George's romance with Monroe Wheeler. Most probably the sexual relationship between Wheeler and Wescott had faded, and a *ménage à trois* was slipped into with little or no discussion. Neither of the two older men wished to disrupt the familiarity of their domestic life together; the easiest solution was to incorporate the young faun from Englewood into their existence. Theirs was the world he wanted to enter. Why make a fuss?

Monroe was called Monie by George, and in turn Monroe called him Giorgio. This nickname was to stick for the rest of George's life. Anatole Pohorilenko, Wheeler's companion in his last years, has said, "George was Monroe's great love." There are many photographs of them alone and together during the years that followed, many on holidays in France, where both bared as much of their bodies as was acceptable. George was unusually slender and beautiful, and Wheeler's falling in love with him is not hard to understand. He was to tell Pohorilenko many years later that George "had the most beautiful waist I have ever seen on a man."

George was twenty. Monroe was twenty-six. They parted, Monroe to Paris and George to New Jersey, where he fell upon his father's neck weeping and told him all about his new love. Poor Reverend Lynes. He always tried to be a good sport about his son and never got overly excited about the sinful or socially unacceptable aspects of his son's life. He probably felt that all the years of effeminate behavior had been leading inevitably to this admission of love for another man. He confided his son's story to a close male friend in Englewood, who then told the entire town. This betrayal *did* anger the Reverend Lynes. Homosexuality was one thing; betrayal of a confidence was something else. *That* was unforgivable. For all their conventional background and position in the church, Reverend and Mrs. Lynes were sophisticated, understanding, and accepting parents.

George wrote regularly to Glenway Wescott in Paris, who never seems to have had any hostility toward the young contender for Monroe Wheeler's affections. George discussed opening a bookshop upon finishing his studies and wrote presciently, "Everything is finished or else everything is just beginning."

The Park Place Bookshop in Englewood was George Lynes's only venture into the bookseller's world, a store that he opened in October 1927 with his parents' financial backing and many misgivings. Curiously, the shop prospered even though, as he wrote to Wescott, "Existence here is like no existence at all. It is so unbeautifully true. Nothing ever quite happens." For a spoiled, precocious young male beauty, a shop in Englewood was obviously not enough, but George managed to make a success of his brief undertaking. He sold it in the spring and made enough profit to repay his parents and buy a ticket on the *Mauretania* for France, with enough left over to live on for a while. He was just twenty-one.

In May 1928, he passed quickly through Paris and continued on to Villefranche on the Mediterranean coast, where Wescott and Wheeler

George Platt Lynes *by Jean Cocteau, circa 1928 (ink on paper, 9¹/₂" x 7³/₄"). (Courtesy of Mr. and Mrs. George Platt Lynes II. Reprinted by permission)*

had rented a villa. Jean Cocteau (who had just finished his famous book *Le Livre Blanc* dealing with his homosexual experiences) and his lover, Jean Desbordes, were living on the waterfront in the Hotel Welcome, indulging in heavy opium habits. And the American navy was in port, which perhaps explains why Cocteau was there. George wrote his younger brother, "Down in the harbor the navy is just anchoring. The *Detroit* is there, and there are destroyers. The boats are terribly pretty, like polo ponies. I like them so much. And I am having such a good time."

He was there ostensibly to write a novel. Glenway and Monroe were to help him, and in his letters an effort to write in a mannered and personal style is quite evident. He also wrote to his brother, "Constance Talmadge is here." The actress was in Villefranche making a movie. Of the twenty-eight-year-old Constance he added, "She is pretty and ancient, black eyes and blond hair . . . her shadow of a mouth opens enchantingly when she smiles." This was the world of the Fitzgeralds and many other expatriate writers on the newly glamorous Riviera.

The American colony, primarily because of the low prices, had made it smart to go to this winter resort in the summer and get a tan. The thrill of being in an exotic foreign country and being allowed to indulge in every kind of excess was heady stuff for many writers of the period. The American dollar went a long way in 1920s France, but the fun and excitement were soon to be swept away by the coming market crash and the Depression. When the exchange rate fell and the financial advantage departed, so did the Americans.

Although it was common for writers such as Dorothy Parker and Lillian Hellman to summer in France during the twenties, and for others such as Hemingway and Fitzgerald and Wescott to take up residence there, most of the American expatriate colony spoke little or no French and knew few French people. Their world was something like a colony on the moon, and they were "Flaming Youth," fireworks that flashed and flared and then burnt out. George Lynes was there for the last fine flickers.

Late in the spring of 1928 he wrote his brother, "I am sitting here well sheltered from the wind, in a little salmon sun room. The view is heavenly. Over Villefranche, as far as the horizon, there are tufted mountains sliding into the tufted sea. And I am at peace."

In the same letter he describes being at Monte Carlo with Monie: "I couldn't begin to describe the people I've seen there: dowagers weighted down with pearls and emeralds, somebody's cousins from Idaho, nobody's cousins from the great beyond. The gambling rooms are deathly still."

The attempt to write a novel was not going well. He isolated himself in the small hill town of St. Martin Vesubi behind Nice. From there he wrote Gertrude Stein: "I have a combination of melancholy, of

George Platt Lynes and Monroe Wheeler sunbathing in the south of France, circa 1928. (Courtesy of Mrs. Russell Lynes. Reprinted by permission)

loneliness, of mysticism (fantasy and fanaticism). I am not unhappy. Save your pity. 'Life is like that . . . a horrid dangerous thing.' "

Back in Paris, he again wrote his brother: "Everybody I see (almost) is so nice and loose. Moyses (owner of the two smartest nightclubs in Paris) brought the dinner (cold lobster, roast chicken, pâté de foie gras, and two quarts of champagne), and we ate at Mary's. The way we carried on would have been an education for someone. Am I horrifying you? Did I write that Beatrice Lillie suggested that Wesson be seduced by her about a month ago in London?"

He certainly had a way with words, but his style of writing at this young age was that of a worldly and world-weary society woman. This was Iris March, the sophisticated, disillusioned heroine of Michael Arlen's sensationally popular novel *The Green Hat*. Or Tallulah Bankhead, who was captivating London audiences playing Iris March on stage, or Louise Brooks, who was taking the type a step further, and making film history, when she played Lulu in the German film *Pandora's Box*. A photograph from this period shows George in drag, wearing lipstick and a cloche hat, and certainly indicates he identified with these young women.

From time to time, George interrupted his work on his novel to attempt a short story or essay, but he was never satisfied with the results.

He never showed his work to either Wescott or Wheeler. To his father, he wrote, "I have not yet learned to depend entirely on myself, which is unfortunate, though I am gradually acquiring a knowledge of my own character and mind. And if only I can control or get rid of my vanity, everything will come out alright. . . . One gets to know one's own faults and to calculate for one's witnesses. . . ."

George Lynes was still only twenty-one. He was not to lose his vanity or his calculation. He partied excessively during his Parisian winter, and in April he departed for the United States on the *De Grasse*, having abandoned his plan to become a writer.

In 1929, he was back in his parents' attic in Englewood, and as was often the case in George Lynes's life, periods of great indecision were punctuated by dangerous illness. Four days after his return to Englewood, his appendix burst, and he nearly died. In later nude photographs of him, the appendectomy scar can be seen.

The ricocheting back and forth to Europe, the dabbling with education and careers, must have been maddening for George's parents—or perhaps they were inured to the willful ways of their beautiful and erratic changeling. George and his parents must have been wondering what would happen next, when destiny appeared—in the form of Mrs. Hope Weil. Mrs. Weil was a petite, good-looking young woman married to a wealthy man. In the preceding year she had decided to be a photographer. Now she was to become a bookbinder. Either Glenway Wescott or Monroe Wheeler suggested to their friend Mrs. Weil that she give her photographic equipment to George, which she did. Later, Wescott and Wheeler each claimed the suggestion was his. It was a good idea, whoever suggested it.

George had shown flair in Villefranche with a borrowed folding Kodak, taking a more-than-a-snapshot picture of Jean Cocteau holding a spyglass on his hotel balcony. Now George put to quick advantage the five-by-seven view camera, plate holders, tripod, lights, and darkroom equipment of Mrs. Weil. A local photographer of weddings and babies taught him how to develop photographs and light subjects. In those days, photographers had no light meters, so this was an important skill for which George showed an immediate knack.

As his teachers had frequently reported, when George Lynes was interested in something, he had more than adequate energy and discipline. Photography interested him. Within the year, his father had bought him additional lenses, an enlarger, and other necessary equipment, and he had made a darkroom of the guest bathroom.

The family was pressed into service as models. He traveled around New York, photographing the George Washington Bridge as it was being built, boats at the Hudson River docks, and shop windows in Little Italy.

During this time, the dashing back and forth to Europe continued, only now it had a different focus. After a year spent in Englewood improving his craft, George planned to return to Monie and Glenway in Paris. He financed this by finding, in his father's country library, an early edition of *Huckleberry Finn* that had been withdrawn from sale because of a misprint. The misprint in an illustration seemed to reveal a large penis on one of the characters in Twain's novel. George sold this book to a dealer in first and rare editions for $450, which was a large sum of money in the spring of 1930, after the stock market crash and with the Depression deepening. That this money was rightly his father's apparently did not bother George. His father was probably relieved that at least he didn't have to lend it.

Within a week of arriving in Paris, George had set himself up in the rue Granacière in the chic Sixth Arrondissement, even to the extent of having stationery printed. Two and a half rooms cost the equivalent of $40 a month. Monroe and he went for a weekend to Senlis, which he wrote was "so charming and lovely I should have been content to stay there longer." Now twenty-three, he still expressed himself in the best society-hostess manner.

George and Monroe had a lengthy romantic and sexual relationship that perhaps endured as long as it did because Monroe had Glenway Wescott as the "wife" and George Lynes as the "mistress." Glenway's career never advanced much further after the entrance of George Lynes into the lives of Monroe and himself. Some connection has to be considered.

In the summer of 1930, George Lynes wrote his brother about meeting André Gide: "The most exciting thing that has happened since I have been here is last Friday's luncheon when I sat next to André Gide. A privilege not only because he is so great a man, but because he makes rather a point of inaccessibility. He was beautifully agreeable and interested, and his wit, which was poignant and kindly, made me think by contrast more than ever of the charlatan antics of Cocteau."

Gide, who was married but whose homosexuality was well-known in literary circles, was enchanted with the young photographer. So much so that one of George's Paris friends wrote to a New York acquaintance about their subsequent encounter: "André Gide . . . arrived unannounced at nine in the morning and consented to every torture in order to turn out an interesting picture, even to lying on the floor with three brilliant lights playing upon him." Now added to his Gertrude Stein and Jean Cocteau portraits was André Gide's.

In addition to pursuing celebrities for his portfolio, George discussed photo-illustration projects for Barbara Harrison's spectacular home outside Paris. Miss Harrison had an equally spectacular Mercedes-Benz sports roadster in which they careened about with her. She invited Monroe and George for a weekend to see this home, despite her own romantic interest in Monroe.

George left for the United States again in September, but this time was different. His visit to France had resulted in a number of important portraits, and he was returning to New York to look for work.

In January 1931, George wrote to Gertrude Stein, "I am sensationally poor." As was the rest of the country. He borrowed money from a stockbroker friend of his parents to pay for photographic supplies and made his home once again in the Englewood parsonage attic. He was busy photographing celebrities and debutantes.

In the summer during his 1931 visit to France, George had posed nude for the photographer Man Ray. Man Ray was the leading Surrealist photographer and a habitué of Gertrude Stein's salon, where the two men most certainly met. The photography session was a commission by Mrs. Mary Barnwell, the wife of an American banker. She was in Paris to pursue a career as a sculptor. Mrs. Barnwell had met George and, as many did, found him extremely attractive and wanted to see him with his clothes off. He refused to pose. However, he did agree to her secondary stratagem, which was for him to be photographed nude so she could work from the pictures. Monroe Wheeler told Russell Lynes, "I have a print of it somewhere. It's not much of a photograph."

But in fact quite a few photos are extant as well as a small study for the statue, which seems never to have been realized. The photographs in the possession of Anatole Pohorilenko are moodily sepia in the style of the early 1930s and show George with his hair bound in a kind of Grecian fillet and taking some Greek athlete poses. The preliminary statuette reflects none of these poses or the hair binding and curiously has socks on George's bare feet, though he did not wear any in the photographs. Perhaps feet were beyond the skills of Mrs. Barnwell.

Curiously, another set of Man Ray photos has a completely different lighting setup and background. George's hair looks fairer because of the early onset of graying, and his front and back poses, some with him holding a gymnasium weight over his head, have a much more art deco

Glenway Wescott, Monroe Wheeler, George Platt Lynes (left to right), circa 1930. (Courtesy of Mrs. Russell Lynes. Reprinted by permission)

look. The two separate sessions even seem distant in time as well in style. Mrs. Barnwell may have been unhappy with the first session or just wanted more glimpses of the beautiful George Lynes body.

This summer George also managed to visit Gertrude Stein and Alice B. Toklas at their country home. There he did a portrait of Gertrude, against a distant landscape, in which her resemblance to a Roman senator is marked.

After his visit to the Stein ménage, George set out on a tour of Germany and Austria with Monroe Wheeler, Glenway Wescott, and Barbara Harrison, all of them in a large Renault touring car driven by a chauffeur. On this trip he photographed baroque churches and landscapes and palaces so lavishly that by the end of the summer and his return to New York he had shot between fifteen hundred and two thousand pictures.

He had been on the *De Grasse* on his way over with the New York gallery owner Julien Levy, and they had liked each other. The prospect of a show in New York seemed good. George left Paris in October of 1931, beginning to feel that New York was more promising as a venue for a career.

His photographs had already been shown at the Wadsworth Atheneum in Hartford, Connecticut, the preceding spring as part of a Neo-Romantic show put together by the museum's director, Everett "Chick" Austin. Austin was showing Pavel Tchelitchev, Christian Bérard, Kristians Tonny, and the Berman brothers, Eugene and Leonid. He had written to ask if George had works by any of these painters to lend the show. George Lynes sent some of his photographs as well as some drawings to Austin for the show. Chick Austin was "extremely enthusiastic," as he wrote back, and the photographs went into the show, too. This was the first museum exhibition of George Lynes's work. That the material in the exhibit was to be sold interested him very much and assured his cooperation.

This Wadsworth Atheneum show was followed the next year by the exhibit at the new Julien Levy Gallery in February of 1932. Lynes shared this show with Walker Evans. The contrast of Evans's haunting views of American life and dilapidated American cities with Lynes's glowing and svelte celebrities must have been very great. It should be noted that neither Glenway Wescott nor Monroe Wheeler was yet living in New York. In contacting subjects for Lynes's camera, they had been helpful, but getting himself shown in a museum and a gallery had been altogether his own doing.

His next museum appearance was in some part due to his Berkshire schoolmate Lincoln Kirstein. Kirstein was a member of the Junior Advisory Committee of the Museum of Modern Art and had conceived of an exhibition, *Murals by American Painters and Photographers*. This was to be the first exhibition in the museum's new quarters in a brownstone at 11 West Fifty-third Street. (This house was torn down and replaced with the present museum building in 1939.) Julien Levy was asked by Lincoln

Male nude by George Platt Lynes, at North Egremont, Massachusetts, quarry, circa 1927. (Courtesy of Mrs. Russell Lynes. Reprinted by permission)

Kirstein to choose the photographers, so George Lynes was a shoo-in. George's entry, for the show was a competition with a prize of some thousands of dollars and an installation in the brand-new Rockefeller Center, was a large collage of views of New York buildings, rural scenes, and a big, double-exposed male nude statue. George didn't win the prize—the trustees had already awarded it to Edward Steichen before the show opened—but the show served the twofold purpose of establishing photography as museum material and of placing George squarely among those photographers considered worthy of the honor.

In 1932 he continued his now-usual pattern by returning to Europe in the spring. Again, he stayed in Wheeler and Wescott's apartment in Paris.

He had been sending pictures to France throughout the winter for the advice and direction of Glenway Wescott. George wrote, "I would like to be assured that someday I am going to improve. Nothing I have done this winter is better than those I did last summer, if indeed as good. And I scarcely know what it is I lack." He had also begun taking nude photographs and, before his departure for France, wrote Glenway, "I am not going to send you nudes. There are too many and too many other non-portrait subjects. I want you to see them all, but will wait until May to take them to you. . . . Besides as far as the nudes are concerned, too much shows in many of them and they might be stopped and confiscated."

In France, George took more portraits, many for paying clients, and again took a long and musical tour of Germany.

The writer Katherine Anne Porter also entered George's life in Paris that summer. She was then forty-two, seventeen years older than George, and their lives were to become entwined. She was yet to become famous, but her first important book, *Flowering Judas*, had been published in 1930, and she was beginning to be known in the literary world. In 1934 Harrison of Paris relocated to New York City and published, as one of its last projects, a fine edition of Porter's "Hacienda," a long story set on a Mexican ranch where a Russian film director, modeled on Sergei Eisenstein, was shooting a film.

George Lynes returned again to the United States in the early autumn to move back into his parents' attic. Now twenty-five, he was likely very tired of living upstairs over the folks.

In December 1932 his father died of a heart attack. His sudden departure at fifty-two was a shocking surprise, but George maintained his calm and took photographs of his father dressed in his surplice on his deathbed.

The family had to vacate the rectory in Englewood. His mother moved to the North Egremont country house in Massachusetts, and his young brother, Russell, moved to New York City. George rented a studio at 44 East Fiftieth Street in New York. The apron strings were cut, just when the young photographer was ready to take on a professional life.

George Lynes had an unusually open and close relationship with his parents and his brother. Shortly before his father's death, when the Reverend Lynes was suffering from arthritis, George wrote, "I had no idea of the real pain you must be supporting. It is perhaps characteristic of me to think, or at least to hope, that misfortune and illness are temporary, and that somewhere, surely, there are remedies. Consequently, it was a shock to me to hear that your pain continued and was mysterious . . . if writing is difficult for you please do not think of writing me. There is small chance of misunderstanding; I know your devotion . . . it is only important that you should become well again. . . ."

Although his letter is largely about himself, it is clear that the love his parents bore him was returned. And George didn't have a problem expressing it. To be loved and then have the source of much of that caring disappear without warning must have been difficult. But his travels in Europe, and his growing circle of friends and professional contacts, seem to have steadied him. He turned to his new life and did not discuss his loss.

Paul Cadmus

We were always very poor.

—Paul Cadmus

Paul Cadmus was a city child. Of the three central subjects of this book, he had the least affluent upbringing. Whereas Lincoln Kirstein was born to true wealth and George Platt Lynes to a pastor's family that lived in a world of wealth, Paul Cadmus was born into an artistic milieu where his father was a not-highly-paid lithographer.

Cadmus was born in New York City on December 17, 1904, more than two years before George Platt Lynes and Lincoln Kirstein. He always kept this slight edge of maturity. At the time of Paul's birth, his young parents were living at Amsterdam Avenue and 103rd Street. In 1910, when Paul was six, they moved to 152nd Street.

His father, Egbert Cadmus, traced his family back to the Netherlands. His ancestors came to America in 1710, well before the Revolutionary War. The Dutch ancestry of these settlers matched the Dutch ancestry of New York, which not too long before had been New Amsterdam. All the most prominent New York families claimed Dutch forebears: the Van Rensselaers, the Vanderbilts, the Lydigs—all were of old Dutch stock.

Maria Latasa, Paul's mother, had a more exotic lineage. The Latasa family was Basque, from northern Spain, and had first emigrated to

Cuba, where they worked in cigar manufacturing. Maria's mother was born in Cuba, but Maria's grandfather transplanted his family to Tampa, Florida, where they flourished, when Cuba was torn with unrest in its battle to free itself from Spain. Many Cubans who manufactured cigars moved to Tampa then and brought that industry with them. The Latasa family was large and very Catholic, and Maria always regretted that she was unable to have more than two children. She came to New York to study and met her husband at the National Academy of Design there.

Paul's sister, Fidelma, was born two years after him, in 1907. Paul and Fidelma grew up to resemble each other physically, although Paul was to inherit the Dutch fairness and Fidelma the Spanish darkness of hair and eye.

Their father supported his family by working as a commercial lithographer in a firm on Jane Street in Greenwich Village. As an artist, he specialized in watercolors. Charming and talented work survives: a small painting of blond, blue-eyed Paul as a child rowing a boat and an interior of Mrs. Cadmus lounging on a kind of pillowed daybed favored by the late Victorians. In Gibson Girl attire with a dark skirt, puffed long sleeves, and small waist, Maria Latasa Cadmus was clearly a lovely woman. In his photographs, Egbert Cadmus cuts quite a dashing figure himself, a handsome man with no obvious fair Dutch heritage. They must have been a good-looking couple—and their love of art created a nurturing and pleasant atmosphere for their children to grow up in, money or no money.

Maria Cadmus illustrated children's books to add to the family's income, but her time was limited with two young children to care for. What remains of her work includes a pretty drawing of Fidelma.

The Cadmus children seem to have had little question about their career paths. During a family summer vacation at Oceanic, New Jersey, Paul Cadmus, age nine, said, "I am going to be a marine painter, and Sister is to be a portrait painter."

In 1919, Paul Cadmus finished his public school education and entered the National Academy of Design. He was to be sixteen the following December, just before midterm. Unlike Platt Lynes or Kirstein, Paul Cadmus didn't start and stop in search of a career. Under his parents' influence, he had always focused on a career as an artist and never caused his parents anguish. Not only was he a good student at the National Academy, he was also one of the most successful ones.

Charles Hinton was the principal instructor of Paul Cadmus when

Paul and Fidelma Cadmus, circa 1910. (Courtesy of Paul Cadmus and Jon Andersson. Reprinted by permission)

he began his full-time art studies. Hinton had also been one of the major instructors for Paul's parents. Charles Hinton had studied in the Gérôme atelier in Paris. A good draftsman and a successful academic painter, Jean Léon Gérôme was a popular teacher and had himself been a pupil of Ingres. So through three preceding generations of painters, Paul Cadmus found himself directly linked to the classical tradition.

For two years in the "antique class," the younger students at the National Academy learned to draw from plaster casts. The academy had no newfangled ideas about art education. Students sat in their places and drew from casts of ancient busts and bodies, in preparation for life class. What was it like for a young Paul Cadmus to go each day to his classes? Educated at home by his artist parents, he must already have been adept with pencil and paper. He has always been deeply interested in the romance of the tradition of painting from the Renaissance to today. And certainly the fact that he was being trained in the same manner as Michelangelo, Poussin, David, Courbet, and Corot must have counted for a lot.

In 1921 he joined the life class for drawing, and in 1922 he was given a bronze medal for the excellence of his work. (One wonders who received the gold and silver medals and what happened to them?)

In 1923 he started learning printmaking at the school. His teacher was William Auerbach-Levy. Cadmus quickly started producing work of a quality that was entered in exhibitions, and the weekly book-review section of the *New York Herald Tribune* began using his work for illustrations. He was paid for this, and since his parents could not support him to pursue a career as a fine-art painter, they must have been gratified at his success.

He completed the Academy of Design curriculum in the spring of 1926, when he was twenty-one. He graduated with a number of prizes for the excellence of his work as well as scholarships for advanced study.

That same spring a former classmate painted a fine portrait of Cadmus. In the portrait, sporting a wonderful green tie, he has his head lowered and is glancing at the viewer with a mix of shyness, sulkiness, and sexiness. As an attractive young man, he must have had many admirers of both sexes while he was a student. Living at home in the nuclear family of his good-looking and understanding parents and his beautiful sister probably only made him shyer. When he laughed in later years there was an echo of that boy who wasn't entirely at ease in an aggressive, competitive world, but who was ready to find out if it would like him.

The shyness and expectancy of his portrait must have very much reflected him.

Paul Cadmus continued his studies at the Art Students League on West Fifty-seventh Street in New York. He supported himself with a series of small commercial positions until he was employed by the Blackman Company in 1928 as an advertising layout artist. Twenty-three, having finished his formal education two years earlier, he was still living at home, although he rented a small studio on West Twenty-third Street in which to work. His sister, Fidelma, also lived at home. Upon finishing her studies, she was employed at the Traphagen Studio designing wallpaper in 1926. Their mother died in 1927.

Paul Cadmus continued sketch classes at the Art Students League with Charles Locke and studied lithography with Joseph Pennell. The most important event while he was studying there, however, was his meeting Jared French. A handsome young man from Rutherford, New Jersey, French was dedicated to becoming an acknowledged artist, even though his days were spent working on Wall Street in a stockbroker's office. French had been educated at Amherst College and was one year younger than Paul Cadmus.

The two men met in 1926 and became lovers. Their daytime jobs, although not badly paid, stood in the way of their devoting themselves to making art, and so a plan was hatched. They continued to work and save their money until the depths of the Depression in 1931. Then, when the dollar would go its farthest, they departed for Europe, where they could live cheaply and find out just exactly who they were as artists.

They left the United States in October 1931 aboard an oil tanker out of Hoboken, New Jersey, and made their way to Paris. In the cathedral town of Chartres they bought bicycles and Paul Cadmus learned to ride, wobbling up and down the bumpy cobblestone streets under the looming cathedral with its famous and amazing windows. The windows, intact from the Middle Ages, were as brilliant and piercing as the blue of Paul's eyes, but they held no great meaning for him. Raised by a Protestant father who espoused no real religious beliefs and a fervently Catholic mother, he had opted to ignore religion altogether to preserve peace in the family.

Touring France and Spain by bicycle, however, led to a good deal of sightseeing in churches, and their religious art began to catch Paul's eyes for its use of color and the placing of shapes in unusual and irregular spaces. In a letter to a collector, Paul Cadmus later wrote, "The contemporaries who have influenced me have been very few. Jerry French, however, really got me started into painting pictures other than just direct painting from life, just composing pictures, trying to be more like the Old Masters. He was a great influence—very important. He persuaded me that I actually could be an artist and that I needn't be a commercial artist, which I had been."

In these lines one can see reason enough for Paul Cadmus's love for Jared French. If the definition of love is to be sincerely concerned for the welfare of another person, Cadmus was much loved by French and was wheeled off across Europe to meet his destiny.

Paul Cadmus considers himself to have truly started painting only when he began work in Mallorca, where the two men took up lodgings after completing their bicycle journey southward from Chartres. In some of this early work, the arrangement of figures in constraining space certainly shows lessons learned from church painting. What Paul Cadmus considers his first real painting, an oil done in 1931 called *Jerry*, has an unusual "looking down" view of Jared French naked in bed looking up, his finger keeping his place in a paper-covered copy of Joyce's *Ulysses*, which he has been reading. The light, which could be from a candle, has some memory of the eighteenth-century portrait painter Quentin de La Tour in it. The difficult nonfrontal position of the body is expertly done. The light, curling hair under the arm, the mustache that doesn't quite conceal a mouth that French probably considered too sensual, the direct look from French's eyes into those of the viewer, make this a painting anyone would be proud to consider his "first" painting.

The second painting Paul Cadmus considers a *real* painting is a self-portrait done in his small, modern apartment house in the Mallorcan town of Puerto de Andraitx. His face is reflected in a shaving mirror. Perhaps he is on a balcony, as the mirror reflects greenery and the bay and mountains in the distance. His head is somewhat lowered in a manner not dissimilar to its position in the portrait done by his school friend. He again looks somewhat retiring, but his full mouth and shadowy eyes have a new sensuality. The schoolboy is gone. Cadmus is now twenty-seven, and is sporting the beginnings of a mustache (like Jerry's), though the shaving brush and razor suggest that he is perhaps considering removing it. Is that a persimmon sitting on the ledge and reflected in the mirror—too knobby to be an apple? His striped sailor pullover under his open-collar shirt speaks of all the young men who launder but do not iron. A pudgy, naked lady darting from a doorway in the background has dropped her towel in surprise, and there is something of interest in those

Paul Cadmus, Mallorca, 1932. (Courtesy of Paul Cadmus and Jon Andersson. Reprinted by permission)

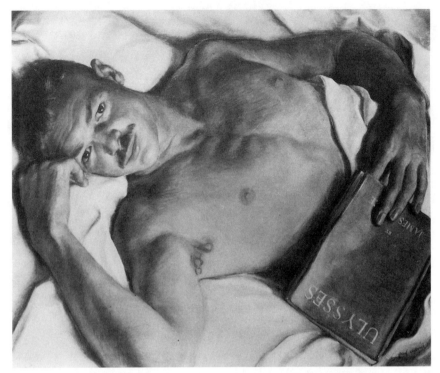

Jerry *(portrait of Jared French) by Paul Cadmus, 1931 (oil on canvas, 20" x 24").*
(Private collection. Courtesy of D. C. Moore Gallery, N.Y.C. Reprinted by permission)

Mallorcan eyes. He *is* attractive. Paul Cadmus the artist is alive and well
in Puerto de Andraitx.

In his 1932 watercolor *Deposition,* five figures surround a youthful,
short-haired Christ lying with his head toward the viewer, the body
stretching across the painting, corner to corner. The surrounding figures surge like a curling wave around the still body. The youth, the old
man, the two Marys, and an additional woman were all posed for by
Jared French. The naked Christ is another portrait of French. His slim,
young body has none of the emaciated asexuality ordinarily used in the
depiction of Christ. Here one truly feels the loss of someone young
and beautiful—a secular feeling that gives a religious image additional
reality.

While in Mallorca, Cadmus did watercolors and oil views of this port
town, but he also did drawings and paintings of the fishermen who lived
there. One portrait, *Juan,* resembles a bust of the Roman emperor Cara-

calla. Cadmus must have seen a resemblance to the emperor in Juan's strong classical features. Other paintings weave figures on decks of fishing boats together in intricate patterns. In his monograph on his brother-in-law, Lincoln Kirstein claims that Paul and Jared posed for all the figures in *Mallorcan Fishermen*, but the faces are obviously portraits of local young men.

The two painters must have been cutting some kind of sexual swath through Puerto de Andraitx, also. A friend from later years has a scrapbook of male nudes that includes a young friend of Paul's, whose photograph had been taken in Mallorca. Supposedly this young man always wanted a mirror placed so he could watch himself in bed, as he couldn't believe anyone would want to make love to him.

Local color soon gave place to other subjects for Paul Cadmus while he remained on Mallorca. His *Bicyclists* (1933) has no inspirational source in American work being done at the time; instead, this canvas harks back to Renaissance wall paintings. One bicyclist is getting instructions from another on a rutted country road; two powerful bodies are interwoven with multicolored wheels. Strong thighs and buttocks and backs point in opposite directions while the cyclists' eyes meet. Their gestures have a feeling of urgency coupled with the sense that the two men are not unaware of each other physically, which is often also true of religious painting. This painting was purchased later by composer Cole Porter.

Though painted while Cadmus was still living on Mallorca, his *Y.M.C.A. Locker Room* has an American theme, a frieze of men of many different types against a framework of green metal lockers. The simplified lockers and the coffered white ceiling overhead with its blossom-shaped light fixtures are typical of commercial spaces, but also echo trompe l'oeil Renaissance frescoes where architecture is only painted on. The moving figures are then fitted into this space, again much as one sees in a fifteenth-century fresco, but the men are distinctly modern and American. Perhaps Paul was beginning to miss New York. Or was he seeking a subject that would allow many undressed men? But his view of these men is scarcely homoerotic. These men are skinny and fat as well as nicely built, and with one exception their attention is not directed toward each other. They are busy getting dressed to leave the gymnasium. The painting is almost like a panning film shot. For a moment we get a glimpse of many different bodies in many different positions. Despite his youth and love of beauty, there is something unforgiving in Paul Cadmus's eye.

Factory Worker: Francisco *by Paul Cadmus, 1933 (pencil on paper, 12⁵/₈" x 9¹/₄"). (Collection of Dr. Leo Lese. Courtesy of D. C. Moore Gallery, N.Y.C. Reprinted by permission)*

About this work the painter has written, "I try to do people with as few clothes as possible. I would rather that they were all nude. . . . I knew the locker rooms fairly well because when I was working in the advertising agency I used to walk up to the Sixty-third Street Y on my way home—I lived on Ninety-fifth Street then. I was thinking of Mantegna (the low perspective) and also of Signorelli when I did it."

In 1933 he also did a painting called *Shore Leave*, showing sailors and young women in New York's Riverside Park. Like a jumble of unthinking young animals, they bounce and clamber, their hormones herding them in an inevitable direction. The young men are stalwart and unaware, while the women appear less attractive and predatory. This painting, also done in Mallorca, and owned eventually by publisher Malcolm Forbes, was an intermediary step toward another painting with the American navy as its subject, and that work was to thrust Paul Cadmus into the national limelight.

While in Mallorca, Paul Cadmus was sent press clippings by Fidelma about the Public Works of Art Project being organized by the new Roosevelt-led government. With the prospect of working for this new organization, designed to assist and encourage American artists during the Depression, the two painters made plans to return to the United States. Climbing back on their bicycles, they toured Germany, Austria, and Italy for a look at the art sheltered in the museums, churches, and galleries in those countries. And in October of 1933, exactly two years after arriving in Europe, they returned to New York. Paul immediately applied to the government project and was quickly accepted. The painting he did for them in 1934, *The Fleet's In!* was a harsher look at sailors ashore and caused a furor, followed and exploited by the press.

The painting was included in a PWAP exhibition at the Whitney Museum in New York, which specialized in American art, and then traveled to the Corcoran Gallery in Washington. Glanced at without comment in Manhattan, in Washington *The Fleet's In!* provoked the anger of Admiral Hugh Rodman, who vented his spleen in a letter to the Secretary of the Navy that was released to the press. The President's cousin, Assistant Secretary of the Navy Henry Latrobe Roosevelt, demanded that the painting be removed from the show. The *Washington Post* replied on May 21, 1934, "As opponents of censorship we can not condone Admiral Hugh Rodman's burst of indignation at the striking canvas *The Fleet's In!* . . . Admiral Rodman has had a long and distinguished career as a sailor. That does not make him an art critic. The PWAP show is an art exhibition, not an enlistment bureau for the Navy." The American press, loving a censorship scandal, spread the news and a reproduction of the painting. Suddenly the whole country knew about Paul Cadmus and his painting that had offended the U.S. Navy.

Secretary of the Navy Claude Swanson had the poor judgment to is-

The Fleet's In! *by Paul Cadmus, 1934 (oil on canvas, 30" x 60"). (Courtesy of Naval Historical Center, Washington, D.C., and D. C. Moore Gallery, N.Y.C. Reprinted by permission)*

sue a statement that said the painting "represents a most disgraceful, sordid, disreputable, drunken brawl, wherein apparently a number of enlisted men are consorting with a party of street-walkers and denizens of the red-light district. This is an unwarranted insult." How unwarranted was it to depict sailors getting drunk and trying to get laid? Sailors were famous for misbehaving, and now Paul Cadmus was, too.

At the time Paul Cadmus was quoted in the press as saying, "I'm going to do the picture as an etching. They can tear up the canvas, but they'll have a sweet time eating copper."

Later he wrote, "I owe the start of my career really to the Admiral who tried to suppress it. I didn't feel any moral indignation about those sailors, even though it wouldn't be my idea of a good time. The girls are not particularly attractive, neither are the sailors as a matter of fact, in this picture. But I always enjoyed watching them when I was young. I somewhat envied them the freedom of their lives and their lack of inhibitions. And I observed. I was always watching them. I didn't know them personally, I was not going after them or expecting any relationship with them, but they were fun to watch."

Another vehement critic simply scrawled a note across a reproduction of the painting and sent it to the artist: "You are a disgrace to art—a moral moron with distorted imagination. Pick your brains up out of the gutter. You damned traitor."

Never mentioned explicitly but certainly one of the triggers of the

outrage was the inclusion of a wavy-haired homosexual offering a cigarette to a tough, droopy-socked marine, who is reaching across his
passed-out pal to accept. Sailors accosting ugly girls on the street was
one thing, but for sailors to let themselves be picked up by other men
must really have bruised the sensibilities of navy brass. The little old lady
with her dog seems to have wandered into the picture from the turn of
the century. A close look reveals that she has the same tough face and
heavy shoes as the rest of her New York cohorts. She is supposedly modeled on an aunt of the painter, and she must have been surprised to have
been included in the sidewalk bacchanal.

As with many of Cadmus's long, mural-like paintings, the scene is
viewed from below. Feet are enlarged, as are lower legs. Buttocks loom
overhead like storm clouds. Movement washes back and forth, with bodies lurching back and swaying forward. No one is beautiful in this picture. The men are as overblown and used up as the women. There was
something funny and a little bitter and misanthropic in Cadmus's view of
humanity as he approached his thirtieth birthday.

It isn't known whether *The Fleet's In!* was returned to the exhibit or
not, but as a government purchase made with public funds, it was sent to
be hung over a fireplace at the Alibi Club in Washington. It slowly de-
graded there for many years, but has now been restored and hangs at the
Naval Historical Center in Washington.

Cadmus's next painting for the Public Works of Art Project was
Greenwich Village Cafeteria (1934), which also displayed the American
public at less than its best. When he came back from his isolated years in
Europe, Greenwich Village must have looked particularly exotic to Cadmus. Large ladies making passes at men without glasses, made-up boys
arranging a rendezvous, a careless woman spilling her purse across the
floor, the wavy-haired homosexual making a return engagement to
glance meaningfully over his shoulder as he heads into the men's room.
Shouting, yawning, wielding lipsticks, these people don't care what you
think of them. Art critic Bernard Berenson compared a Caravaggio
painting to this Cadmus: "It is a scattered composition. A delightfully
balanced arrangement with each performer individualized. As I enjoy
frivolous parallels, let me bring to notice a composition of today, perhaps its direct descendant, although unaware of its distant ancestor. It
is Cadmus's *Greenwich Village Cafeteria* in the New York Museum of
Modern Art."

Cadmus painted another unlovely mob in *Coney Island*, also in 1934.
He was working prodigiously upon his return to the United States. Each

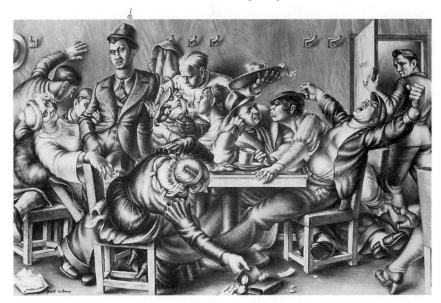

Greenwich Village Cafeteria by Paul Cadmus, 1934 (oil on canvas, 25¹/₂" x 39¹/₂"). (The Museum of Modern Art, New York, Extended loan from United States Public Works of Art Project. Photograph © 1999 The Museum of Modern Art, New York. Reprinted by permission of The Museum of Modern Art. Courtesy D. C. Moore Gallery, N.Y.C. Reproduced by permission)

painting is crammed with detail, each person is clearly an individual, and Cadmus is particularly aware of clothing. Starting with *Shore Leave*, the women's dresses are real clothing. The long, red lace skirt and the flat-heeled shoes on the cuddling girl in that painting could only have been seen on someone observed. Those kinds of clothes one doesn't dream up, though he must have done some fancy remembering when he painted *Shore Leave* on Mallorca. The dresses, hats, bags, and shoes in *The Fleet's In!* and *Greenwich Village Cafeteria*, and the endless varieties of bathing suits in *Coney Island*, show that the painter's eye was alert to porkpie hats and ladies' toques, drooping ruffles, spats, two-toned "co-respondent" shoes, and men's white-belted swimming trunks. Not only are subjects caricatured, but their clothing is caricatured too, and that is one of the reasons these paintings are so vividly real.

Cadmus's final paintings for the Public Works of Art Project presented the human body in a more flattering manner, hearkening back to the opulence of the Rubens period, except that these opulent bodies are male. *Horseplay* (1935) presents three young men changing clothes in a bathhouse. A swirl of clothing and towels frames one young man toweling his back, though he doesn't seem to be enjoying the horseplay as much as his friends. Although Lincoln Kirstein points out in his Cadmus monograph that many paintings have a homoerotic undertone, these nudes have no feeling that they are appealing in any way and just present pleasant flesh, sunny and ample.

The bodies are more mature in the painting *Gilding the Acrobats.* Here acrobats are preparing for a performance by gilding their bodies with large paintbrushes, and the main acrobat is actually gray-haired. Kirstein believed that Jared French posed for this central naked figure, but the curvy legs and strong upper body bear little relation to photographs of French in the nude. Again, it is the swirl and movement of clothing being removed and brushes being wielded that gives this 1935 work the rich and almost impromptu feeling of painting in the early seventeenth century. Neither of these paintings have any kind of bitter comment to make about human beings in the 1930s, which marks a kind of change in Cadmus's work.

By the middle of the 1930s, Paul Cadmus was recognized as a more-than-promising young artist. He shared a studio in St. Luke's Place with his lover, Jared French, and both men were meeting many creative people in the lively New York scene. Cadmus had come a long way from the young commercial artist of only five years before.

Lincoln Kirstein

*I had no dynasty; I had no family. My father gave me the idea that any-
thing was possible. I mean that nothing was possible for him but anything
would be possible for me.*

—Lincoln Kirstein

Kirstein was born in Rochester, New York, but he did not stay there
long. The date was May 4, 1907, three weeks after the birth of
George Platt Lynes.

Kirstein's statement that "I had no dynasty; I had no family" is somewhat misleading. Lincoln Kirstein was not born into one of the elite
New England families, but he came from a close-knit and supportive
Jewish family. Perhaps in his mind you were without family if you did
not come from an elite background. The Middle Western Rockefellers
would probably have disputed that.

George Platt Lynes, too, was concerned about family antecedents and
made the most he could of his interior-decorator ancestor, English-born
George Platt. Of the three men, only Paul Cadmus seems to have risen
above these concerns, believing that his connection through his painting
to the great artists of the past was enough of a background to claim.

Kirstein's father, Louis Kirstein, through his marriage to Rose Stein,
had connections. The family was in Rochester at the time of Lincoln
Kirstein's birth because Louis was working there for his wife's family.
This was not a success, and he moved his wife and children on to Boston.
After an experiment with owning a baseball team and working for an op-

tical company, Louis Kirstein found his niche at the William Filene Sons company, a major Boston retailer.

Louis Kirstein was a handsome and even dashing man despite early balding and a tendency to portliness. Both he and Rose Kirstein had a taste for beauty and comfort, and despite his father's early false starts in business, Lincoln Kirstein never lived in anything approaching poverty.

His father quickly prospered in his position at Filene's, becoming a partner in the department store and its chief executive, and it was this money that allowed the younger Kirstein, who never had to hold a job, to devote his life to the development of the arts in America. Lincoln had an older sister and a younger brother with whom he shared this family fortune, with which, though it was never on the scale of the Rockefellers' or the Whitneys', a great deal was accomplished.

Lincoln Kirstein well remembered his childhood home. He was impressed as a child with the foyer of the town house on Commonwealth Avenue in Boston. It was a large room done in Napoleonic style, the walls hung in olive-green silk. His own silk-hung drawing room later in New York may have sprung from this early memory. The Boston home was a rented house on a relatively grand scale with equally grand furnishings. The authentic antique pieces and the somewhat authentic period paintings were typical of a late-Victorian idea of decor, but must have created an ambience of art and its appreciation that had an effect on young Lincoln.

Lincoln, like Platt Lynes, was never a good student. The schooling he most enjoyed was at summer camp. His interests were artistic, and his parents always had difficulty keeping him in a reputable school. In this he was very unlike his older sister, Mina, who was always an admirable student and eventually made her way to Oxford in England. Although Lincoln Kirstein claimed he had no family to advance him in his life, Mina was well entrenched with the Bloomsbury group when he visited her in England, and he made important literary and artistic acquaintances through her.

At sixteen, after an academically troubled year at Phillips Exeter Academy, he was sent to the same school that George Platt Lynes was attending, and to achieve the same goal: scholastic grades good enough to qualify for an Ivy League college. At the Berkshire School, Lincoln wrote a bit for the school magazine, made a papier-mâché suit of armor for an art project, and fooled around with the other boys—though not with the same success as George Lynes, he grumpily noted in later years. He failed to graduate and was given a trip to London to help him forget

Lincoln Kirstein (left), his brother George, and their mother, circa 1925. (Courtesy of Jensen Yow. Reprinted by permission)

L. E. Kirstein, father of Lincoln, by George Platt Lynes, circa 1930. (Collection of Jensen Yow. Courtesy of Mr. and Mrs. George Platt Lynes II. Reprinted by permission)

Mina Kirstein Curtiss, sister of Lincoln, circa 1930. (Courtesy of Jensen Yow. Reprinted by permission)

it. It was during this trip abroad that he first saw the Diaghilev company. Kirstein took no notice of George Balanchine in *The Firebird*, though their destinies were to intertwine. (In Boston he *had* taken notice of Ted Shawn, who danced "nearly naked—what I chiefly recall is his gilded jock-strap, a suggestion of molten bronze.") Although his manner was often brooding, he must have mustered a fair amount of charm and intelligence in talking with his sister's friends, for he made many of the Bloomsbury notables into friends of his own. This trip gave him an international perspective on literature, theater, and art, which was to guide his steps as he proceeded through college.

Helped by private tutors and cram courses, Lincoln took the entrance exams a second time and was accepted at Harvard. He began his studies there in 1926. With other freshmen, he listened to a welcoming address from Harvard's president emeritus who gave them this advice: "Flee introspection." Kirstein didn't think that most Harvard freshmen needed much urging to avoid self-examination, and he was quick to set himself off from those well-bred, sports-minded, frolicking lads. But was he actually that different? Throughout his life he examined the people and the art and the dance around him incisively, but he seems to have avoided reflecting on the nature of his own confusing and conflicting personal activities.

What Lincoln Kirstein studied at Harvard seems to have left less impression on him than did the people that he met there, and his projects had little to do with the college curriculum. In his book of collected essays *By With To & From*, he remarks upon a favorite art teacher, Martin Mower. Mower must have been a treat. He used words like *saucy* to describe pictures and suggested that perhaps Cézanne was all thumbs, Derain awkward, Frans Hals flashy, and Rubens beefy. For someone enamored of art, these must have been alarming opinions from a respected art teacher, particularly one who wore a "burgundy scarf secured by a big garnet." Here were the very opinions of his father's friends (if they could only express themselves so well) echoing from an art expert. This kind of questioning of the sacred positions held by others in the art world must have stood Lincoln Kirstein in good stead, for in later years, when the taste in modern arts suddenly veered sharply away from his own, he was in no way deterred. Dismayed perhaps, but not deterred.

Mower was a portraitist and a great pal of Boston's leading patron of the arts, Isabella Stewart Gardner. Fenway Court, the museum-mansion that she built there, still stands as a flamboyant, sensual Venetian example of what a great house can be even in the uptight, small-roomed, low-heating-bills architecture of Boston. How a rather plain lady came to have such a sure taste for beauty is inexplicable, but she did, and she contributed energetically to make the arts flourish in that city's austere and chilly atmosphere. It was she who encouraged and helped pay for the education of Bernard Berenson, a quite beautiful Lithuanian boy who later became a wrinkled little old man and the most influential art expert of his time, living in a villa outside Florence and putting his seal of approval on art for American dealers.

Because Mrs. Gardner had been painted by artists such as Sargent, Whistler, and the then well-known Anders Zorn, Lincoln got it in his head that he wanted his portrait done by her friend Martin Mower. Mower probably found young Kirstein rather sexy, as he surely was, and duly painted a full-length portrait vaguely inspired by Sargent's famous (and subtly homoerotic) portrait of the willowy Graham Robertson. Lincoln was in riding clothes, crop in hand, hand on hip. The head was the least successful part of the painting, and the artist decided to cut the portrait down to focus more on the head—an unfortunate decision, as photographs, which are all that is left of the full-length painting, show a sinuous, rather elegant young man. It makes an interesting contrast to the later lumbering, hunched-over figure in a black suit that was the older Lincoln Kirstein. The one continuity over the years was the Roman-senator haircut. That was always a Kirstein trademark, even in his college days.

His first intellectual adventure while at Harvard was the founding of a magazine, *Hound & Horn*, in the spring of 1927 with Varian Fry. (A handsome classmate of complex sexual identity, Fry could read and write six languages when he entered college, and in 1941 was sent to Europe by a relief committee to rescue artists and writers from the Nazi terror.) The magazine was well thought of and published early stories by John Cheever and Katherine Anne Porter, as well as the poetry of Stephen Spender and articles by Sergei Eisenstein, T. S. Eliot, Gertrude Stein, and Edmund Wilson. Yet later on Kirstein was vexed with himself for failing to publish Hart Crane. Kirstein and the other *Hound & Horn* editors declined to print "The Tunnel," the last section of Crane's major work, *The Bridge*, rejecting it as "confused, self-indulgent, inchoate," although they did condescendingly admit it had "some good lines" and was "promising." Crane's suicide by drowning shortly thereafter (he leapt from a ship that was bearing him back to unappreciative New York) must have made the rejection seem even more of a wrong decision, and

Kirstein could only console himself by noting that the other literary magazines had rejected "The Tunnel" also.

The magazine continued seven years, long after Kirstein and his fellow publishers left Harvard. Finally it was closed because Kirstein felt it had become too concerned with philosophy and politics, neither of which interested him at all. He admits that he found the kind of material later editors wanted to include boring, and when he wrote pieces for the magazine himself, he thought they were frivolous in comparison to other, weightier subjects in the contents. Kirstein's interests, then and later, were "frivolous" if one defines this as being amusing, interesting, loving, and interested in the concerns of most people. Lincoln Kirstein was of excellent intelligence, but he was not an intellectual. He was not amused by ideas that had no purpose except to exercise the mind. He liked real things such as painting, sculpture, architecture, and most of all dance. Writing and reading about real things was what he found interesting in literature.

Hound & Horn was primarily of service to him as a vehicle of exploration. The famous people he met, such as Eliot (who terrified him), and the subjects he investigated led him to ascertain directions that *did* finally interest him. In these early years he was a prototype of the wealthy young man who does not know what he wants to do. But this period was brief. He was only twenty-six years old when he saw an evening of George Balanchine ballets in Paris, and from that time forward, his course was set.

His interest in becoming a painter himself withered away while he was at Harvard. He did a large and relatively successful mural for the Harvard Liberal Club during his college years, but his critical faculties did not fail him. He was able to compare himself to the artists he admired and found himself wanting. Nevertheless, his interest in painting and sculpture remained strong, and his most influential activity while at Harvard was undoubtedly the founding of the Harvard Society for Contemporary Art. This society was founded with three others: Bryn Mawr graduate Agnes Mongan; fellow student Edward Warburg, who was wealthy and eager to be involved in the arts; and John Walker III, another Harvard student, whose contribution lay in his vast social connections. Agnes Mongan had a cool, dispassionate, and truly sophisticated eye for modern art, Warburg and Walker between them mustered up backers and membership from the upper strata of society, and Kirstein had the enthusiasm and organizational skills. Very much like George

Platt Lynes, he was already too mature for college when he got there, and much of his collegiate life was devoted to activities one would have expected from an older and more sophisticated person.

Their first exhibit at Cambridge, in rented quarters, presented for the first time in the Boston area Thomas Hart Benton, John Marin, Georgia O'Keeffe, Gaston Lachaise, Alexander Archipenko, and Edward Hopper, as well as others. If they expected to stir up a great flap among the staid Bostonians, they were disappointed. The reviewers pretty much liked what they saw and congratulated the young people on their efforts.

For the next show they organized, they tried even harder to set the public's teeth on edge, but achieved very much the same approving results. Their exhibition was called *The School of Paris*, and it brought to the United States Georges Braque, Giorgio de Chirico, Aristide Maillol, Raoul Dufy, Juan Gris, Man Ray, Amedeo Modigliani, Jules Pascin, Georges Renault, Chaim Soutine, Maurice de Vlaminck, and Constantin Brancusi. An impressive roster when one considers that it was anyone's guess as to which contemporary artists would survive in public opinion. For many of these artists, it was the first time they were shown in the United States. If Agnes Mongan was displaying great taste and judgment, Lincoln Kirstein was learning fast and showing marked ability at securing the cooperation of artists, as well as physically bringing all this art together in one place and on schedule—not to mention shipping it back.

More than anything else Kirstein achieved at Harvard, it was the founding of the Harvard Society for Contemporary Art that gave him excellent credentials when he arrived in New York after graduating from college. He was accepted as being far more knowledgeable about art than one would expect of a young man who had just received his degree. While still at Harvard, he had been introduced, or had introduced himself, to many of the literary and artistic figures in New York. Prohibition was still in effect, but it was easy to buy liquor, and groups of intellectuals met regularly to talk and drink in the city's apartments and town houses. As a freshman, Kirstein had attended an evening at the salon conducted by Muriel Draper. This larger-than-life lady brought writers and painters together with wealthy socialites at large parties in her home, and many useful contacts were made there. To be fair, she arranged these introductions and meetings largely for her own pleasure and for the advancement of art—the moneymaking possibilities of these new friendships she left to others. Mrs. Draper was a bohemian and didn't care about social conventions. At her salon, guests could be open

Lincoln Kirstein by Walker Evans, circa 1929 (gelatin silver print, 12.4 cm x 9.8 cm). (The Metropolitan Museum of Art. Gift of Myriam and Harry Lunn, 1995. © Walker Evans Archive, The Metropolitan Museum of Art. Reprinted by permission)

about their sexual interests. "She was fond of molding young men," notes the cultural historian Steven Watson, "and particularly homosexual young men like Lincoln Kirstein. . . . " There are reports that the young Kirstein was one of Muriel Draper's lovers, and he probably was. Given the complex issues of sexuality, nothing is impossible.

Lincoln Kirstein met Carl Van Vechten at Muriel Draper's home in 1927. Van Vechten was wearing a fireman's red shirt, and as "throwaway chic" was unknown to the young student, he thought the well-known critic and novelist was in fact a fireman. A large, fair, charming fireman who knew a great deal about music and dance, Van Vechten was discreetly homosexual and had married an actress. He introduced Kirstein to Harlem and the music and art world that existed there in the 1920s. The black community was welcoming creative white people who were interested in African-American energy and originality. Kirstein wrote in an article on Carl Van Vechten that for the downtown group he knew in New York "Harlem was far more an arrondissement of Paris than a battleground of Greater New York." He adds, "It was a Harlem then oddly unresentful, open and welcoming to . . . all writers and artists who recognized in its shadows the only authentic elegance in America." Ever after, Kirstein was interested in and appreciative of the inspiration and elegance black Americans brought to the arts. Carl Van Vechten had taught him to open his eyes and take a look about him.

In 1927 Lincoln Kirstein spent some time studying with the mystic Gurdjieff. Born in Russia of Greek and Armenian parents, Gurdjieff emerged in France between the wars with a brand of theosophical thinking that attracted a number of society women and artists. In his book *Mosaic*, Kirstein writes about his experiences with Gurdjieff and his group at Fontainebleau, just outside Paris. His recounting of his summer trying to get in touch with himself is as wreathed in mystery as the teachings of Gurdjieff himself. Essentially, Gurdjieff taught that if we are ever to free ourselves from the endlessly repetitive patterns of our behavior, we must study our actions minutely and change them, tiny detail by tiny detail. This kind of spiritual study is linked to oriental systems, in particular to Zen Buddhism. Kirstein seems to have adopted the disciplines of meditation and self-examination, but he always found Gurdjieff inexplicable and did not continue his studies for long.

Perhaps the Gurdjieff method was designed for those who feel a deep desire to change themselves, something that it is unlikely that Kirstein wanted. What he seems to have desired was an artist's talent to match the artistic interests with which he was born. Exploring his various talents, Kirstein found no real personal gift for painting or writing and was finally to focus his enormous energy and enthusiasm on promoting the talents of others.

While searching for the right direction in life, Kirstein had an affair with a writer–merchant seaman, Carl Carlsen. (Kirstein "came out" in

1982 when he wrote an article for a "little" magazine called *Raritan* about his relationship with Carlsen, which took place in the early 1930s. He subsequently illustrated this article when it was reprinted in his book *By With To & From* with a 1947 George Platt Lynes photo of handsome Hollywood gym owner Harvey Easton, and one has to wonder where truth leaves off and fantasy begins. Perhaps Carl Carlsen, thirty-five or forty at the time, wasn't handsome enough for his lover to be proud of their relationship. More likely, Kirstein had no photograph of Carl Carlsen and didn't want to disappoint readers.) When Bertha, Carlsen's companion or wife, was out of town, the merchant seaman entertained his young admirer in the spare little house he occupied in the backyard of a house in Chelsea. Carlsen aspired to be a writer and had been a close friend of the poet Hart Crane, whom he admired very much. Kirstein tried to interest himself in Carlsen's writing as much as in the sailor's body. He describes Carlsen in his memoir *Mosaic* as "a sleek, hard, almost hairless male; easy, self-confident and deliberate." But evidently he found no way to convince himself that Carlsen's short stories were of any real value. Carlsen himself didn't seem to care one way or another whether he was published by *Hound & Horn*.

Whatever may be true or embroidered romantic memory, an exchange just before the two men went their separate ways has a ring of actuality. Carlsen asked Kirstein, "Why didn't you like Hart?" To which Kirstein replied, "Carl, why the hell do you always have to bring Crane into it?" Carlsen answered, "Why, you silly son of a bitch. If it wasn't for Crane, I wouldn't have given you the sweat off my ass."

Kirstein remembered seeing Hart Crane thrown out of a party for excessive drunkenness. Crane later returned to the party with the cabdriver he had been unable to pay when he reached the bar he was heading for. No one seemed to want to pay the cabdriver his round-trip fare, but the driver stayed at the party for a few drinks and left with the contrite and sober Crane, one hopes to take him to his destination free of charge.

Lincoln Kirstein wrote that Crane had the demeanor of a small child who has been bad and is sorry for it. Kirstein aspired to be a poet and Crane couldn't help but be one. This was an enormous difference that Carl Carlsen, awkward and incompetent writer or not, recognized. As his parting remark to Kirstein shows, Carlsen obviously allowed Kirstein to know him because Kirstein's connection with Hart Crane's milieu had established him as someone of merit literarily. That was his only interest in Kirstein.

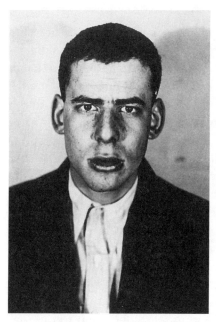 

"Public Enemy" photograph of Lincoln Kirstein by Walker Evans, circa 1932. (Collection of Jensen Yow. Courtesy of the Metropolitan Museum of Art, © Walker Evans Archive, The Metropolitan Museum of Art. Reprinted by permission)

Kirstein had met Carlsen through Walker Evans, whose artful documentary photographs had appeared in *Hound & Horn*. After a photo session that resulted in Evans's "mug shot" portraits of Kirstein, Kirstein stripped to the waist, and the two men started to box, a sexually charged encounter that seemed to satisfy neither of them, but this episode in no way affected Kirstein's high regard for Evans's photography.

At this time Lincoln Kirstein considered himself a writer, having abandoned his idea of being a painter. He wrote a highly autobiographical novel, *Flesh Is Heir*, which was published in 1932. Kirstein's Jewishness plays an important role in the novel as the central figure explores the WASP world of boarding school and then expatriate life in Europe. Though his book met with little success, he next considered writing a biography of Nijinsky in collaboration with Romola Nijinsky, the great dancer's wife.

Romola Nijinsky was a well-born Romanian woman who was famously difficult to deal with. In her youth she had been a kind of ballet groupie. Although not an accomplished dancer, she had joined the Ballets Russes before World War I because of an infatuation with Diaghilev's leading male dancer, Vaslav Nijinsky. She was with the company when it embarked for a tour of South America without Diaghilev, who, having been told by a fortune-teller that his death would be by water, from that point on refused to travel by boat. For the first time since Diaghilev had begun to manage his life and career, Nijinsky was free to establish some contacts of his own. Although Romola and he spoke no common language, he knew of her infatuation for him through other members of the company, and as their ship approached Buenos Aires, he asked her to marry him. They were married soon after the ship docked. When Diaghilev was notified by wire, he immediately fired Nijinsky.

Romola said that sleeping with Nijinsky was like sleeping with a god. She was fortunate that her marriage had some pluses, as there were many negatives. World War I soon broke out, and by the time the war was over, Nijinsky was insane and spent most of the remainder of his life in a Swiss sanitarium. Despite Romola's occasional claims of improvement, he was to die in London in 1950 without recovering his sanity.

In the early 1930s, Romola was doing her best to make a career out of being the famous dancer's wife. Diaghilev had died in 1929 in Venice, at the Excelsior Hotel on the Lido ("by water," as the fortune-teller had prophesied, although not on a ship), battled over to the end by his last lover, Serge Lifar, and his indispensable secretary, Boris Kochno.

Curiously, Lincoln Kirstein was in Venice at the time and saw the mourners at a distance. The stars and other dancers of the Diaghilev troupe soon scattered to other ballet companies, and there was a great surge of interest in the now-vanished Ballets Russes. Its contribution to the European art world was beginning to be appreciated as the lack of any replacement became evident.

Lincoln Kirstein had gone to London in 1933 to see Romola Nijinsky and discuss their book project. Romola was charming and hospitable one day, distant and whimsical the next. There would be meetings and discussions, and then she would have to leave London for mysterious reasons. Kirstein was providing her with money to maintain herself, and to more seasoned outsiders, it must have been clear that Romola saw no reason for this project to move rapidly to a conclusion. The more confusion she could engender, the longer the project, and her income from it, would last.

During one of her absences from London, Kirstein crossed the Channel to Paris, most likely to visit George Platt Lynes, Monroe Wheeler, and Glenway Wescott, and other friends. When Kirstein wanted Romola

Lincoln Kirstein, in front of a painted backdrop of Venice, pretending to be a gondolier; photographed by Max Ewing, circa 1932. (Courtesy of Bernard Perlin. Reprinted by permission)

Nijinsky to come to Paris to continue working on their project, Romola, for some reason, preferred meeting in Holland. Kirstein demurred, but their professional relationship still lingered on for a short time.

With George Lynes he visited the studio of Pavel Tchelitchev, the Russian painter, whom he was to admire greatly and help later with his career in New York. More important, he saw Les Ballets 1933, the dance company that had been formed by a wealthy Englishman, Edward James, to display his new wife, the Austrian dancer Tilly Losch. George Balanchine, recently a dancer and choreographer for the Diaghilev troupe, had been hired to mount the ballets presented by the new company. This company also presented for the first time the "baby" ballerinas: Tamara Toumanova, Irina Baronova, and Tatiana Riabouchinska. These three young girls were expatriates raised and trained in Paris. Their teachers were former Imperial ballerinas, and they had a direct heritage from the St. Petersburg tradition. They were all beautiful and, although still in their early teens, had a glamorous Parisian manner. Their presence was fortunate for the credibility of the company, as the prima ballerina, Tilly Losch, was long on beauty and self-confidence, but extremely short on dance technique.

Edward James had brought together a company that was the first to provide some of the thrills of innovation that had been lost at Diaghilev's death. George Balanchine choreographed the entire repertoire, which included the first performances of Kurt Weill's *Seven Deadly Sins*. Pavel Tchelitchev created the sets and costumes for *Errante*, with a remarkable cape for Tilly Losch of miraculous clouds of floating gauze, and André Derain and Christian Bérard provide the décors for the ballets *Fastes* and *Mozartiana*. Bérard, who was Boris Kochno's longtime companion, would also design sets for *La Machine Infernale*, Cocteau's chicly modern retelling of the Oedipus myth, in the following year.

Kirstein had first seen Balanchine's choreography in 1925 when Tamara Geva danced an "Etruscan" *pas de deux* that the young Bostonian found "perverse, pornographic, and passionately interesting." In 1929 he had attended London performances of *Apollo*, *The Prodigal Son*, and *Le Bal*. Now he became completely infatuated by Balanchine's creations, and although he was yet to realize it, his hesitations in the choice of a career were over. He was to become a ballet impresario. Picking up the cloak dropped by Diaghilev, he was to carry the great tradition of classical ballet to the United States, aided and abetted by George Balanchine.

Kirstein's diaries of this summer of 1933 in Paris make perhaps the most interesting reading of anything he ever wrote. They are not premeditated, they have no planned point of view to communicate, and he was yet to know where his contacts with the famous and yet-to-be famous in Paris would lead him. The diaries fascinate because they reveal Kirstein's personality in its embryonic stage, amidst the witty and glittering whirl of the international beau monde. He apparently knew everybody, went everywhere, and in a few choice words in these diaries he captures the brilliant spirit of those times, which were soon to be extinguished by World War II.

On June 7 he lunched with a prominent American lesbian couple, Romaine Brooks and Natalie Barney. Barney had been in Paris since well before World War I and was known as La Belle Amazone for her striking appearance riding sidesaddle in the Bois de Boulogne. She had had a much-talked-about affair with the famous courtesan Liane de Pougy. Fortunately, Barney had a fortune of her own and didn't have to depend upon the kindnesses of others. As did Mademoiselle de Pougy, who later got religion and was painted in a beautiful pose as Mary Magdalene.

Natalie Barney's lover at the time was the painter Romaine Brooks, also an American with an important family inheritance. She was of a dark and brooding manner, as opposed to the ebullient and auburn-haired Natalie. At this lunch, Lincoln asked, "'Are there no friendships in Paris?' . . . Miss Brooks said Paris is a continent in itself; there are only alliances, no *amitiés*."

Also present at the luncheon was Dolly Wilde, the lesbian niece of Oscar Wilde, who Lincoln thought bore "a fascinating resemblance" to her portly and stately uncle. The diary recounts, "I recalled what Wilde said on his release from prison: *'Plus des amis, plus que des amants.* (I have no more friends, so then I'll have lovers.)'"

That same evening he attended Les Ballets 1933. After describing the ballets, he adds, "Too much Balanchine for one evening, but two out of three knockouts, not bad." Little did he know how many full evenings of Balanchine he would eventually sit through. (In later years, the New York dance critic John Martin wrote of Balanchine's *Symphony in C* when it was first performed, "We had Mr. Balanchine's ballet again, this time to Bizet." Like Martin, many balletgoers have felt they were seeing Mr. Balanchine's ballet again as the years went by, but Lincoln Kirstein was never one of them.)

Virgil Thomson was a good friend, and in Kirstein's diaries there are many comments and criticisms by this gay composer that tell us much about the young man who was soon to become a ballet impresario. On June 8, for example, Thomson talked at length about Kurt Weill and the fact that he was Jewish, which strongly affected what he was interested in composing. Thomson told Lincoln, "Jewish culture is always practical, concerned with action. The Jew, when he sins, apologizes. The

Gentile has not only to repent but to send flowers if late for dinner." Kirstein wrote, "Virgil says I resist this separatist definition of Jewish art (I objected to his flowers-being-sent; I always send flowers), because I was brought up in a first generation without persecution, hence want to prove Jews are the same as everyone else."

It would probably be safe to say that Kirstein *did* want to contribute to American culture and society by developing the arts, and he wanted to be recognized for it, though it was primarily a gentile-dominated society. What he failed to realize was that most moneyed gentiles cared little for development of the arts, and his acceptance would have to come from the world of art and artists, people who liked him and had great respect for him.

On June 9 he attended a rehearsal of Balanchine's *Errante* at nine o'clock in the morning. This ballet had been designed by Pavel Tchelitchev and featured a long cape worn by Tilly Losch. Kirstein wrote, "Some startling effects à la Loie Fuller [a turn-of-the-century dancer who barely danced, but flaunted great lengths of silk to great success]. Tilly Losch's ten-foot, sea-green satin train, hard time managing it." Later in New York, Tchelitchev was to talk of this ballet and his amusement one evening when a rebellious French corps member stepped on Tilly's train and tore it off. He remembered, "She was off the stage, got to her dressing room, and reappeared in her rehearsal cape in ten seconds, I swear. Ten seconds. It was amazing." Miss Losch obviously had her professional qualities.

The next night, Kirstein went to the premiere of *Errante* and wrote, "Stupendous climax with the falling chiffon cloud. Virgil says this is the private life of Pavel Tchelitchev: love, revolution; tempestuous love affairs, etc. Tchelitchev looking like an angry, intelligent horse; with Edith Sitwell swathed in white chiffon, with a white-and-gold mobcap and huge gold plaque."

Kirstein was leading quite an action-packed life in Paris. On June 11, Virgil Thomson was quoted as saying, "He asked how my education was proceeding; said if I spoke French better, I'd get further." Thomson was evidently an exception to the floods of American expatriates in Paris between the wars who spoke little or no French.

Kirstein went to a private concert in the afternoon where he argued with Maurice Grosser, a painter and Thomson's companion. "I complained about the sensibility of Tchelitchev and Bérard. I am interested in subject matter, not sensibility. He said I was talking about preference, not taste. Taste was a serious business *dans tous les sens*, particularly in

Paris. There is virtue in sensing and directing the mode, not alone in fashion, but in ideas and manners; the French had provided taste for the rest of the world for three centuries. Maurice says I am simply put off Paris because I have never been part of it and its social dimensions are beyond me."

This may have been true, but Paris was certainly giving him the opportunity to learn a lot. His objections are interesting, since both Tchelitchev and Bérard were to become artists he championed greatly in the United States. He would come to learn that style could be content. It is worth noting, too, that the finale of the New York City Ballet production of *Orpheus* in the 1940s owed a great deal to the early production of *Errante* and its descending silk cloud that he saw during this summer.

The writer Katherine Anne Porter was also in Paris that summer, and on June 14, he called for her and took her to see Serge Lifar dance *Le Spectre de la Rose* at the Opéra. He writes, "Perfect archaeological reconstruction . . . if I had not known something of what it had been, would not have been interested." He did find Miss Porter interesting, however, and discovered that she had once written the libretto of a ballet for Anna Pavlova, *Xochimilco*. She had spent time in Mexico and was fascinated by it. They also talked about homosexuality. He notes, "Spoke a long time on why it was American artists can't endure being, at one and the same time, men *and* women: Whitman, Melville, Henry James; most recently Hart Crane." Porter had seen Crane often during his last six months in Mexico but would only say enigmatically that his life there was a "horror; will never tell what happened to a living soul." Kirstein may have been able to talk knowledgeably about artists who couldn't confront conflicting sexual interests, but of all his circle he was the least able to do so. He was one of the few in his circle to marry for social reasons, and the only one who joined the army.

During this summer, Kirstein also met the brothers Eugene and Leonid Berman, both painters, and wrote in his diary, "[Met] at Virgil's, Eugene Berman, a Russian painter trained as an architect; complaining non-stop, no one will let him design a ballet. Consoles himself knowing good painters don't take ballet seriously. Berman would like to design big open-air ceremonies; public funerals. Unhappy little man; hates everybody." As with many people Kirstein met in Paris in 1933, he was to come to know the Bermans better and think differently about them. Or perhaps his thinking didn't change, but he didn't speak so frankly when he knew them better.

On June 16, Kirstein lunched with Monroe Wheeler, who was publishing fine editions at the time. For Kirstein as for almost everyone else who talked to him, Wheeler was a great catalyst. This time he explicated clearly for Kirstein the situation in the world of ballet. Who was capable of managing what, and what potential there was for ballet. Wheeler asked pointed questions to ascertain how interested Kirstein truly was in serving as an impresario for ballet. Wheeler's time and attention were amply rewarded later when Kirstein was influential in obtaining the job of publications director for him at the newly opened Museum of Modern Art in New York.

In an interesting entry on June 17, Kirstein notes that Ballets 1933 is about to leave for London. He has yet to meet Balanchine, and the painter Christian Bérard tells him that Balanchine "is entirely mysterious, invisible offstage, unhealthy—TB; nobody seems to know him. He is held captive by a demon called Dimitriev, an ex-croupier, ex-singer, ex-soldier, most sinister type. Balanchine is in love with Tamara Toumanova, whose mother says he is old enough to be her father (at twenty-nine?). He never goes out or accepts invitations; there is simply no point in trying to see him. He is slightly mad, really cares nothing for the ballet, is only interested in playing the piano, keeps taking music lessons from some old Russian lady, a pupil of Siloti and Rimsky." All this mystery, however, couldn't have helped but intrigue the impressionable and romantic Kirstein. One feels that his attitude toward Balanchine never developed much from this early fascination with the choreographer's strangeness. Balanchine *was* elusive. On June 22 Kirstein wrote "no one willing to see me or talk about possibilities for ballet."

Kirstein got a straightforward talking to by Virgil Thomson on June 18. One can imagine the very large Kirstein all hunkered down, hands between his knees, as the diminutive Thomson blazed forth. "Virgil said I was silly, more affected than effective. I had no mind, I mistook myself for an intellectual but was by no means a man of taste (like Philip Johnson; an admirable interior decorator), but was first of all a worker, the artist part is incidental." Thomson would not have talked so frankly or even brutally to Kirstein if he hadn't sensed that Kirstein was capable of a great deal and needed to stop floundering.

On June 21 he writes that he paid a visit to Pavel Tchelitchev's studio and found "George Lynes (the photographer), Glenway Wescott (the novelist) already there. Tons of beautiful sketches in heaps, rejects from *Errante*, he pressed one on me, like an idiot I was too slow accepting it, so he gave it to George Lynes, 'Oh, so it's not good enough for you?'"

A French painter, Jacques Mauny, tells Kirstein on June 24, "It is all very well for the American (me?) to vaunt his innocence but naïveté is no excuse for not getting things done." Everyone seems to have been getting on Lincoln's case. He must obviously have been an intelligent, capable person in search of a calling.

During this summer Kirstein was also seeing much of the poet e. e. cummings, whom he always refers to as "Estlin Cummings," and his beautiful wife, Marion Moorehouse, one of the first "name" models. (Natalie Barney described Marion Moorehouse's clothes as being like "the guts of a rainbow.") Kirstein evidently did not care greatly for cummings, who once told him, "French poetry is nothing but paper patterns." Kirstein was tempted to say, "You should know."

Political tensions in Europe resound in Kirstein's diary on June 27 when he has lunch with an American, Barbara Sessions, who had been living in Berlin with her husband, composer Roger Sessions. She tells Kirstein that "every Jew should leave as soon as he can." This is 1933: Hitler had come to power five months before. The Nazis had already closed Magnus Hirschfeld's research institute and burned its library of books about homosexuality.

By July 4 Kirstein was back in London waiting for Romola Nijinsky, who was still in Holland spending his money. She wired for more at regular intervals with no explanation of what she was doing there. He went to meet her train, but she was not on it. Returning to his hotel, he found a telegram asking for more money to pay her hotel in Holland so she could leave. She held little enchantment for him at this point; however, he paid her bill. Evidently, Romola's way was to push her luck to the point where no one wanted anything to do with her.

He had lunch in London with the ballet critic Arnold Haskell and Tamara Toumanova and her mother. Toumanova interrupted her domineering mother to say that "Balanchine was actually a brilliant dancer, and she has seen him turn and jump like no one else can, but that he cannot appear since he has only half a lung and will die within two years." There was much talk then of Balanchine's health. In 1930 Balanchine had spent several months in a sanitarium in the Alps recovering from tuberculosis, which collapsed one lung and somewhat damaged the other.

On July 8, Romola Nijinsky finally arrived in London, and Kirstein took her to a performance of Ballets 1933. Romola was never one to mince words. "She said Toumanova was too big and slow and should still be at school; some of Balanchine's adagio ideas not bad; the whole evening like a school demonstration, a sort of *salade russe*." Afterward, backstage, Balanchine came out looking haggard and tired. Romola said he had actually to make the very theater dance, since he had no dancers. She added, "Old Pa Diaghilev would be pirouetting in his grave." It depressed Kirstein, and one wonders how much validity Romola's remarks had. That American audiences had never seen any of the great Russian ballets certainly helped Balanchine and others choreographically. Americans couldn't compare the new ballets to anything they'd seen before, and they wouldn't recognize anything taken from a ballet performed earlier in Russia.

Finally, on July 11, Kirstein had a long talk with George Balanchine at an evening party given by the Kirk Askews. Balanchine said that one must never revive ballets, adding that his own *Prodigal Son* would seem hopelessly old-fashioned if revived. (One can only wonder how he felt about *The Prodigal Son* remaining in the New York City Ballet's permanent repertory for decades.) Balanchine expressed an interest in coming to the United States with a small company. Kirstein concluded his entry, "Balanchine seemed intense, concentrated, disinterested; not desperate exactly but without hope. I like to imagine we got on well; he said nothing about meeting again."

In Kirstein's book of memoirs, *Mosaic,* he recounts how it happened that Balanchine came to the United States. Clearly, Balanchine chose Kirstein; *he* didn't choose Balanchine. The Ballets 1933 season was ending in London, with no further plans for that company. Balanchine was without prospects. At a dinner alone with Kirstein, he mapped out his requirements for moving to the United States. He would have to come with his manager, Vladimir Dimitriev, with the dancer Tamara Toumanova and her mother, and also the dancers Pierre Vladimirov and his wife, Felia Doubrovska. The last couple would direct and teach at the school that it would be necessary to establish.

Kirstein was overwhelmed. His own finances would not permit underwriting this venture, but he couldn't explain this to Balanchine. After pursuing the choreographer so avidly without any real plan of action, suddenly the choreographer's plan was placed before him. Action was necessary. He left Balanchine and went to his hotel room, where he wrote a sixteen-page letter to Chick Austin, the director of the Wadsworth Atheneum in Hartford, Connecticut. In part, the letter reads:

> This will be the most important letter I will ever write you as you will see. My pen burns my hand as I write: words will not flow into

the ink fast enough. We have a real chance to have an American ballet in three years' time. When I say ballet—I mean a trained company of young dancers—not Russians—but Americans with Russian stars to start with—a company superior to the dregs of the old Diaghilev company. . . . Do you know George Balanchine? If not he is a Georgian called Georgei Balanchanavidze [*sic*]. He is, personally, enchanting—dark, very slight—a superb dancer and the most ingenious technician in ballet I have ever seen. . . . I'd stake my life on his talent.

He could achieve a miracle—and right under our eyes; I feel this chance is too serious to be denied. . . . Please . . . rack your brains and try to make this all come true . . . we have the future in our hands.

Austin had been experimenting with presenting entertainment and music at the museum he directed and seemed to have his board of directors mesmerized. As the Depression deepened, he must have seemed one of the few possibilities for the establishment of a home base for a ballet school and company.

Kirstein's friend Virgil Thomson arrived in London from Paris and told him that his opera *Four Saints in Three Acts* would soon be performed at the Wadsworth Atheneum. Gertrude Stein had written the libretto, and much excitement surrounded the planned production. Kirstein said nothing to Thomson about his own plans, for fear Thomson would think he was trying to have available funds used for his project instead of Virgil's.

Balanchine had already returned to France when Kirstein received a cable from Hartford:

GO AHEAD IRONCLAD CONTRACT NECESSARY START-ING OCTOBER 15 SETTLE AS MUCH AS YOU CAN BRING PUBLICITY PHOTOGRAPHS MUSEUM WILLING CAN'T WAIT.

Kirstein departed immediately for France to find Balanchine and organize his party of dancers, teachers, and the choreographer for departure for New York.

Once in the United States, Kirstein accompanied Balanchine and Dimitriev to Hartford for a reconnaissance trip, and the two Russians decided immediately that it would be impossible to have a ballet company and school in this small city in the center of Connecticut. How Chick Austin felt about being abandoned after making a great effort to launch ballet in America is not known. Perhaps he was relieved and immediately turned his attention to the Thomson-Stein opera. Certainly the board of directors must have felt no regrets.

The money to establish the ballet school came first from Edward Warburg, who had joined Kirstein in organizing art exhibitions at Harvard, and later from Kirstein's father, while Lincoln Kirstein gathered funds from Nelson Rockefeller and other well-to-do society friends. That Balanchine and his party were already in New York must have carried some weight.

Kirstein had arrived in October 1933 with his ballet contingent, and by January 1934 the School of American Ballet had opened on the second floor of 637 Madison Avenue between Fifty-ninth and Sixtieth Streets. George Platt Lynes was soon to have his studio directly across the street. George Balanchine had the title of artistic director and maître de ballet. Lincoln Kirstein's title was secretary-treasurer and director of the Division of Theatrical Sciences.

By June 1934, the students at the new ballet school were ready for a public showing. This troupe was called the Producing Company of the School of American Ballet, and Edward Warburg presented them at his family's estate in White Plains, New York, to celebrate his twenty-sixth birthday. The dancers were to premiere Balanchine's *Serenade* at an elaborate evening party, which was unfortunately rained out. However, the Warburgs rallied to the occasion and invited all 250 guests to return the next evening, where they ate, drank, and saw Edward Warburg's birthday gift: an evening of ballet.

This company, with Chick Austin's cooperation, made another appearance in December 1934 at the Wadsworth Atheneum's Avery Memorial Theater in Hartford. They performed a ballet called *Transcendence* with a libretto by Lincoln Kirstein. He was quickly emerging from his secretary-treasurer role to become part of the creation of ballets.

The Thirties
1935–40

Glittering Prizes

*It's 1937. You have been invited to a party at the apartment of the fashion pho-
tographer George Lynes. His apartment is at the corner of Madison Avenue
and Eighty-ninth Street.*

*You haven't really been invited. You're going with a handsome young friend
of yours, Richard Roehmer. Richard works as a sometime model for artists, and
he has recently been posing nude for George Lynes, who is planning a series of
photographs with mythological subjects. All this Richard has told you. He also
says he'd just as soon you didn't tell everyone that he poses nude. You wonder
who you could tell that would be surprised. Richard seems to know his way
around New York very well.*

*You're excited. You've just come to New York from Sandusky. Or Keokuk.
Or Painted Post. Does it matter? That's all behind you now. You're young and
good-looking and smart, and New York holds out its glittering prizes to you.
This party is your first step toward the glitter. Famous people will be there.
Beautiful people will be there. The party that George Lynes has once a month is
known for its mix of socialites, artists, and beautiful young people. Mostly beautiful young men, true, but beautiful young women are not unwelcome if they
are wealthy and well-connected. But that's not crucial. Beauty is.*

*Many artists will be at Lynes's party, always looking for handsome young
faces to draw and paint and perhaps fall in love with.*

*You arrive at eight-twenty. Richard has explained to you that in New York,
you always arrive twenty minutes late. If you arrive on time, you will probably
find your host or hostess coming out of the shower.*

*When you arrive at the building, you see that it is not new, but probably
built at the turn of the century when New York was booming and not struggling
out of a depression. There is a doorman in uniform. You are impressed. There
are no doormen in uniform down in the Village where you live—or at least*

damned few. Richard explains that you are visiting George Lynes, which the doorman seems to expect. Other people in the building probably don't give large parties with the great regularity that George does. The doorman only nods as you pass him by.

The elevator operator is in uniform, too. He is young and good-looking with dark hair slicked tightly back. Everyone in New York seems to be young and good-looking. The operator looks at you as though he knows you or knows something about you; you wonder what.

A dark and dashing man answers the door. Richard introduces him as Mr. Wheeler. "Please," the man says, "call me Monroe. I'm not that much older than you." Mr. Wheeler is elegantly dressed in a dark blue jacket and a navy silk ascot with white polka dots. You've never actually seen anyone before in an ascot, a look you've only noticed in fashion illustrations in men's magazines like Esquire. *You get a little more excited now that you've met Monroe. You wonder how he learned to tuck that ascot so perfectly into the neck of his white shirt. His dark hair is slicked straight back. How old is he? Thirty-five, forty, somewhere in there. He has a kind of devilish look about him until you look in his eyes, which are dark brown and friendly, something like a spaniel's.*

"Just go in and introduce yourselves," he says. "I have to stay here by the door. George will get you a drink."

The apartment isn't large, and quite a few people are already there. So much for the fashionable twenty minutes late. Some of the guests look as if they have been there for hours, slumped into armchairs and seeming quite drunk. The living room has unusual paintings on the wall—not trees and fields, as they do in the better homes in Sandusky. Most people back home have a lithograph of The End of the Trail, *the well-known dead Indian on a sick horse. The paintings here are in bright colors. The people don't really look like people, but they look good. You don't know what they're about, but you know they're modern, and you approve. You will learn about them. You're a quick learner.*

Richard guides you toward a table across the room. A man with white hair is standing with his back to you. Mr. Wheeler's father? He turns. You stare a little. He is young and handsome. Very. Although it is early spring, he has a tan. He has brilliant blue eyes and very white teeth. He smiles and holds out his hand, saying, "Hi. I'm George Lynes." You will know him for a good many years, and you pay little attention when he makes a change around 1940 and begins calling himself George Platt Lynes.

He is friendly, not at all haughty as you expected someone on their way to being famous might be. He asks you what you'd like to drink, gesturing at the table that has been set up like a bar. You hesitate. "Let me make you a Manhattan," he says. "A Perfect Manhattan. It's the only drink I know how to make well besides a Martini. And somehow you don't strike me as a Martini person." He rattles on. You are enchanted. "Actually Monie makes a better Martini than I do. He just waves the cork of the vermouth bottle toward the glass." You have no idea what he is talking about but you love it. And him. You're glad you wore your navy blue suit.

A beautiful dark-haired woman is standing not far away in a burgundy velvet dress. George sees you looking at her and says, "I know, it's a little late in the season for velvet, but it suits her. She's a very velvet kind of person. Come over here and meet Fidelma." He hands you your glass of dark reddish brown liquid. It goes well with the beautiful woman's dress.

George Lynes introduces you to the beautiful woman, whose name is Fidelma Cadmus. She seems a little uneasy. Perhaps because she is so beautiful. Very dark with enormous eyes. She introduces you gently to her brother, who is standing beside her and who has just turned in your direction. He resembles her in a fair-haired way. He fixes you with the same large eyes, but in sapphire blue. Also very intense. You begin to feel a little dizzy. Is everyone here going to be wonderful-looking? You were considered good-looking in Sandusky, but this is something else altogether. The brother's name is Paul Cadmus. He has the same gentle manner as his sister. "Tell me something about the paintings," you say, feeling you have said the right kind of thing at a party like this.

Paul Cadmus turns, "Well, this is one of mine," he says, waving at a smallish painting of a man's head with dark, wavy hair.

"He's very handsome," you say.

Paul says, "I like it. I think I did a good job. I did it in Mallorca." He peers closely at the painting. "It needs dusting with a damp cloth."

"Don't do it yourself," his sister warns, pulling him away by one arm. They are a wonderful couple. Something like a grown-up Hansel and Gretel.

A tall man with a brush-cut hairstyle, similar to the one Paul is sporting, is telling a story to a group near you. He has an unusual way of speaking, as though he were from England but not quite. You mention this to Paul, who laughs and says, "He is from Wisconsin, which is very much like England." And laughs some more. The tall man is saying, "But she has the sharpest knee," and everyone surrounding him laughs. "God, not that tired old tale again," someone says near your ear. "Glenway should get some new jokes. I've been hearing that one since 1933."

"Lincoln," Paul says, "you don't know my sister. Fidelma, this is Lincoln Kirstein." Paul politely introduces you, also. Fidelma doesn't seem to quite know what to do with her glass but finally extricates her hand and shakes the big man's hand. He shakes yours also, but he is obviously not interested in you. He is big, this Lincoln. Almost lumbering. But handsome. Something like a Roman

senator in a black suit. You're pleased with yourself for thinking up that comparison.

With Lincoln is a handsome, dark young man who looks like Tyrone Power, you think. Could it be? He reaches around from behind Lincoln and says, "My name is Pete Martinez." You like him immediately. He has fantastic eyelashes and is wearing a suit with, you notice, suspenders under his open jacket. "Are you having a good time?" he asks. You tell him far more than that. You ask him what he does. He says he dances. Your first dancer, and a male one at that. This is the major leagues.

Pete is from Mexico. He is charming. He drags you away to talk to "some young people."

You pass a man with curly hair piled up on top of his head and a nose like—what? A perfect triangle? He is speaking quickly in French with the man called Glenway. "Come on," Pete says. "Jean Cocteau. You won't get a chance to talk anyway." You're impressed. You thought Jean Cocteau was a woman whose name was pronounced like that of Jean Arthur, the actress. Now you know it's pronounced to rhyme with dawn. *You do not tell Pete Martinez this. You ask him who Glenway is as you follow him across the room. "Famous writer. He's one of your hosts. Doesn't actually write. Just talks."*

"Pete, darling, come here a moment," a pointy-faced man with bright eyes calls out as you pass. Pointy faces and bright eyes seem to abound tonight. Mr. Pointy Face is accompanied by a large black man. Handsome, of course. Before you can be introduced the black man says, "Let's go, Sess, there's nobody here." "But I'm here, darling, isn't that enough?" the fair-haired man trills in response. It obviously isn't and the black man wanders away into the mob. You're sorry. You've never spoken to a black person or shaken a black hand before. You have only seen them at a distance in Sandusky. The pointy-faced man with light hair says, "I'm Cecil Beaton," taking your hand. He has a rather kind expression and seems to want to make up for his rude friend. "Ignore him," he says, gesturing with his head toward the black man's back across the room. "He's just miffed because he thought Josephine Baker was going to be here. She's in town and he thinks she's going to put him in her next revue at the Folies-Bergère. Fat chance."

"I think she is here," Pete says. "Over there in the yellow."

"Oh, God, and Lester went in the other direction. Excuse me, I have to go find him and drag him over there, or there won't be any fun for Mother later tonight." Cecil smiles and shakes your hand politely before pushing his way toward his friend through what is now a serious throng.

"Want to look around?" Pete asks. You nod. You're feeling kind of speechless. All these famous foreigners in all these different colors. You walk down a hall.

You pass several bedrooms. One with a double bed. One with a single one. "Who lives here?" you ask Pete, who is in the door of the kitchen at the end of the hall. "George and Monroe and Glenway," he answers. Before you can ask your next question, he says, "Monroe and George sleep in the same bed. Glenway sleeps alone. He used to sleep with Monroe, but that was a while ago."

George's back is to you as he gets something out of the refrigerator. Over his shoulder he says, "Quite a while ago—1928 to be exact." Pete doesn't seem embarrassed. Neither does George, who asks Pete to take a large plate of stuffed hard-boiled eggs into the living room. You don't feel embarrassed anymore either. Perhaps it's the Perfect Manhattan.

George says, "I'll bet you'd be fun to kiss." You can't believe it when you hear yourself say, "They didn't think so in Sandusky."

"Sandusky doesn't know what it's missing," George says as he pushes by with a second platter of stuffed eggs. "Come on, have another drink."

You do. You meet many more good-looking young men. Some beautiful women, too, but they are definitely outnumbered. George nods to a beautiful blonde and says, "Say hello to Helen. She's my favorite model." You do. Helen is actually quite a lot of fun. As you talk, you realize you've seen her photograph in every magazine you've picked up for the last year. And here she is. A real person. Somehow you thought models were like paper dolls that are tucked away in a drawer when not in use, but Helen is definitely a real person, having a drink on upper Madison Avenue. You get excited all over again.

Across the room, you notice Lincoln Kirstein saying something to Paul Cadmus. Paul's blue eyes fly open in surprise; he says something back to Lincoln, who laughs and goes over to talk to Fidelma, seated in a chair nearby talking to no one. "Who is Lincoln?" you ask Pete, still by your side. "My boyfriend," Pete says. "He runs the School of American Ballet and he put a ballet company together this year for the Metropolitan Opera. That's where I'm working. And he's on the board of directors of the Museum of Modern Art. My God, everyone is here." Pete points me toward the door. "There's Frederick Ashton." You don't know who Frederick Ashton is. You look blank. "The English choreographer." Pete sounds a little put out with you. Mr. Ashton looks a lot like Cecil Beaton, only shorter. Cecil himself is now in the doorway with his black friend and an exotic lady in a yellow lace dress. She has to be Josephine Baker. Despite the spring weather she is carrying a large fox-fur. She is glamorous. "We're going up to Harlem to Small's Paradise," Cecil screams across the room to no one in particular.

"Poor Small's Paradise," Pete mutters to himself behind you. He doesn't seem happy. He keeps eyeing Lincoln talking to Fidelma. A tall man passes behind you and presses himself against you rather insistently. He seems to have an

*erection. You say, "Pardon me, am I in your way?" He goes away. You're get-
ting the hang of things.*

*Later Richard Roehmer comes over and says he's planning to go downtown
with the tall man who pressed his body against you. Do you want to go along?
You say no, but he can drop you off if they're taking a cab to the Village.*

*You thank George Lynes and Monroe Wheeler and Glenway Wescott, who
says archly, cocking his head to one side, "But we didn't even get a chance to
talk. And you look as though you'd be so interesting." He has probably said that
to hundreds of people, even some this evening, but even so it is nice to hear. No
one has ever said that to you before.*

*You leave. Your hosts have invited you to come again, and George Lynes has
gone so far as to take your telephone number. You will in fact see them all many
more times. You will almost sleep with Monroe Wheeler once, but change your
mind because you'd be cheating on so many different people. You understand
that Monroe likes to sleep with someone slim and blond and young, but despite
his sexual adventures, no one will replace George at the center of his love.*

*You will never go to the country house the three men share, Stone-blossom.
You feel that would be pushing your luck with Monroe. Of them all, he is the
most attractive.*

*But right now you know none of this, this spring evening in 1937. The taxi
takes you down Park Avenue. It isn't truly dark. The sky is a dark gray behind
the Grand Central tower at the foot of the avenue. A long chain of green lights
simultaneously change to red far down the slope ahead of you. The buildings
that line the avenue are only about ten stories high, but they seem clifflike to
you, full of twinkling lights.*

*The streetlights change to green and you are sailing down the avenue again.
This is glamour. This is New York. You are on your way to a tiny apartment in
Greenwich Village, but you congratulate yourself. You've made it to the city.
Where everyone is. Where everything is. Where everything is possible.*

—∞∞—

George Platt Lynes

*He was a man of great sensitivity, extraordinary beauty, made
like a Greek statue, super-real.*

—*Lisa Fonssagrives*

If George Lynes and Lincoln Kirstein did not renew their schooldays
acquaintance at Kirk and Constance Askew's salon, they strengthened
it there. All the young movers and shakers in the New York art world
made a point of visiting the Askews at their Sunday-afternoon parties.
These parties were known as "the Askews' saloon" since the cocktails
served there made it seem more of a drinking resort than a true salon.
But it served a salon's purpose.

Kirk Askew was assiduous in matching up artists with other artists,
artists with potential patrons, as well as artists who could use a new lover
and lovers who could use a new artist. Askew himself was the director of
the Durlacher Brothers Gallery and primarily dealt in Old Masters.
Later he had his own gallery and extended his representation to artists
he had come to know at his "saloon."

Constance Askew was blond and unaggressive and had a surrealistic
quality to her personality: dreamy and speaking in a manner that was
frequently hard to follow. Of course the Surrealists loved her, and she
was often painted by them. Her portrait by Pavel Tchelitchev is one of
his best.

In *No Intermissions*, the dancer and choreographer Agnes de Mille had this to say at a slightly later date: "Kirk Askew, a gallery owner, and his wife, Constance, gave parties in their brownstone on East Sixty-first Street. Couples might be interracial or hetero or homosexual and the *mariage blanc* (Paul and Jane Bowles, Lincoln Kirstein and Fidelma Cadmus, Carl Van Vechten and Fania Marinoff, Marc Blitzstein and Eva Goldbeck) were [*sic*] accepted, but flirtations were discreet. Homosexuals had tremendous power in the theater of the day but there was no camping at the Askews and it was considered bad form even to allude to the subject openly." She doesn't say that Mr. Askew was among the homosexual married men, though his marriage may have been a *blanc* one.

In the early 1930s, the Askews had competition from Muriel Draper, whose parties served more truly as a salon. Draper was not solely devoted to hustling for her friends and was actually interested in meeting and helping develop talent.

George Lynes was in need of the contacts he met socializing. In 1933 he embarked on fashion photography, as it had become evident that portraits were never going to cover his bills. He had a friend, Fredericka Fox, who knew her way around the fashion business in New York, and she became a kind of unofficial agent who brought him work. Although he hadn't planned to go to Europe that summer, he did go unexpectedly when Barbara Harrison offered to pay the rent on his apartment/studio while he was absent. The wealthy Miss Harrison must have enjoyed her jaunts around Europe with Monroe Wheeler and had evidently found the jaunts went better when George was present.

During this summer, George's brother, Russell, was also in Europe touring with friends and was involved in an automobile accident in which one of their party was killed. Stranded while sorting out accident reports and body shipping, Russell spent a lot of time with another member of the party, Mildred Akin. This friendship resulted in their marriage in May 1934. George's path crossed with theirs in Salamanca, and Mildred wrote her husband later, "I thought when I first saw that handsome young man with the brilliant eyes that in some way, he would play a part in my life. It had nothing to do with love. I don't know what it was. I was furious not be asked to go on the picnic"—a picnic that had been organized by George with Monroe and Glenway.

Back in New York, Fredericka Fox was replaced by Mary Conover Brown as an unofficial agent. In those early days fashion magazines and society overlapped. Pretty debutantes were often asked to model. It was all rather casual, and photographers had to know the right people. Evidently Mary Brown was one of "the right people." She built George Lynes's business rapidly and later married Paul Mellon, whose father had donated the funds to build the National Gallery of Art in Washington and his own collection to fill it.

With his business growing, Lynes moved to 214 East 58th Street, a former speakeasy. (Prohibition had been repealed in 1933, but the state liquor authority could revoke a bar's license if it served homosexuals.) Despite the new studio's low ceilings, Lynes managed to work photographic wonders there. It was at this time Monroe Wheeler, Glenway Wescott, and he decided to share digs, and it was Lynes who found the apartment at 48 East 89th Street. He wrote his mother in August 1934, "We will have seven rooms, six windows on Eighty-ninth, and though it is not a modern building, there are all modern improvements so desirable in kitchen and bathroom." It was furnished with Wheeler and Wescott's furniture from Paris and the best of Lynes's parents' furniture. His mother, in moving to their country house in North Egremont, Massachusetts, seems to have relinquished her antiques without a murmur. Since most of them were the work of her husband's ancestor George Platt, she may have had little interest in them. Her son used these antiques to advantage in his decoration. Photographs of the interiors where he lived show antique tables, chairs, and bookcase mixed with more modern furniture and paintings. He had an unconventional taste and must have been among the first to decorate in a neo-Victorian style.

George exchanged letters with Katherine Anne Porter during this period, and one reveals his basic attitude toward photography: "In general, at present, I am hating photography, all the necessary and commercial faces of it, to which, thanks to my economic disorder, I am having to devote my energies. I like to photograph for fun, for the hell of it. And just lately I have turned out some jobs that have satisfied not even the purchasers. I have always had my ups and downs, and, though I may never reach the point of doing consistently good work, I will probably strike a richer vein and for a while produce something I like. Not really pathetic, not yet."

In October he had a show at the Julien Levy Gallery, which included his portrait of Miss Porter and other celebrities, some outdoor scenes, and two nudes, one female and one male.

In a letter to Gertrude Stein at this time he wrote, "I have been remembering my devotion to you and the inevitable influence you have

George Platt Lynes in his apartment at 48 East 89th Street, N.Y.C., circa 1934. (Courtesy of Bernard Perlin. Reprinted by permission)

had on my life, the valuable or merely pleasant hours I have spent with you, that I met you at the critical age of eighteen and am now at the somewhat critical age of twenty-seven." It was true that the period of trying to find himself was over. His career was now truly launched. He never wrote to Gertrude Stein again.

George Platt Lynes and George Platt Lynes II, his nephew, 1938. (Collection of Robert W. Bishop. Reprinted by permission)

From this time on the true George Platt Lynes took form. As his finances prospered, so did his debts. Probably with no real intention of doing so, he styled himself on the young Regency rakes of a century before. He spent money on art he could often not afford and had to resell later. The work of some of his closest friends he kept: such as Cadmus's portrait of his mother and the painting of Glenway Wescott, Monroe Wheeler, and himself under a tree in front of the Stone-blossom house; drawings of himself by Jean Cocteau and Pavel Tchelitchev; and a large portrait of him by Tchelitchev that was never finished. But his Marsden Hartleys, Yves Tanguys, Paul Klees, and his Picasso came and went.

He furnished his residence with great style and spent large sums getting the paint and paper exactly right. He loved giving gifts and entertaining. In sum, he had an exact idea of the effect that he wanted to create, the personality he wanted to be. The glittering spider in the center of a fascinating web, into which those who amused him were drawn. Once there, they also amused themselves very well. He was no snob, in that he didn't want to know people simply because they were wealthy or famous, unlike his competitor Cecil Beaton. Because he believed himself to be special he wanted only to be surrounded by those who appreciated him. He had no great eagerness to please unless he found the other person pleasing. It is almost wonderful that he had the successful career that he had, and as long as he had it. Clearly, he always considered "himself" to be the fascinating center of his life, not the fact that he was a "famous photographer."

George Lynes's career as a photographer of ballet began at the same time as his fashion photography took off. He had already done his first portrait of Balanchine in 1934. In 1935 he photographed the ballet *Errante* for the newly formed American Ballet, as the Balanchine/Kirstein company was then called. *Errante* had originally been created for Ballets 1933 in Paris with "costumes, lighting, and dramatic effects" by Pavel Tchelitchev. Tchelitchev re-created the ballet, and Tamara Geva and William Dollar danced the leads. Geva had begun life as Tamara Gevergeva and had been the first of Balanchine's many wives. At this time, she was no longer Mrs. Balanchine, which did not seem to interfere with her enthusiasm as the prima ballerina of this new company.

His ballet work didn't improve Lynes's finances. He did his photographs for cost, which was to lead to a major falling out with Lincoln Kirstein in the years before the photographer's death.

The romantic event of 1935 was the marriage of Barbara Harrison to Glenway Wescott's younger brother, Lloyd. Barbara Harrison had followed her friends from Paris to New York. There she met handsome Lloyd Wescott and they fell in love. The wedding was a quiet one, and after a honeymoon in Europe the newlyweds installed themselves on a large estate in New Jersey. They planned to develop a model farm, raising prize breeds of cows as well as other farm animals.

Some felt Wescott and Wheeler had dangled the handsome Lloyd in front of the heiress's nose to insure that her fortune did not fall into hands that would spirit her away from them. Jacques Guérin, Wescott's

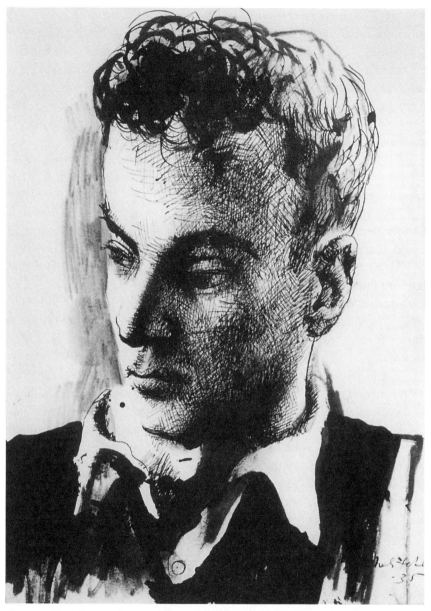

George Platt Lynes *by Pavel Tchelitchev, circa 1934 (ink on paper, 13" x 9¹/₂").*
(Collection of Mr. and Mrs. George Platt Lynes II. Reprinted by permission)

former lover, felt Barbara Harrison was becoming romantically interested in him and that she had been encouraged to come to New York
with the idea of incorporating her into the Wescott family.

Jerry Rosco, currently writing a biography of Glenway Wescott, was told a different version of the events by Wescott himself, which is probably closer to the truth. In the summer of 1929, Jacques Guérin broke off his relationship with Glenway Wescott while Wescott was making a long family visit to the United States. Guérin's intention was to court Barbara Harrison and marry her in Wescott's absence. Guérin then wrote Wescott that his attempts at heterosexual lovemaking had been a failure and that he wanted Wescott back.

Guérin's attempt to woo and win Barbara Harrison was widely separated in time from the heiress's visit to New York in 1934 when she met Lloyd Wescott and they fell in love.

Glenway Wescott did return to Paris and resume his relationship with Guérin before subsequently moving to New York. This entire sequence makes Guérin's claim that Barbara Harrison was spirited away from him by Wescott and Wheeler highly dubious. It also ignores the fact that Barbara Harrison was a woman with a will of her own; a woman used to making her own decisions. It is likely that she and her husband were truly in love and she probably welcomed the idea that she would be even more closely linked to her longtime friends once married to Lloyd Wescott.

George Lynes's first assistant, Jane Kemper, had just been replaced with a Princeton freshman, James Ogle. Ogle worked for Lynes until 1940 when he married Jane Kemper and struck out on his own as a photographer. Shortly after becoming Lynes's assistant, Ogle had aroused the interest of Lincoln Kirstein, who invited him to the ballet and other outings. He saw being squired about by Kirstein in an innocent light until finally one day Lynes said to him, "You have to stop acting like a damned chorus girl," and it dawned on Ogle that he was being courted, which ended the matter there and then.

Some of the lessons James Ogle learned from George Platt Lynes were these:

"The nose shadow is either directly under the nose or clearly on one side. Nothing in between."

"There can only be one reflection in the eye."

"Print for the highlights."

He remembers a discussion between Lynes and Wheeler about the difficulty of seeing through a new ground-glass Rolliflex lens. The photographer had experimented with improving the transmission of light by coating the lens with Vaseline. Wheeler said, "A new use for Vaseline," and Lynes blushed bright pink.

Self-portrait by George Platt Lynes, circa 1935 (silver print). (Courtesy of Peter Hiler. Reprinted by permission)

Ogle also remembers Lynes saying to his sister-in-law one day while she was visiting his studio, "Mildred, I have to take your picture while you still have your figure." By this he meant a nude portrait. Which he did, recording her magnificent figure magnificently. Ogle also remembers his boss drinking green tea exclusively in the studio, to remain slim, when he first came to work for him.

The big event for George Lynes and his assistant in 1936 was the fabled Paper Ball, also called Le Cirque des Chiffonniers, held as the final event of a festival concocted by Everett "Chick" Austin, the director of the Wadsworth Atheneum. Called the Hartford Festival, it was sponsored by a group called the Friends and Enemies of Modern Music and the Wadsworth Atheneum. Gene Gaddis, the museum's historian, has written, "This marked the height of the museum's reputation in the 1930s." Lynes was engaged to do portraits of the artists involved.

The festival began with "Music of Today from Connecticut Valley," followed by a series of films arranged by Iris Barry called "Early Masterpieces of Cinematographic Art." Then there was a performance of Stravinsky's *Les Noces* and the American premiere of Erik Satie's *Socrate* with "mobile" sets by Alexander Calder. *Seranata*, a ballet by Balanchine, was also introduced. (The same ballet was referred to as *Magic* by Pavel Tchelitchev, who designed the costumes and sets.) Eugene Berman designed a set for the background of one of the concerts, which included music by Virgil Thomson.

All of these artists had their portraits done by Lynes for a lavish souvenir program. The museum queried if Lynes had a photograph in which Eugene Berman looked other than "a little bit pathetic," as they put it. Lynes replied, "The photograph of Berman was his choice and mine. I am afraid he always looks rather pathetic."

The museum also asked Lynes to lower his fee for the pictures, which he did not do.

The Paper Ball—or the Ragpickers' Ball, which would be a more accurate translation of its French title—was held on the closing evening of the festival in the Avery Memorial Annex. Newly built in the Bauhaus style, the annex was transformed by Tchelitchev, using newspaper. Austin himself wrote that magically the artist made "the court of the museum . . . into a sort of newspaper heaven of incredible delicacy, shimmering with extraordinary color." Finished, it was a florid eighteenth-century opera house with cartoonish occupants peering from opera boxes, separated by twisted paper columns and paper balustrades. Paper garlands hung from the ceiling of the glass-topped courtyard. It must have been quite something, this thrilling kind of magic environment where the cream of Hartford society frolicked with many New York guests, all wearing paper costumes.

The ménage à trois that Platt Lynes now shared on East 89th Street was functioning well. Glenway Wescott had settled down to write a book as well as a ballet scenario about the ornithologist Audubon. He won a prize in a contest (organized by Lincoln Kirstein) with his scenario, but neither his book nor the ballet ever saw the light of day.

Wescott's own career never fully recovered from his move to New York. He spent an enormous amount of time writing letters, talking at great and brilliant length at parties, but wrote only a few books after this time. Did his writer's block stem from Lynes's presence in the life Wescott had once shared with Wheeler alone? As Lynes's career flourished, Wescott's diminished. Perhaps they both needed Wheeler to guide and encourage them, and he didn't have the resources to inspire both. Or perhaps Wescott, who also became romantically attached to Lynes, assumed a mentor's role for the younger man and depleted his own creative abilities.

Monroe Wheeler, on the other hand, through his contact with Lincoln Kirstein, became a member of the Museum of Modern Art's Junior Advisory Council, then director of the museum's publications, and soon after director of its exhibitions, a post he held until his retirement.

The sexual relationship among the three men, however it was worked out, was not exclusive. Lynes evidently had a romance with the children's book illustrator Clement Hurd. (Hurd was to become well-known later for the book *Goodnight Moon*.) Lynes photographed Hurd's handsome body both nude in his studio and sprawled naked over a large rock in the woods.

In 1937, Lynes, Wheeler, and Wescott began spending their weekends at the house provided for them by Lloyd and Barbara Harrison Wescott on the five-hundred-acre farm they had purchased in Clinton, New Jersey. The old colonial house was refurbished by the Wescotts and given the romantic name Stone-blossom by Glenway Wescott. George wrote to Katherine Anne Porter in 1938, "You would never know Stone-blossom. There is an acre of lawn, and a little newly-planted flower garden, and there are new stone walls and new trees. Why aren't you here?" The wing George added to the house was called the Bombay Wing, as it had been paid for with the profits from a major photo shoot done for a businessman from that city.

Other expenses for the new country home were met by Lynes's boring but lucrative job photographing the three hundred members of the Vassar graduating class for their yearbook. His money paid for all the landscaping and the antiques and the primitive oil paintings that decorated the house. Of the three men, George Platt Lynes seems to have been the only one who felt he owed the Wescotts something for their

Stone-blossom in the snow, George Platt Lynes in foreground, circa 1938. (Courtesy of Bernard Perlin. Reprinted by permission)

Daybed with needlepoint cover, petit point by George Platt Lynes, design by Jared French. (Collection of John Connolly and Ivan Ashby. Photo by Ethan Winslow. Reprinted by permission)

generosity, and he spent large amounts of his own money improving their property. Wescott and Wheeler seem to have accepted it as their due, having lived so long already from the largesse of others. The attitude of Wescott, as an artist, is easier to understand; there are many precedents for wealthy patrons supporting the arts. Wheeler is more difficult to comprehend. Intelligent and charming as he was, he seemed always to be sharing benefits that were intended for others. (Many years later, after Glenway's death, he was to be ousted from the home provided by the Wescotts, so perhaps resentment *had* been felt through the years.)

The three men were to remain together in New York and at Stoneblossom until 1943, when George ended his relationship with Monroe Wheeler and moved out.

During those six years, the house served as a much-loved weekend retreat for the men and their friends. They commissioned a painting by Paul Cadmus, called *Conversation Piece* (1940), of the three of them lounging under a tree in front of the house. In the painting are many of the small clues to this happy time in their lives: a copy of *U.S. Camera* magazine with a photo by George on the cover, a copy of *Time* with Monroe's friend the pianist Elly Ney on the cover, a print of a pilgrim hawk (Glenway had written a short novel titled *The Pilgrim Hawk*).

George had taken up needlepoint during this period and his chef d'oeuvre was a large daybed cover, designed for him by Jared French. Two lovers (male and female) lie intertwined, having obviously just made love. This daybed cover still exists, now owned by John Connolly and Ivan Ashby, as well as a number of pillows and chair coverings done by Lynes.

In terms of income and stability, these were Lynes's golden years. He was the leading fashion photographer in the United States, and he was also doing portraits of all the most famous and fashionable people in the country. In addition, he was photographing the increasingly successful ballet companies and productions launched by Balanchine and Kirstein, as well as adding to his ever-growing collection of nudes. His nude studies include some females but were largely males. These male studies were, of course, unpublishable in the climate of the time.

His life in the late 1930s was glamorous and fashionable. He had gone to Paris for the collections in 1937 and made contact with many old friends. Jean Cocteau, who had visited him in New York with his lover Marcel Khill, was there, of course, as were Edith Sitwell, Man Ray, Jacques Guérin (the fragrance baron), and many others. Lynes toured an

Lillian Gish by George Platt Lynes, circa 1938. (Collection of Bernard Perlin. Courtesy of Mr. and Mrs. George Platt Lynes II. Reprinted by permission)

international exposition in Paris and wrote that the new Trocadéro "looks like anything that might be built for an American University," and finished by declaring "everything else very hard and bleak and German-looking." He was no friend to modern architecture.

Upon his return that spring, he moved to a much larger studio at 640

Madison Avenue between Fifty-ninth and Sixtieth Streets in a two-story "tax-payer," as these low buildings on prime real estate were called. In his biography, Russell Lynes describes this studio: "The space George rented was (or he made) ideal. Its center was a large, high-ceilinged, squarish room, a studio with space for constructing substantial backgrounds and for props stacked in the corner. There were things from the flea market, stuffed animals from a taxidermist, rectangular boxes in various sizes painted white and strong enough for a model to stand on or lean against, pieces of driftwood, a paint-stained ladder [which he used as a prop for Jean Cocteau and Gloria Swanson and others], a piece of Victorian iron fence, egg crates, anything that took light handsomely and added ornament or character or entertainment to a sitting. In another corner was a jukebox that filled the studio with Gershwin and Cole Porter and the voices of his favorite jazz singers."

From *The Complete Photographer*, a book of the period, we have this description of his equipment: "In this new studio he used lights of a size, intensity and flexibility he had not worked with before, and he supplemented them with a skylight he had installed. Mr. Lynes' equipment included a trough light for stage effects and backlighting, a 5,000 watt spot which is used in combination with other lights in photographing groups or as the sole source of illumination on single models, three 2,000 watt spots, one of which is fixed on a boom, one flood and one movie flood which is used for backlighting." The descriptions of his studio and his equipment suggest that the major-league photographer's studio originated with George Platt Lynes, right down to the mood music.

His brother adds, in his comments on this studio, "He had two darkrooms, one for developing and one for printing, but he farmed out orders to commercial laboratories for publicity prints-by-the-dozen and out-size blow-ups." He also describes Lynes's office, which he says the photographer redecorated regularly as the "whim" took him. At one point it was covered in dark green wallpaper and was graced with a large blowup of a postcard of Ingres's painting *Oedipus and the Sphinx* with conductor Leopold Stokowski's profile montaged over Oedipus and Greta Garbo over the Sphinx.

There was no air-conditioning in New York in the 1930s, and in summertime the photographer's work was arduous. With only fans to cool the studio, the hot lights kept it degrees hotter than the sweltering outdoors. George wrote to his mother, "Friday . . . we consumed two dozen Coca-Colas and fifty pounds of ice . . . the models sweat, the dresses wilted, everybody felt a little sick." Studio photographs show Lynes and

George Platt Lynes's studio office at 640 Madison Avenue, N.Y.C., circa 1938. (Private collection. Reprinted by permission)

the retoucher Bob Bishop naked from the waist up. They must have enjoyed showing off their excellent bodies.

When it came time to do fur coats in August, Lynes devised a wall of blocks of ice to photograph against. When the shooting was over, his assistant, James Ogle, simply threw the ice out the window onto an adjoining roof, which, unfortunately, was a movie theater. The ice bombardment emptied the theater, to the manager's ire.

On the artistic side, Lynes had four photographs included in the Museum of Modern Art show *Photography: 1839–1937*. His portrait of Jean Cocteau with the familiar paint-spattered ladder was reproduced in the catalog. This wasn't Lynes's first appearance at the Museum of Modern Art. He had done a photomural in 1932 (which had wound up in the men's room at the Wadsworth Atheneum), and his airbrushed montage photo called *Sleepwalker* had gotten a lot of attention in the 1935 *Fantastic Art, Dada and Surrealism* show. Lincoln Kirstein and Monroe Wheeler had a lot to do, of course, with his appearances in these exhibitions.

The 1937 show, however, was probably the first to legitimize photographs as museum exhibition materials. It was the first one of its size (891 prints), and, what was especially important for Lynes, it was considered a kind of retrospective of all American photographers to be taken seriously as artists.

Lynes always preferred to do his fashion shoots with models whom he liked personally. Two important models of the prewar period were Lisa Fonssagrives, then married to the dancer and choreographer Ferdinand Fonssagrives (they were both Danish and she had begun her career as a dancer), who was later to marry the photographer Irving Penn, and Liz Gibbons, who became a Condé Nast editor and worked with Lynes in Hollywood in the 1940s. Laurie Douglas was another important model, one Lynes largely created. He did photographs of her when she first arrived in New York in the late thirties and they immediately made her a top model.

All models who worked with him were impressed by his beauty and the physique he maintained with regular workouts at the gym. Fonssagrives has remembered him working "stripped to the waist . . . he moved like a dancer. Unlike most people, his feelings were written on his forehead. He was a man of great sensitivity, extraordinary beauty, made like a Greek statue, super-real."

He often worked in a denim mechanic's coverall, in which he was painted by Tchelitchev, and sometimes in dark pants and a much unraveled, out-at-the-elbows, dark red Berkshire School sweater. Both Tennessee Williams and Cecil Beaton were photographed in that very recognizable sweater, as was a male nude.

Liz Gibbons remembered posing for him in a night class he taught in photography. One of his students, Clifford Coffin, was obviously enamored of his teacher, much to Lynes's irritation. Coffin went on to a major fashion photographer's career and also did many male nudes.

George Lynes was also fond of photographing the beautiful face of the actress Ruth Ford. She was part of the "family" of Lynes's friends, which included her brother Charles Henri Ford, who was Pavel Tchelitchev's longtime lover. She was a favorite model for the painter as well as for the photographer. Ruth Ford recalls, "It was the greatest thing that ever happened to me when George wanted me to come over to the studio and photograph me. I never had more fun in my life. . . . Pavlik [Tchelitchev] adored him."

She lived with her mother and brother at this time, and the photographer Henri Cartier-Bresson slept on their living room floor on his first

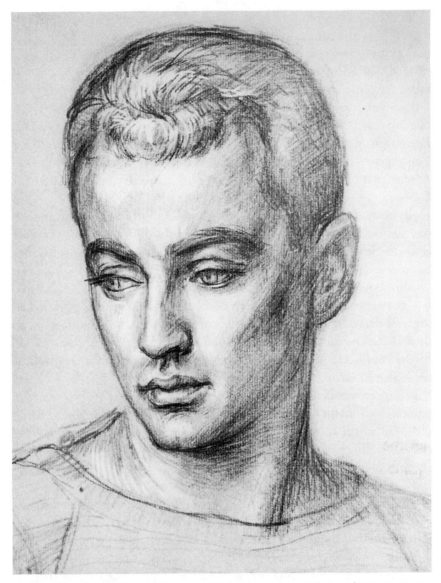

George Platt Lynes *by Paul Cadmus, 1938 (ink on paper, 11¹/₂" x 8³/₄"). (Collection of Mr. and Mrs. George Platt Lynes II. Courtesy of D. C. Moore Gallery, N.Y.C. Reprinted by permission)*

visit to New York. Then a beautiful young man, Cartier-Bresson was photographed by Lynes soulfully looking over a large cow's femur.

When Christopher Isherwood arrived in New York in 1939, he also posed for the photographer, whom he described in his diary as "prematurely grey haired, with the arrogant profile of a late Roman coin. . . ." The portrait shows the British novelist "peering out from behind a wooden property-pillar," and, according to Lincoln Kirstein, looking like "the rat with the nervous breakdown."

Judging from the quality of the reminiscences about George Platt Lynes, he obviously held a unique and exciting place in many people's lives. His brother remembered him in his apartment surrounded by beautiful and interesting people, giving them stringent directions on how to conduct their lives successfully while he worked on his needlepoint. He had all the necessary instincts and desires for conducting a salon.

In 1938 Lynes began a private project of photographing mythological scenes. The mythological series allowed the photographer to strip down young men and pose them as gods, the only way the public was likely to accept male nudes. Another explanation came from Monroe Wheeler, who claimed that this series was done at the urging of Barbara Harrison Wescott. She had always wanted to publish the photographer's work in some form, and her brother-in-law Glenway Wescott was writing his own version of myths, much as he had done earlier on the lives of the saints in *A Calendar of Saints for Unbelievers* in 1932.

Lynes wrote his mother in February 1938, "I have a studio full of stuffed animals, skunks and squirrels and rabbits and a raccoon and a woodchuck and a bluejay, which look extraordinary. There are plaster clouds hanging from the ceiling and marbleized drapery on the wall and a thicket of apple branches in one corner." He had a passion for stuffed animals, and Katharine Hepburn must have wandered in during this period because there is an unlikely photograph of her in a *Gone with the Wind*–style ruffled ballgown, with branches behind her and the stuffed raccoon at her feet. She also consented to have deer antlers attached to her head in one shot—the same antlers Lynes used on a male nude in his *Acteon* mythology photograph. Hepburn evidently did not find the proofs of these pictures amusing, though there are prints in private collections.

Only Russell Lynes in his biography mentions his brother's musical interests. The photographer, who could not carry a tune, was only interested in sopranos. He liked Lily Pons, renowned for her "Bell Song" in the opera *Lakmé*. Lily was fashionable, slender in a way few singers are, and also well-known for her jewels. George came to know her when he photographed her for *Town and Country* magazine. He also favored the heftier singers Kirsten Flagstad and Lotte Lehmann and photographed Lehmann very much to her advantage during his stay in Hollywood. He admired the compositions of Richard Strauss and liked to listen to Elizabeth Schwarzkopf singing Mozart.

Typical of Lynes was his pleasure at being loaned a recording of the singer Ninon Vallin singing Fauré art songs and his unwillingness to return it to his brother, saying, "This means more to me than it does to you." With remarks like this, a certain George Platt Lynes mind-set emerges.

In his work with the world of fashion, George Lynes encountered many people like the editor Diana Vreeland, whom he photographed in her home. Both Vreeland and he represented a new type in New York: people with a lot of drive who substituted taste for money in order to enter the world in which they wanted to live. The same thing could be said for Glenway Wescott and Monroe Wheeler, the painter Pavel Tchelitchev, and Cecil Beaton. Because of them, society became café society. Finally, because so many of these new types forced their way in, some people called it "Nescafé society." Old money for the most part retreated completely, and society came to be made up of these newcomers.

Glenway Wescott

What happened to Glenway Wescott? Many of his friends and lovers must have asked themselves that. At an early age, he was hailed as an important figure in the American literary world. With his first novel, *The Apple of the Eye* (1924), he was immediately recognized as an unusual talent, and his second novel, *The Grandmothers*, gained him the Harper Book Prize in 1927 and what seemed to be a firm position in a group of writers that included Hemingway and Fitzgerald. Yet this more than promising beginning was to wither away into years of little or no productivity. Gertrude Stein had already written perceptively about Wescott in 1933, saying, "He has a certain syrup, but it doesn't pour." A prophecy is a prophecy is a prophecy.

The Pilgrim Hawk was published in 1940; a short novel about a troubled marital relationship, it is, according to the poet and critic Bruce Bawer, "perhaps his most nearly perfect work—taut, subtle, and exquisitely ordered." In 1945 *Apartment in Athens*, a bestselling novel about a Greek family during the German occupation, was praised by *The New Yorker*'s Edmund Wilson and reintroduced Wescott to the American reading public. Yet five other novels were begun . . . and abandoned, and Wescott was to be known for the better part of his life as an inveterate partygoer, loquacious raconteur, and extra man about town. A president of the American Academy of Arts and Letters, he was an expert literary gamesman, and was regarded as a minor celebrity who loved to know other celebrities, not as a serious and important writer. His lack of enduring success as a writer must have eaten away at his self-esteem and was a great disappointment to his lifetime companion, Monroe Wheeler. Wheeler would have much preferred being linked to a great writer than a great party animal.

Also, Wescott always had grave misgivings about his sexual appeal because of his small penis. When Jared French painted his triptych of the three partners-in-love—Wescott, Wheeler, and Lynes—their nude figures were accurate frontal views, sexual parts and all. Wescott never failed to point out to others the difference in size between himself and the other two men. In French's triptych the difference doesn't seem all that great, actually, but size evidently loomed large in Wescott's mind.

Of the three members of the ménage à trois, Glenway Wescott seems to have been the most accommodating and the most determined to maintain his relationship with the others. In the early 1930s, before leaving Paris, he had an affair with Jacques Guérin, the wealthy owner of the Bourjois fragrance company. Guérin had for some time been a source of entertainment, dinners, parties, and travel for Wescott and Wheeler. Although the Frenchman was Wescott's lover for several years, there was never any question of Glenway leaving Monroe and George.

In this ambisexual society, Jacques Guérin seems to have thought it entirely reasonable to pursue the beautiful American heiress Barbara Harrison, once he had broken off with his American writer lover, and he was piqued when she married Lloyd Wescott, his former lover's brother.

We also know that Lloyd, before his marriage to Barbara Harrison, shared an apartment with George Lynes in New York and evidently had a brief liaison with the photographer. The shifting sexual preferences of this group were unusual for this or almost any period. Jealousy seems to have had low priority. Friends who visited Lloyd and Barbara Wescott's country home in New Jersey when George Lynes was present report that Lloyd and George were often demonstrative of their former affection for each other.

When Glenway Wescott and Monroe Wheeler took an apartment with George Lynes, Monroe and George shared a double bed and Glenway slept by himself. However, in the latter part of the 1930s, Wescott seems to have developed a passion for Lynes, which acquaintances seem to think may have been consummated but in the most nonchalant way possible on George's part. (Glenway was proud of his fellatio expertise, and his romance with George seems never to have been more than this occasional service.)

Monroe and George evidently regarded this activity as a temporary aberration on Glenway's part, one that would pass and allow the even tenor of the three-way to resume. Which it did. To the outside observer, Monroe and George were the true romance in this trio, and Glenway was the odd man out. The best comparison for this relationship might be to a traditional Chinese home where wives are added, not dismissed, and the first wife has to like it or lump it. Glenway did his best to like it.

One clue to the mystery of the three men's relationship lies in a letter George Lynes wrote to Glenway Wescott as early as October 1929: "It is more than affection that makes me want for you, and more particularly for myself, all the quality, the sureness and inquietude, the farewell kiss and the future blessing, of our brotherhood. You are the nourishment and no one of us has failed."

From this it would seem that Glenway provided support and inspiration for the young, not-yet photographer, and although Glenway was not to share George's body with Monroe, he had his share of George's attachment. In a curious way the two older men together provided what George wanted: sexual excitement and a great deal of attention. Wheeler seems to have been satisfied with his share of the bargain, but Wescott had to have felt somewhat left out.

Glenway Wescott had a unique public persona, one of great intensity. He spoke in torrents of unusual verbiage in an accent concocted from years on the Continent. He was surely far different from the boy who had left Wisconsin years before. The painter Bernard Perlin remembers visiting the studio of Paul Cadmus in the early 1940s with a friend. Glenway was evidently without a lover at this time and was called on the telephone by Paul to come down and inspect the young visitors. He duly arrived and, taken with Bernard, turned on his formidable charm. It worked on Perlin, who soon visited the writer for a weekend at Stoneblossom and became Glenway's lover for a time. This was a heady and interesting world for a young painter to gain admittance to, and Glenway must have seemed a fascinating entry to it.

As Glenway drifted ever more away from a major writing career, he also drifted into a confirmed habit of sexual voyeurism. In his journals (published after his death under the title *Continual Lessons*), he tells of this interest. He was probably pushed even further into this "outsider" relationship to sex when his sister took his lover Mark Pagano away

Glenway Wescott (right) with Fred Danieli at a rehearsal of the ballet Billy the Kid, *Ballet Caravan, 1938. (Courtesy of Anatole Pohorilenko. Reprinted by permission)*

from him in the mid-1940s. In this unusual family, his sister did not seem to feel any remorse or that her behavior was inappropriate. Glenway, in his journals, expresses little more than resignation and makes an effort to understand his sister's behavior.

In this entire network of friends, relatives, and lovers, not disrupting the relationships seems to have been the paramount consideration. Soon after her marriage to Lloyd Wescott, Barbara Harrison Wescott was supporting many members of the large Wescott family as well as providing a country home for Glenway and his outreach dependents: Monroe Wheeler and George Lynes. Her money kept her husband's never-profitable showplace farm afloat, his brother and his friends in relatively palatial surroundings, and an endless string of relatives with hard-luck lives afloat. By all appearances, these demands on her largesse seem never to have bothered her unduly.

Glenway's passion for celebrities led to a close relationship with the English writer and poet Edith Sitwell. They exchanged letters frequently and spent much time together when she was in New York. Lank and attenuated, Edith did not evidently turn any romantic attentions his way, though she had earlier been infatuated with the artist Pavel Tchelitchev, an equally poor choice for female affection. For some reason, at the peak of their friendship in the mid-1940s, she and Glenway gave a reading of *Macbeth* in semi-costume at the Museum of Modern Art. Those who attended found it difficult to understand, as both readers had affected but dissimilar accents. Even more difficult to understand was why they had wished to do the reading in the first place. It did little to enhance either performer's reputation.

When Dr. Alfred Kinsey entered Glenway Wescott's life, it was, in a way, a godsend. They met in 1949 and Wescott wrote in his diary: "Kinsey is a strange man, with a handsome, good sagacious face but with a haunted look—fatigue, concentration, and (surprising to me, if I interpret rightly) passionateness and indeed sensuality." The doctor's research *was* essentially voyeurism, and Glenway was of enormous assistance to him and his Institute for Sex Research at Indiana University. Wescott told Kinsey's biographer, James H. Jones, that he and Wheeler agreed to let the institute's photographer film them as they had sex. Kinsey observed the couple and noted the intensity of Wescott's orgasm, which caused his body to jackknife. Friends of the couple during this period find it hard to believe that Wheeler and Wescott had intercourse for the doctor to preserve on film, as their sexual life together had long been over. But, perhaps, some kind of sexual activity took place.

In New York and in New Jersey, Glenway set up orgies where the large, placid bulldoggy doctor would sit impassively on a couch in his three-piece suit and tie and watch the naked proceedings around him. One young man who attended a weekend orgy remembers being interested in another participant, and after the orgy proper they agreed to share a bed that night. Dr. Kinsey said, as the young men mounted the stairs, "Now, if you get into something during the night, be sure to call me." (The man recounts that he and his partner got into plenty during the night and they did *not* call Dr. Kinsey.) However it was, Glenway's interest in sex seems to have increased as his ability to concentrate or produce as an author declined. Friends also report that it was very possible that Glenway was, for a time, Dr. Kinsey's lover and that Kinsey also had a relationship with the beautiful William Christian Miller. Recent Kinsey biographies certainly suggest that neither of these eventualities was impossible.

During his involvement with Dr. Kinsey, Glenway Wescott moved more or less permanently to Haymeadows, the house provided for Monroe Wheeler and him on the new Wescott farm. From there, he commuted frequently to conduct his sexual revels in New York. Later, he and Monroe purchased a small apartment on Fifty-first Street, where

Monroe lived during the week and where Glenway stayed when in the city.

After his popular success with *Apartment in Athens* in 1945, his only substantial published work was *Images of Truth* (1962), a collection of essays about his literary friends Somerset Maugham and Katherine Anne Porter and other writers. In the country he occupied himself with his journals and letter writing. His correspondence was massive, and some friends thought that his creative energies were drained away by literary busywork, but more likely, he was filling time in what must have been a lonely existence in the isolated farmhouse, particularly during bleak New Jersey winters. The writer had lost his way, and Monroe Wheeler, unhappy with the sexual direction Glenway's life had taken, distanced himself from any hands-on attempt to give him guidance.

Russell Lynes wrote that Glenway Wescott "was a year younger than Wheeler, and though they shared and pursued many interests and enthusiasms, literary, artistic and otherwise, they were very different in bearing and manner. Glenway, a young man at the top of his literary form and reputation when George first met him, was tall, slender and blond, and handsome in a more conventional way than Wheeler. He spoke in a way that was mannered, a confected accent and rhythm that belied his rural Wisconsin origins and upbringing—a made-up, carefully nurtured sort of speech that was obviously pseudo-something but not at all clearly what. This deliberately cultivated, somewhat rococo manner of speaking was off-putting at first, but was quickly forgotten because of the quality of his conversation—witty, explicit, often gossipy and sometimes socially wicked. His intelligence was bullet-quick and accurate, and his perceptions, both personal and intellectual, were never predictable. He was a man who enjoyed scheming simply for its own sake, and he could create a character and manipulate it as readily and amusingly as he could assassinate one. Whichever he was doing, creating or manipulating, it was never tiresome; a parlor game, not an intellectual contact sport. He had a way of almost giggling when he was at his verbal naughtiest. He was the best, most invigorated conversationalist I have ever known, an opinion I shared with a great many of his friends. He was magic to listen to and converse with, and in my experience, as he was in George's, a loyal friend and sturdy advocate."

Glenway Wescott died on February 22, 1987, at eighty-five years of age.

Monroe Wheeler

Regarding a personality in retrospect, we often assume that a person *is* the image he projects; the image that most of the people who have known him in their lifetimes have agreed upon.

But as new information is assembled, as more and more pieces in the puzzle come together, another view sometimes emerges. This is certainly true of Monroe Wheeler. Monroe was seen as the dark, handsome, and calm presence who reigned behind the lives of Glenway Wescott, George Platt Lynes, and many others. He was intelligent and was sought out for his good counsel. He did not have perceptible problems, did not suffer from the inability to work that hounded Glenway Wescott or the inability to manage a career financially that plagued George Platt Lynes. Yet what would Wheeler's life have been if he hadn't had the opportunity to give shape and order to the helter-skelter arrangements made by his talented, creative lovers?

Monroe was obviously the dark and brooding "top" to the effervescent blondness of his lovers, who—whatever they may have been with others—were "bottoms" for him. He was still sexually active with much younger lovers when he was eighty. There was no doubt that Monroe always had a lot of sexual magnetism, and it is interesting to observe how he used it.

His first major liaison was with Glenway Wescott, whom he met in Chicago in 1919. Glenway must have been a budding, blushing, beaming farm boy in that epoch, brimming with talent and very, very ambitious. It was Glenway's talent that opened doors to the publishers of "little" magazines and to the art world that existed in Chicago. Monroe had no real career at this time, but moved in these bohemian circles because he was Glenway's companion.

Their move to New York City and then to France was supposedly prompted by Monroe's discomfort at being half of a recognized homosexual couple in the same city where his parents lived. So in 1925 they installed themselves in Villefranche and quickly became popular with the expatriate community.

A few years later Monroe caught the eye of Barbara Harrison, a wealthy and beautiful young American woman living in France. Who had the idea of creating a publishing house to issue special and finely made books is not known, but Harrison of Paris was founded in 1929, when Miss Harrison was twenty-five. It evidently ran on Barbara's money, Monroe's direction, and Glenway's literary advice and contributions, and it gave Monroe a career, Glenway a Paris publisher, and Miss Harrison something to do—and a reason to see Monroe regularly.

In a letter some years later, George Lynes described her home in the suburb of Rambouillet: "Her house is interesting. Made out of three small houses and decorated in the modern manner. The living room is . . . the largest room I've seen in a private house; all in white plaster and dark woodwork and hung with Courbets and Gauguins. The dining room is hung with Picassos and Derains. My room was silver and green and glass; a great many fish swam behind a panel in the bathroom; a poor Van Gogh hung above the bed." Although Lynes derides the sumptuousness, Barbara Harrison lived in enormous style worthy of her enormous fortune.

Monroe was the "brains" behind this publishing venture in which someone else was the more visible presence, a role he was to play many times in his life. Barbara Harrison was a beautiful, elegant, and self-assured young woman. She could play the role of the president of an interesting avant-garde publishing house perfectly. She seemed to want this role because of her interest in Monroe, which never came to anything, but also was never clearly and forthrightly rejected.

Her cars, her holidays, and her friends were all shared with Wheeler and Wescott, and the lavish lifestyle the two enjoyed while in France was due to her. Perhaps something of a "fag hag," she seemed to enjoy traveling and socializing with homosexual men and didn't mind being put on some kind of endless "hold" in her relationship with Monroe.

The style of the period made it unlikely that anyone ever discussed anything openly. Barbara Harrison probably never embarrassed herself by telling Monroe how she felt, and Monroe never jeopardized his situation by clarifying his feelings about men. Glenway, who talked endlessly and excruciatingly about everyone he knew, seems never to have brought up the fact that he was largely supported by Barbara Harrison during his lifetime.

In Wheeler's relationship with George Lynes, the young man declared his love to Monroe, and the somewhat astonished Monroe acquiesced. He guided George through an abortive attempt to become a writer and on to his career as a photographer, but at no time abandoned Glenway Wescott.

In the Depression, Wescott and Wheeler left Paris and moved back to New York, at the time Lynes was becoming well established there. They made the move in part because publishing costs had become less expensive in the United States. Shortly thereafter Wheeler found work as the director of publications at the newly founded Museum of Modern Art. It must have been through his connection with Lincoln Kirstein, who had seen something of Wheeler in Paris in 1933 and was a member of the museum's Junior Advisory Council. Wheeler had no museum experience or art-exhibition background, but was knowledgeable about trends in modern art and highly skilled at maneuvering through the shifting shoals of museum boards and art patrons. Someone who knew Wheeler during this period has said he was generally well liked, although a few people referred to him as "that snake." Kirstein was not wrong in placing Monroe Wheeler in his new position, but he probably would not have used his influence if he had not known Lynes since their Berkshire School days. Again, Monroe Wheeler's life took its shape and direction as the result of his lover's.

Wheeler remained at the museum for the rest of his working life, becoming director of exhibitions in 1941. He was never highly paid, but he had a structure to his life that Wescott and Lynes never had. Other than a brief flurry of interest in the German pianist Elly Ney in Europe in the early 1920s, he always had male lovers. His fling with Elly Ney may have been the result of a brief interest in assuming a heterosexual lifestyle, but given the pattern of his life, it is hard to believe that the affair would

Monroe Wheeler *by Paul Cadmus, circa 1940 (ink on paper, 8³/₄" x 11¹/₂"). (Collection of Paul Cadmus and Jon Andersson. Courtesy of D. C. Moore Gallery, N.Y.C. Reprinted by permission)*

have happened if Miss Ney had not been famous, well-connected in the art world, and in pursuit of him. In later years he had a series of young and lissome blond lovers such as Bill Miller and Ralph Pomeroy.

Monroe Wheeler and his intimates had little to offer except talent and charm. They had no money but plenty of ambition. Their ambition, however, was to be successful in the world of art and artists, not in the more commercial fields of advertising, publishing, banking, or law. These generally more lucrative endeavors would have required an ability to endure routine and boredom, and charm and beauty usually have little bearing. Monroe Wheeler preferred touring the South of France in Barbara Harrison's fabulous Mercedes-Benz roadster, meeting Jean Cocteau and Coco Chanel, or making reputations with his exhibitions at the Museum of Modern Art to drudging at a high-paying but humdrum office job.

He was never to have any money except that sent his way by wealthy friends. To an outside viewer, Monroe Wheeler was a handsome and seductive male presence who played a largely passive role in the lives of others, with his more flamboyant and energized lovers creating his opportunities and the structure of his life.

Monroe Wheeler was unable to return to Haymeadows after Glenway Wescott's death as the house had been sold by Lloyd Wescott. Wheeler had understood that he would have some use of the house, but this was not to be the case. The new owner, John Connolly, had no wish to share Haymeadows. Certainly with the acquiescence of Lloyd Wescott. Monroe Wheeler was never to see the house again, nor the many possessions he had shared with Glenway Wescott. The remainder of Wheeler's life was spent in the apartment in New York that he had shared with Wescott.

Monroe Wheeler died in 1988 at eighty-nine, and to the end he remained sexually active. At this level of intimate interaction he was not passive. This vigorous sexual appetite is perhaps the motivation behind the series of young lovers Wheeler had throughout his life. Sexually, he was always the dominant partner. Socially, he was the second-fiddle éminence grise.

Paul Cadmus

Paul Cadmus is a contemporary Hogarth and an artist whose work is not cluttered up with refinement.

—Henry McBride, art critic

The personal life of Paul Cadmus was never flamboyant. He has always lived quietly, sometimes with a partner, sometimes without, dedicating much of his time to his art. Although charming and gregarious, he seemed to have enjoyed solitude as much as the company of other people.

In the 1930s he lived in New York in a St. Luke's Place apartment, shared with Jared French, which both men used as a studio. Even when French married and moved to an apartment in the Chelsea neighborhood of New York, he continued to spend each day with Cadmus in his St. Luke's Place studio.

Cadmus was concentrating intensely on his work in the 1930s. He drew and painted in a number of different manners and techniques, drawing upon his strongly classical training and interests, and he arrived at the end of the decade at a style that was intensely his own, a style he maintained to the end of his life.

In 1935 he began work on a project for the Treasury Relief Art Project called *Aspects of Suburban Life*. Cadmus did several preliminary paintings, in a mixed oil-and-tempera technique, for what were to be murals. The first two, *Commuter Rush* and *Regatta*, are more loosely painted on

Two Boys on a Beach, No. 2 *by Paul Cadmus, 1938 (etching, edition of 75, 5$^1/_8$"*
x 7$^1/_8$"). (Author's collection. Courtesy of D. C. Moore Gallery, N.Y.C. Reprinted by
permission)

paper and have the look of preliminary sketches for more finished work
to come. The murals were to decorate a post office in Port Washington,
on Long Island's North Shore. As Lincoln Kirstein points out in his
book on Cadmus, this is *Great Gatsby* country, and everything F. Scott
Fitzgerald saw as insincere and nouveau riche in this world is Cadmus's
subject as well. That the murals were never completed is no surprise. It
would be hard to imagine that the locals would enjoy seeing themselves
parading on the walls of the post office as Cadmus saw them. The first
two paintings have a frenzied quality, but the four final submissions are
much more biting. Painted on wood and jammed with figures viewed
from below, the paintings of 1936—*Main Street, Golf, Public Dock*, and
Polo Spill—show overdressed, overweight, and overexcited citizens at
play. No one looks good except some of the working-class people, who
are obviously not there to take part in the fun. These paintings eventually wound up in a billiard room at the American embassy in Canada.
According to Kirstein, *Main Street* was ultimately returned to Paul Cadmus as being "unsuitable for a federal building," while the others went
into storage at the Smithsonian Institution.

A similar, smaller-scale painting of 1936 could easily have been called *Tennis*, but is instead titled *Venus and Adonis*. In it, a handsome, bare-chested, spoiled-looking tennis player is pulling himself out of the arms of an overweight, older, blond lady in a playsuit and sandals. Cupid, who is always part of the classic vocabulary in this kind of painting, is replaced here with the blond lady's squalling baby. Done in a loose, classical manner on canvas, this marked the end of Cadmus's working in this style.

In 1937, he did a beautiful painting of his sister, Fidelma, lying down with her dark hair spread about her. This painting on linen over board is all tenderness and consideration for the subject and is painted in great detail.

Paul Cadmus's life changed in 1937 when Jared French, his lover for a decade, married Margaret Hoening. Margaret had met both men at the Art Students League. They all shared similar interests in art and became friends. Acquaintances of that period have suggested that she had originally shown interest in Paul but had been quickly disillusioned about romantic possibilities in that direction. She was not rebuffed by Jared French. Paul Cadmus, when queried about this, said, "Margaret would have married anyone to get away from home."

Paul Cadmus never exhibited any hostility toward the woman who had married his lover, and the three were inseparable for many years to come. With Margaret's Leica camera, they created studies of people and objects on the beaches of Fire Island and Provincetown. Because they all took turns creating the photographs and pressing the camera button, their photographs are attributed to PaJaMa, an acronym using the first two letters of each of their first names. They also took an interesting series of photographs in Margaret's baronial New Jersey homestead before it was torn down. Velvet draperies create capes and heavy oak paneling a background for beautiful and eerie pictures.

Both Paul Cadmus and Jared French continued working for the Works Progress Administration throughout the Depression. Paul Cadmus did a large mural, *Pocahontas and John Smith* (1938) for the Parcel Post building in Richmond, Virginia. This mural, oil and tempera on canvas, used Fidelma Cadmus as a model for the lithe Pocahontas and Jared French as the half-naked Captain John Smith. Lincoln Kirstein posed for the totally naked Indian holding the captain's feet. One Indian's fur loincloth had to be repainted, as officials felt it too closely resembled genitalia. Cadmus's mural, as well as one done by Jared French for the same building, have both just been restored after years in storage

Pocahontas and John Smith *by Paul Cadmus, 1938 (mixed technique: oil and tempera on canvas, 82" x 162"). Mural for the Parcel Post Building, Richmond, Virginia; restored and currently displayed in the Lewis F. Powell Jr. United States Courthouse, Richmond, Virginia. Fidelma Cadmus posed for Pocahontas, Jared French for John Smith, and Lincoln Kirstein for the kneeling Indian (right foreground). (Courtesy of the U.S. General Services Administration, Public Buildings Service, Fine Arts Program, and D. C. Moore Gallery, N.Y.C. Reprinted by permission)*

and they are now installed in the federal courthouse in Richmond.

Pocahontas must have been in the air in those years, as Lincoln Kirstein had already produced a ballet on that subject for his dance company, Ballet Caravan. A small, experimental touring company that he had created with George Balanchine, the troupe had premiered the ballet, which had choreography by Lew Christensen and music by Elliott Carter, in 1936. George Lynes shot the photographs of the ballet production.

Paul Cadmus first met Lincoln Kirstein in 1937, and Cadmus was asked to design the sets and costumes for a ballet called *Filling Station.* At this time neither Balanchine nor Kirstein was interested in the classical repertoire of the past, and their small company performed ballets they felt were topical and would be of interest to a public that had no preparation for viewing ballet. Cadmus observed classes at the School of American Ballet before designing his set and costumes for the new ballet.

Filling Station had a score by Virgil Thomson, Kirstein's friend from his 1933 summer in Paris, and choreography by Ballet Caravan's one important classical male dancer, Lew Christensen, who, with his older

Costume design for role of the Rich Girl for the ballet Filling Station. *Design by Paul Cadmus, 1937 (tempera, watercolor, and pencil on paper, 12¹/₈" x 10¹/₄"). (The Museum of Modern Art, New York. Gift of Lincoln Kirstein. Photograph © 1999 The Museum of Modern Art, New York. Courtesy of D. C. Moore Gallery, N.Y.C. Reprinted by permission)*

Costume design for role of the Truck Driver for the ballet Filling Station *(opposite). Design by Paul Cadmus, 1937 (tempera and pencil on paper, 14¹/₂" x 8"). (The Museum of Modern Art, New York. Gift of Lincoln Kirstein. Photograph © 1999 The Museum of Modern Art, New York. Courtesy of D. C. Moore Gallery, N.Y.C. Reprinted by permission)*

Charles Daugherty *by Paul Cadmus, circa 1938 (ink on paper, 8³/₄" x 11¹/₂").*
(Collection of Paul Cadmus and Jon Andersson. Courtesy of D. C. Moore Gallery.
Reprinted by permission)

brothers, had danced in vaudeville. He had been seen there by Kirstein
and was appropriated for the new ballet company. Christensen wore the
clear plastic filling-station attendant's coverall designed by Cadmus.
Since he wore only a dance belt under the see-through costume, every
movement of the dancer's body could be clearly seen. The architectural
blueprint of the inside of the filling station matched the see-through
concept, and a red neon sign added the right edge of modernity.

In 1938, Cadmus added one more painting to his U.S. Navy series,
this one called *Sailors and Floosies.* Again it is worth noting Cadmus's interest in the clothing worn by his subjects. He had to have had a good
deal of interest in his own clothes. In the later portraits of both Cadmus
and Jared French by Platt Lynes, one is struck by their original-looking
and well-fitting sports shirts, sweaters, suits, and ties. This interest in the
right look can be seen in his painting of the sailors and their girls. The
big, blond floozy is bursting out of her red blouse, a twisted silk-cord
crown holding down her overbleached and permanented hair. Her

Seeing the New Year In *by Paul Cadmus, 1939 (mixed technique: oil and tempera on linen on pressed wood panel, 30" x 38"). (Forbes Magazine Collection, N.Y.C. Courtesy of D. C. Moore Gallery, N.Y.C. Reprinted by permission)*

friend wears gloves and a stylish beige toque and carries a purse, which she retains as her burly, redheaded sailor burrows his head between her breasts. These are real women wearing real clothes of 1938. The drunken sailors, on the other hand, are much more beautiful specimens, continuing the theme of previous sailor paintings: boozed-up, handsome young men as the prey of much less attractive women. This painting, too, was taken out of an exhibition, the Golden Gate International Exhibition in San Francisco in 1940, but was put back by the director of the Palace of Fine Arts museum, who said, "If every picture to which some may object is removed, none would remain."

While doing his much publicized gallery paintings, Cadmus was also doing many sensitive portraits of his new friends, handsome young men and celebrities he was meeting. Then in 1939 the artist returned to his theme of Greenwich Village excesses with *Seeing the New Year In.* Not only are the men drunk in this painting, *everyone* is drunk, very drunk, except for the two homosexuals lingering in the doorway. This painting was inspired by a rowdy narrative poem, *The Wild Party* (1928) by

Joseph Moncure March, but even more by Cadmus's own experiences. (Cadmus said that he was the despairing young man with his face buried in his hands in the painting's lower right corner.)

It is little wonder that Paul Cadmus got so much attention in these early years of his career. He was clearly asking for it. The public did not regard these unattractive people whooping it up as funny. In the 1930s this kind of behavior was considered sinful and perhaps just what would be expected in Greenwich Village. His reviews uniformly indicate that the critics found it hard to understand why he wanted to paint these subjects. Writing about *Seeing the New Year In*, Henry McBride, an art reviewer for New York newspapers, commented, "One assumes that Mr. Cadmus is a moralist; yet even so, it is difficult to get the intention back of his picture." And later, McBride wrote about Cadmus's painting *Hinky Dinky Parley Voo*: "I never can quite make up my mind whether he is, or is not, a moralist. This time, I have just about decided that he is. He must paint these dreadful scenes in order to do us good."

Hinky Dinky Parley Voo (1939) is a scene reflected in a round barroom mirror. A drunk veteran of World War I is singing loudly, surrounded by two whores, an even drunker young serviceman in uniform, the bar bouncer, and a quite removed accordion player. The Cadmus genius is to arrange all these faces, costumes, gestures, and wrinkles into one High Renaissance style. Everyone objected to Cadmus's constant hurling of himself against the hypocrisy of the American lifestyle, not the manner in which he painted. Americans did not want to acknowledge that servicemen frequently got drunk, veterans could be bores, and women could be whores. None of this existed in popular philosophy, so why did Paul Cadmus have to keep bringing it up? Perhaps not so much to play the moralist as to portray reality. Most homosexuals do not like to play a double game of pretending to be someone they are not. Certainly, Cadmus never did. With his work, Cadmus was only asking the rest of the world to face up to a little bit of the reality that he was facing up to every day of his life.

His realist and brutal *Herrin Massacre* (1940) was done for *Life* magazine, which commissioned sixteen artists to paint significant events. Also known as the Lester Strip Mine disaster, the massacre took place in 1922 when striking miners in Illinois killed twenty-six men who had been hired as strikebreakers by the mine owners. Cadmus certainly knew how to pick an unpopular subject. With the country on the brink of war, *Life* magazine scarcely wanted to bring up an unpopular subject like the brutality of strikers.

Paul Cadmus *by Jared French, circa 1938 (ink on paper, 11¹/₂″ x 8³/₄″). (Collection of Paul Cadmus and Jon Andersson. Courtesy of D. C. Moore Gallery. Reprinted by permission)*

Cadmus painted the subject in an almost religious way, illustrating the mindlessness and bloodlust of human beings once they set out to kill. The naked and bloodied bodies stretching into the foreground, the thrown-down floral cross, the blood-spattered stone lamb on the child's grave—all refer to Christ on the cross. Violent and disturbing, it is one of his most powerful and beautiful paintings. Little wonder the magazine refused it.

Herrin Massacre would be the last painting Cadmus would do with his mixed technique of oil and tempera on pressed wood panels. From 1940 on, he would use the more demanding technique of egg tempera; a revival of an early Italian method. Urged to try this technique by Jared French, Cadmus would continue for the rest of his career painting in this time-consuming technique. It resulted in paintings, large and small, that have perfect enameled surfaces and are very resistant to the passage of time. The egg tempera technique was a fitting one for an artist who considered himself to be in a direct line of descent from the painters of the Renaissance.

Pavel Tchelitchev

I am only a mad, lonely turtle that hears the sublime sound of the harmony of the spheres [and sees] the incredible beauty of its revolving lights—the forms not seen . . .

—*Pavel Tchelitchev to Parker Tyler, 1956*

Pavel Tchelitchev was born on September 21, 1898, on an estate near Moscow. His father, somewhat older than his mother, had been married before, and the young Pavel was brought up with a group of doting older half sisters. He was a fanciful child educated by governesses, but his interest in drawing and the arts was much encouraged by his mother. He was also interested in fashion and advised his sisters on how to dress and wear their hair. He was treated like a young prince, which his father grew to resent. Tchelitchev's childhood nickname was Panya, but when his father used it in addressing him, his inflection made it clear that they both understood that in Romanian *panya* meant "miss" or "mademoiselle." His relationship with his father, never close, became more distant because of this hostility. Sent to Moscow to pursue his studies, Tchelitchev lived with an indulgent aunt. In addition to his art classes, he began studying ballet and wanted very much to become a dancer, but when his father heard of this, he was called home and told to forget those dreams.

Shortly after this incident, the Russian Revolution took place, and Doubrovska, the family estate, was commandeered and turned over to the peasants who had worked on it. The family remained for a time, but

as the civil war drew near, they fled south to join the family of one of the
older married half sisters. The family divided up, and in 1918 Tchelitchev found himself in Kiev, behind the White Army lines. Since many
Moscow and St. Petersburg artists and theater performers had fled to
Kiev and opened schools and theaters, he was able to study art and theater design. The work he did for an avant-garde theater in Kiev was the
beginning of his career designing stage sets. As the war worsened, he was
forced to flee south to Sevastopol on the Black Sea, and from there he
was evacuated to Istanbul along with the White Russian troops and
many civilians. For a short time, Istanbul was filled with Russians, and
again Tchelitchev was able to find work in the theater, designing sets.
But with many other Russians, he soon set off for Berlin, where he lived
and worked in the theater, remaining there from 1921 to 1923.

In Berlin, he met the American pianist Allen Tanner, and they became
lovers. They spoke French together and in the summer of 1923 they decided to move to Paris as they were beginning to feel resentment stirring
in Berlin against the Russian émigrés. Paris, they believed, would be a
happier place to live.

Pavel Tchelitchev continued to pursue work in theater design while in
Paris, but he also began to paint and draw more regularly. His work was
noticed by Gertrude Stein and Alice B. Toklas; they had seen a small
painting of strawberries at the Salon d'Automne and sought out the
artist. Tanner and Tchelitchev became regulars at the Stein and Toklas
salon, and his career was much assisted by Stein's interest. He drew real
attention at the Galerie Druet in a group show that opened on February
22, 1926. In the show were also Christian Bérard, Eugene Berman and
his brother Leonid, and Kristians Tonny. A critic called them Neo-
Romantics and a school of art was born.

Tchelitchev's theater design career developed side by side with his
growing recognition as a painter, and in 1928 he created an extremely
modern decor for the ballet *Ode*, which opened the Paris season for the
Ballets Russes. Diaghilev himself was taken aback at Tchelitchev's use of
film projections and neon lights and unadorned white body tights with
no additional cover-ups, as well as by Massine's minimalist choreography, which involved little dancing. Years ahead of its time, *Ode* caused an
enormous stir but little enthusiasm in the ballet world. In the 1970s, reflecting on his friend's penchant for controversial stage productions,
Lincoln Kirstein wrote, "Tchelitchev was so seductive a talker, so apt a
wit, so ingenious a diplomat that he could make his most insane project
sound normal and possible."

At this same time Pavel Tchelitchev met the young George Lynes. They were both habitués of Gertrude Stein's salon and established a friendship that would last until the photographer's death in 1955. Through these years they would share many of the same friends and attitudes. Tchelitchev's art would have a major effect on Lynes's photography, and Lynes's photographs of male nudes were of great interest to Tchelitchev.

When Pavel Tchelitchev decided in 1934 to move to New York, he was aided by George Platt Lynes, Monroe Wheeler, and Glenway Wescott. More important, his settled relationship with Allen Tanner had been unsettled by his encounter with young Charles Henri Ford in 1931. Tchelitchev's passion for the elfin, twenty-one-year-old Ford was the decisive factor in the move. At the time, Charles Henri was still shedding his baby fat and was round-faced, adorable, sprightly, and very sexy. When he was introduced to *Vogue* editor and hostess Marie-Louise Bousquet by Tchelitchev, she opened her arms and shrieked, *"Il me plaît!"* Charles Henri pleased all of Paris, but didn't want to remain there. Tchelitchev followed him to New York with Allen Tanner in tow, but it was understood that their romantic relationship was over and the painter's new love was Charles Henri.

Tchelitchev's interest in Charles Henri Ford was certainly sexual. Charles Henri has said, "Pavel told me that he would never have fallen in love with me if I hadn't been so well hung." But most important, their relationship, which was to last until Tchelitchev's death in 1957, was something beyond a friendship or a marriage. It was a kind of bonding through their common interest in the new world of art that was emerging in this period.

The new art world shared by the Surrealists, the Magic Realists, and the Neo-Romantics was in direct descent from the art of the Renaissance, but the painter's skill in depicting reality was now devoted to revealing a greater reality beneath the surface of what is seen. The artist's work pursued the reality of dreams and revealed the emotion and the psychology below the images of everyday life. Charles Henri Ford is devoted to this philosophy in his art, photography, and poetry, and he feels he was very much formed by his life with Tchelitchev. His unabashed interest in eroticism also had to have had a strong effect on his Russian lover. Allen Tanner had been a refined and diplomatic force in Tchelitchev's life. Charles Henri Ford was a randy bad boy. Although there is only one seminude drawing of him by Tchelitchev, his presence probably freed Tchelitchev to draw his homoerotic works without guilt or compunction. While Allen Tanner would have been uneasy about this

Pavel Tchelitchev in his studio with Jonathan Tichenor, by George Platt Lynes, circa 1944. (Collection of Jensen Yow. Courtesy of Mr. and Mrs. George Platt Lynes II. Reprinted by permission)

kind of artwork, Charles Henri Ford relished it. Indeed, Ford's gay novel, *The Young and Evil* (1933), written with Parker Tyler, was declared obscene and confiscated by customs officials when the Paris publisher shipped copies to the United States.

The other important relationship for Pavel Tchelitchev in the prewar period was with Edith Sitwell, the English writer and poet. From a distinguished family, Miss Sitwell was tall and not considered beautiful. She and Tchelitchev shared a kind of fascination for each other. She was in love with the Russian painter, but there was never any physical aspect to their relationship, much to her regret. Their mutual affection flourished more in their letter writing than anywhere else. When they were together, Tchelitchev often became difficult, perhaps from his reluctance at sharing the spotlight with Edith.

During the 1930s and for the remainder of his life, Pavel Tchelitchev was recognized as an important modern painter. In Paris in 1933 he had met Lincoln Kirstein, who liked his work and was of great assistance in New York. Kirstein, as well as Monroe Wheeler, used his position at the Museum of Modern Art to help Tchelitchev's career. As a result, his work was included in exhibitions at the museum, and his large painting *Hide and Seek* was purchased for the museum in October 1942.

Tchelitchev also continued to design for the stage. When Kirstein and Balanchine produced Gluck's *Orfeo ed Euridice* at the Metropolitan Opera in 1936, Tchelitchev designed the sets and costumes. In this production the singers were in the pit with the orchestra while the dancers mimed their roles on the stage. The painter's style was expressed in gauzelike grave windings, veils, surrealistic ladders mounting to nowhere, and large wings of real feathers on the dancer playing Amor, who somehow managed to dance in them. The production was short-lived, but the romantic and magical Tchelitchev designs were long remembered and influenced later ballet productions.

In 1941 Tchelitchev designed the sets for Balanchine's ballet *Balustrade*, danced to Stravinsky's violin concerto. The composer admired Tchelitchev's stage designs and found his compatriot interesting to observe. "Tchelitchev had a queer and difficult character," Stravinsky noted in *Dialogues and a Diary*, "for though lively and very attractive as a person, he was also morbidly superstitious, and he would wear a mysterious red thread around his wrist or talk hieratically about the Golden Section, the true meaning of Horapollo, etc."

At this point in the mid-century Tchelitchev was becoming a famous name in the art world. His gigantic painting *Phenomena* with its hidden and unflattering portraits of the famous gained great attention. As did his erotic *Lion Boy* and his beautiful portraits, particularly those of the Ford siblings, Charles Henri and Ruth.

In the latter part of his life, Pavel Tchelitchev's explorations of the reality beneath apparent reality led him to paint in an "X-ray" style that revealed the veins, muscles, and interior elements of the body. Portraits were of staring eyeballs and a web of tissue in glowing, luminescent colors. From this kind of revelation of the interior human, he then moved to entirely abstract work, devoted only to light and color. His efforts to make his subjects reveal their emotional substructure resulted finally in paintings that were highly geometric and completely abstract.

Pavel Tchelitchev moved to Italy and died in Rome on July 31, 1957. His "darling Charlie" was with him to the end.

Lincoln Kirstein

*How can Kirstein be a director of a ballet company? He took some ballet
lessons from me and he can't get his feet off the floor.*

—*Michel Fokine*

Lincoln Kirstein burst into 1935 with a newfound sense of purpose. His earlier days when he had considered being a painter or a writer or staging art exhibitions, while having only a vague fascination with the ballet, were now behind him. Now he was a ballet impresario, pure and simple.

But as it turned out, his new career path was not so simple. In 1935 he published a book called *Dance: A Short History of Classic Theatrical Dancing.* He had not abandoned writing after all, which was fortunate, as his books and articles would do much to prepare the public for his ballet companies. He also published his first book of poems, *Low Ceiling.* In one poem, called "Organizer," he wrote:

Now, have in mind a different sort of man . . .
He is a quiet man, of quiet men.
He is a simple man, of simple men.
He is without reward; they are without reward
For their time and place . . .

Perhaps that was how he felt about his new role in promoting and organizing other people's creative work.

In addition to ballet and writing, Kirstein's art interests included the French sculptor Gaston Lachaise. He had seen Lachaise's work in Paris and had encouraged him to move to New York. He found patrons and various commissions for Lachaise, and in 1935 he helped arrange a retrospective exhibition of the artist's work at the Museum of Modern Art and wrote the catalog for the exhibit. Strong-bodied, Kirstein had also posed for Lachaise, who made two casts of a walking figure, one with gold added to the bronze while in liquid form, which resulted in a gold-flecked statue. Lachaise had been commissioned—in part, perhaps, because Kirstein knew Nelson Rockefeller—to do large bas-relief plaques for Rockefeller Center, which was being built at the time. For these, Kirstein also posed. Lachaise favored large-breasted and large-buttocked female forms, and tall, big-muscled Kirstein was an obvious choice as an accompanying male. Lachaise also did a number of male nude drawings that are thought to be of Kirstein.

In March 1935 the first season of the newly named American Ballet Company was presented at the Adelphi Theater in New York. In October the company went on its first American tour. It eschewed classic ballets for the most part and presented a program of one-act productions, many on American themes. This company, organized with the best-trained young dancers Balanchine and Kirstein could find around New York, was short on male dancers, and often female dancers took "trouser" roles to partner other young women in the corps de ballet.

At this time, Balanchine and Kirstein discovered classic ballet's first major male American dancer, Lew Christensen. There were three Christensen brothers: William, Harold, and Lew, the youngest. The brothers were handsome and athletic, and had formed a dance unit to tour vaudeville, as Ruth St. Denis and Ted Shawn had been doing for some years. Lew Christensen was appearing in New York when he was called to Kirstein's attention. He had a beautiful body, and because he had had good training, he was able to perform classical male leading roles immediately. He was to be the most important American male star for Balanchine and Kirstein until he left for the U.S. Army in 1941.

Another male dancer added to the company was José "Pete" Martinez, with whom Lincoln Kirstein maintained a liaison until his marriage. Martinez was from Los Angeles, where he had received his early dance training, and had entered the School of American Ballet as soon as he came to New York. Kirstein and he lived together, and when Lincoln Kirstein married Fidelma Cadmus in 1941, she moved into their apartment with them temporarily.

Lincoln Kirstein *by Paul Cadmus, 1937 (pencil and pen and ink on paper, 6" x
9¹/₄"). (Collection of Paul Cadmus and Jon Andersson. Courtesy of D. C. Moore
Gallery, N.Y.C. Reprinted by permission)*

Lincoln Kirstein and his sister, Mina Kirstein Curtiss, circa 1935. (Collection of Jensen Yow. Reprinted by permission)

José Martinez, who died in 1997, less than a year after Lincoln Kirstein, was a droll and witty young man of Mexican origin. Those who knew the two men in the 1930s said he was capable of endlessly amusing his lover, and that of all the men in his life, Martinez was the man that Kirstein most likely loved the most. Kirstein loved gossip and other men's tales of their sexual exploits, and this love of storytelling drew him to Martinez. In addition, Martinez was handsome, and many artists painted, drew, and photographed him. Fidelma Cadmus drew him, Paul Cadmus drew and painted him, and George Platt Lynes created a beautiful series of photos of him nude in a windowlike aperture, wearing a large straw hat.

Martinez was a member of Ballet Caravan. Organized by Kirstein, this company toured the United States, visiting many smaller cities as well as large ones. Their repertoire was very different from the classical companies, Colonel de Basil's Ballet Russe and the Ballet Russe de

Pete (José Martinez) *by Paul Cadmus, 1938 (mixed technique: oil and tempera on linen on pressed wood panel, 12" x 9"). (Collection of the Estate of José Martinez. Courtesy of D. C. Moore Gallery, N.Y.C. Reprinted by permission)*

Monte Carlo, the two offshoot companies from the original Diaghilev companies. Other young male dancers added to the company during this period were Nicholas Magallanes and Francisco Moncion, both of Latin

American origin and both of whom were to remain with Balanchine and Kirstein throughout their long careers. Magallanes was discovered by Kirstein's painter friend Pavel Tchelitchev, roaming the streets of New York. Tchelitchev not only used him as a central figure in his large painting *Phenomena*, but brought him to Kirstein to study dance. He immediately showed talent and became one of the leading dancers of what eventually became the New York City Ballet.

Francisco "Frank" Moncion said that as a young teenager he was walking down the street minding his own business when Lincoln Kirstein passed by and shouted, "Hey, kid, want to be a dancer?" Kirstein undoubtedly had an eye for talent, for Moncion was also to become an important lead dancer with the company.

Balanchine and Kirstein were desperately trying to maintain a regular company, and, to do this, they needed to find employment for their dancers and pay salaries. They arranged with the Metropolitan Opera in New York to provide the ballets for operas and also to perform individual ballets from time to time. This arrangement, begun in the fall of 1935 and continued until the spring of 1938, was never a satisfactory arrangement for either the opera or the fledgling ballet company. The opera management felt uneasy about the modern ballets that were staged by this company, and Balanchine and Kirstein were irked by the lack of opportunity for their dancers to perform more frequently, to say nothing of Balanchine's desire to choreograph more often and more excitingly. During this period Balanchine also choreographed for several Broadway shows by composer Richard Rodgers and his quick-witted, hard-drinking, cigar-smoking homosexual lyricist Lorenz Hart. For *On Your Toes* (1936), which spoofs classical ballet, Balanchine created the gangster dance sequence *Slaughter on Tenth Avenue*, which was performed by Ray Bolger and Tamara Geva, Balanchine's first wife. This collaboration was followed by three more hit musicals, *Babes in Arms*, *The Boys from Syracuse*, and *I Married an Angel*, which starred Vera Zorina, the breathtakingly beautiful dancer who became Balanchine's second wife.

To give the company some true opportunities to dance, Kirstein organized Ballet Caravan, a touring division of the American Ballet. This company specialized in ballets with American subjects. Their first performance was at Bennington College on July 17, 1936, and this company toured until 1941. It employed the talents of the choreographers Lew Christensen, Erick Hawkins, William Dollar, and Eugene Loring. Composers who created music for the company were Elliott Carter, Paul

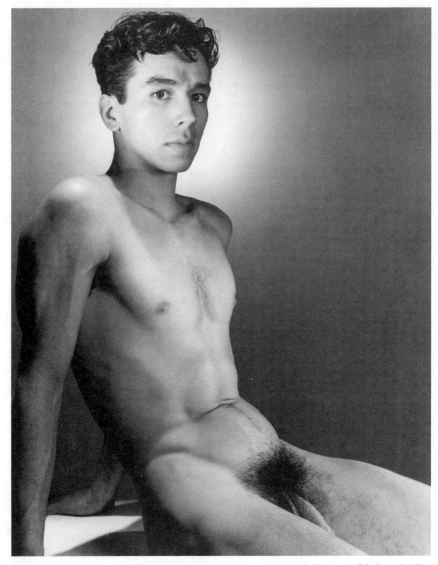

Nicholas Magallanes by George Platt Lynes, circa 1938. (Collection of Robert Miller Gallery, N.Y.C. Courtesy of Mr. and Mrs. George Platt Lynes II. Reprinted by permission)

Bowles, Robert McBride, Virgil Thomson, Aaron Copland, and Henry Brant. Many luminaries in the dance and music world found early work with this company. Any opportunities that Kirstein could find were used to keep Ballet Caravan on stage. In August 1936, for example, the company performed dances in a summer-stock production of *The Would-Be Gentleman* at the Country Playhouse in Westport, Connecticut.

In New York the American Ballet Company mounted an innovative production of Gluck's opera *Orfeo ed Euridice* for the Metropolitan Opera's 1936 season. It was staged by George Balanchine, and Tchelitchev designed the sets and costumes in a style that combined romantic fantasies with surrealism. Lew Christensen and Daphne Vane danced the title roles, and William Dollar, Amor. Ballet aficionados loved it, opera lovers resented it, but with this astonishing production Kirstein and Balanchine established the company as an important cultural force in the public's mind. George Lynes did some of his most beautiful photographs of this production, and in a few he convinced Lew Christensen to appear nude.

Lincoln Kirstein added another important position to his workload in December 1936 when he was appointed the head of the Work Projects Administration Federal Dance Theater. The photographer Walker Evans had introduced him to Harry L. Hopkins, the administrator of the WPA and a close friend of President Roosevelt's. Kirstein's dream of a national ballet company made it possible for him to speak convincingly of his plans for his company, and his new position enabled him to enlist the help of important people.

Two years later Kirstein was able to repay his debt to Evans, who had introduced him to Hopkins. When the first major exhibition of Evans's work was held at the Museum of Modern Art, Kirstein wrote the text for *Walker Evans: American Photographs.*

In April 1937 the American Ballet Company presented a Stravinsky Festival at the Metropolitan Opera. All the ballets were danced to Igor Stravinsky scores, and all choreography was by George Balanchine. The festival included the premiere of *Jeu de Cartes*, whose score Kirstein had commissioned from the Russian composer. "*Jeu de Cartes* was my first commission from Lincoln Kirstein," Stravinsky recalled in *Themes and Episodes.* "Kirstein was a young giant then, who wore a fierce expression and who matched it with a bellicose dedication to the beautiful and a contempt for the sham." The festival's productions presented advanced ideas in choreography, music, sets, and costumes. The conservative opera public, which made up the bulk of the audience, was at a loss as to what to make of this modernism, but the festival's contributions to future ideas about ballet, music, and decor were enormous.

That same year, Lincoln Kirstein was painted by Pavel Tchelitchev in three poses in a single painting. In the center foreground, he stands arms crossed and wearing a brilliant red-and-black athletic-team jacket,

Balanchine's staging of Orfeo ed Euridice *at the Metropolitan Opera, 1936: Lew Christensen (left), Daphne Vane, and William Dollar; photographed by George Platt Lynes. (Collection of Bernard Perlin. Courtesy of Mr. and Mrs. George Platt Lynes II. Reprinted by permission)*

staring steadily out of the painting. On a panel forming the right background, he is naked except for boxing gloves, one of which is strategically placed to cover his privates. In the background at left, he is sprawled on a black-and-white-striped plain that stretches to a horizon,

George Balanchine by George Platt Lynes, circa 1938. (Collection of Bernard Perlin. Courtesy of Mr. and Mrs. George Platt Lynes II. Reprinted by permission)

a somewhat ungainly figure in his customary black clothes, here in trousers and vest with a white shirt. He is reading a newspaper and wearing striped socks that echo the background. As with many Tchelitchev works, the painting is almost cinematic with its close-up, medium shot, and long shot, none from precisely the same angle. The portrait captures different facets of Kirstein's character, if not all of them. There is the handsome young man in an athletic jacket, almost an undergraduate; there is the strong, naked athlete; and there is the business executive, conservative in his attire and intent on reading the day's news.

About this time Lincoln Kirstein worked out a formula for his wardrobe. He was sensitive about his height—he was six feet two inches tall, and seemed even larger—and general demeanor among the darting butterflies of the ballet world and decided he would only wear black. Thenceforth his wardrobe only included black suits, white shirts, and dark ties. Black silk in warm weather, black wool in cold. He never varied from this strict regime.

Kirstein asked Charles Rain, who had designed the costumes for Ballet Caravan's *Yankee Clipper* (1937) to introduce him to Cadmus. Rain took Kirstein to the artist's studio, where Cadmus was preparing his first one-man show for a midtown gallery. Kirstein promptly bought the painting *Mallorcan Fishermen* before it was hung in the show. Shortly thereafter, Kirstein asked Cadmus to design the sets and costumes for a new ballet, *Filling Station*. Also at this time Kirstein first met the artist's beautiful sister who was herself an artist. Upon meeting Fidelma Cadmus, Kirstein told Paul he wanted to marry his sister, and eventually he did.

Ballet Caravan went to Havana in 1938. Shortly after they returned, the company premiered the ballet *Billy the Kid* in Chicago. Kirstein himself wrote the libretto, the choreography was by Eugene Loring, and the score, which had been commissioned for the ballet, was by Aaron Copland. This was the first ballet created to explore American folklore that was an immediate and major success. It established the reputation of Eugene Loring as a choreographer and has remained in the repertory of a number of ballet companies ever since.

At the start of 1939 Lincoln Kirstein extended himself into yet another area of the art world. With the collaboration of Lee Strasberg, Jay Leyda, Mary Losey, and Robert Stebbins, he created a journal for the motion picture industry called *Film*.

In March, Christopher Isherwood dined with Kirstein, "that somber, electric creature," whose "hair is cropped like a convict's, and his eyes, behind austere tin spectacles, seem to be examining you through a microscope." Perhaps Kirstein's many projects were putting a strain on him since the novelist comments in his diary that Kirstein "looks like a mad clipper captain out of Melville."

Nevertheless, in the same year Kirstein published *Ballet Alphabet: A Primer for Laymen*, which had explanatory drawings by Paul Cadmus. Also in 1939 the American Ballet Company took part in a Stephen Foster festival sponsored by a millionaire devotee. As ever, Lincoln Kirstein was relentless in seeking opportunities for his company to perform.

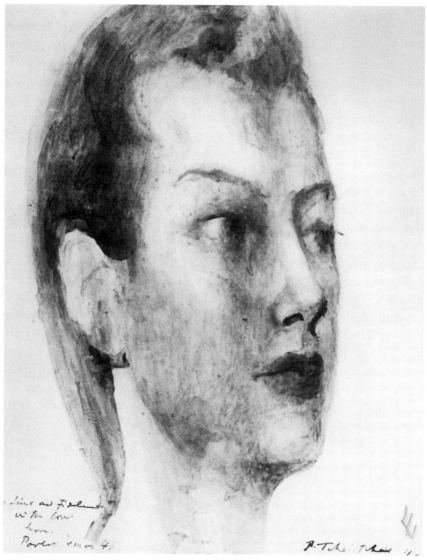

Fidelma Cadmus Kirstein *by Pavel Tchelitchev, circa 1941 (ink on paper, 13" x 9¹/₂"). (Collection of Paul Cadmus and Jon Andersson. Reprinted by permission)*

He was equally relentless in his efforts to educate the public and enhance the position of ballet in the United States. In 1940 he helped create an archive on dance at the Museum of Modern Art, donating more than five thousand books and documents on dance from his own collection. This archive was later the foundation of the Dance Collection of the New York Public Library, now housed in the Performing Arts Library at Lincoln Center. Perhaps as the war spread across Europe, Kirstein was feeling even more pressure to solidify his efforts and Balanchine's to make dance an important part of American culture.

In 1940, he was able to get Ballet Caravan a solid six months of work performing in a production for the Ford Motor Company at the New York World's Fair. Called *A Thousand Times Neigh!* it must have had to do with the replacement of the horse by the automobile. In his later years, José Martinez was asked if he remembered Robert McVoy, a fellow dancer in the company. All he could remember was that McVoy had been the back half of a dancing horse and he himself had been the front. The state of ballet in the United States as the economy emerged from the Depression was such that classically trained dancers were delighted to dance at a world's fair and a choreographer of Balanchine's talent was relatively happy to create dances for it.

During this five-year period, the interrelating of lives began for Lincoln Kirstein, Paul Cadmus, and George Platt Lynes, both professionally and personally. The engine behind all this activity was Kirstein. He created the dance companies that were photographed so imaginatively by Platt Lynes, he involved Cadmus in designing sets and costumes, and he ceaselessly wove the art web that helped photographers get exhibits, artists obtain museum and gallery shows, composers commissions for new works, and dancers opportunities to appear in ballets. Through all these new performances, exhibits, and writings his influence was to reverberate far beyond his immediate circle of friends and acquaintances.

Everett "Chick" Austin

The house is just like me, all facade.

—*Chick Austin*

In 1927 handsome, young Arthur Everett "Chick" Austin, Jr., was appointed to the enviable post of director of the Wadsworth Atheneum. The Atheneum was the center of cultural life in wealthy Hartford, Connecticut, and was supported by the city's most important families.

How had dashing, avant-garde Chick Austin come to be the director of this austere, conservative museum? As a favored pupil of Edward Fowler's at Harvard, Austin had done exemplary archaeological studies, and it was at his professor's recommendation that he had been offered the job.

Chick Austin had been a spoiled only child and knew it. The son of Arthur Everett and Helen Austin, his mother believed him to be a genius and helped him prove it to the world. By the time he was eighteen and entering Harvard, he was international, quadrilingual, and bisexual. In addition to his unusual preparatory education, he was extremely personable, leaving little reason to wonder why his professors adored him.

But not everyone at Harvard admired Austin. One morning in his dormitory, a cleaning lady surprised him by walking in on him while in bed with another young man. Not wanting to ignore the incident and relying heavily upon his charm, as he passed her later in the corridor, he said, "Oh, Mrs. Riley, you must think I'm awfully spoiled." She replied, "Hmmph, you can't spoil a bad egg."

Professor Fowler, who directed Austin's history and archaeology studies, helped arrange for him to be part of an important dig in Egypt in 1923. His mother was thrilled at her boy's success, and when his ship sailed for Europe, he found that she had not only come to see him off but had taken the adjoining cabin and was going to accompany him on the dig. Soon she was in the adjoining tent in the Egyptian desert.

Chick Austin's ambition to become a museum director was fulfilled a few years later, again with the help of his Harvard professor. The dowdy Atheneum was soon treated to a new concept of museum activities. A large costume ball was given immediately upon Austin's assuming the directorship, a Venetian fete with one thousand guests. Powdered wigs and panniers were rented or whipped up locally, and the night rang with revelries never before seen in Hartford.

In 1929 Chick Austin married Helen Goodwin, the niece of Charles A. Goodwin, head of the Atheneum board. She was two years older than he, beautiful and quiet. The newlyweds built a home in 1930 that was a model of what would now be called postmodern architecture. Styled on an eighteenth-century château but built of wood, the house's streamlined classicism outraged the Austins' neighbors. The Austins subsequently had two children, who must have enjoyed very much their father's skill as an amateur magician. As a child, he had called himself Professor Marvel when he performed for family and friends. After 1932 he called himself the Great Osram.

Thanks to his many trips to Europe as a child and teenager, Chick Austin was fascinated with baroque art, a period ignored by most museums at that time. In 1930 he curated the first exhibition in the United States on the baroque art of Italy, Germany, and France. Many contemporary European artists, unknown in America, were also given shows at the Atheneum. The artists often visited Hartford with their work, and Hartford was beginning to gain an international reputation for its interest in the arts.

The expatriate set in Paris at this time was well-known to Chick Austin, and Virgil Thomson's opera *Four Saints in Three Acts*, with a libretto by Gertrude Stein, was given its world premiere at the Wadsworth Atheneum in 1934. The all-black cast, which contained many gospel singers, and the advanced sets and costumes in see-through cellophane by Florine Stettheimer, added a great deal to this extremely

A. Everett "Chick" Austin, Jr., by George Platt Lynes, circa 1936. (Collection of
Wadsworth Atheneum Archives, Hartford, Connecticut. Courtesy of Mr. and Mrs.
George Platt Lynes II. Reprinted by permission)

avant-garde production. Frederick Ashton was imported to create the dances. George Lynes photographed the English choreographer, impeccably dressed in a tailored suit, with his three principal male dancers, impeccably undressed.

One of Austin's great contributions to the arts in America was his sponsoring of George Balanchine and a small group of dancers, which enabled Kirstein to bring them to the United States. Chick Austin and Lincoln Kirstein were friends, sharing a Harvard background, and Kirstein had the idea that the Wadsworth Atheneum should be the home of a national ballet school and company. What Austin thought (or told the trustees of the Atheneum) when Balanchine departed after three days in Hartford has not be recorded. Obviously he was a good sport and knew when to cut his losses.

The apogée of his career at the Wadsworth Atheneum was the Paper Ball of 1936. The Atheneum had recently added an ultramodern wing, and Tchelitchev converted the court of this wing into an opera house by covering its walls with newspaper and painting the opera boxes and their occupants thereon. Then the guests appeared, entirely costumed in paper. Each guest was grandly announced as he or she swept into the large hall and swirled around the grand baroque fountain in the center. Many of the guests had come on a special train from New York. The beautiful young actress Ruth Ford was borne in on a palanquin as an Indian princess, her bearers including her brother Charles Henri Ford and his pal, the writer Parker Tyler. They were dressed in paper cowboy costumes, and later in the evening, it is claimed, they threw themselves into the fountain, where their costumes disintegrated. They emerged largely nude. This was daring at any time of the year in Hartford, but especially in February. Lincoln Kirstein, who was among the contingent of New Yorkers who attended the ball, wrote later that it was "the last public party in America designed as an illustration of the dominance of a certain scale of grandeur in taste and manners."

Magician, archaeologist, and museum director, Austin now became convinced that his true career lay in becoming a professional actor. To that end, he staged *Hamlet* at the Atheneum in 1941 with himself in the lead role. But when 1943 rolled around, his choice of vehicle was the Jacobean tragedy *'Tis Pity She's a Whore*, with himself in the role of the incestuous Giovanni. The title, surely more than the play, pushed the trustees over the edge. When the Atheneum canceled the production, he left the museum and his family, and departed for Hollywood with a young male lover in tow.

His attempt at a film career proved futile, and by 1945 he had relocated to Florida as the director of the Ringling Museum in Sarasota. In his new role, Chick Austin maintained his contacts with his earlier life, inviting Pavel Tchelitchev to be a guest speaker on Gertrude Stein and sponsoring similar activities.

Austin died in Florida in 1957. His wife remained in the beautiful house in Hartford until 1985. It is now an adjunct to the Wadsworth Atheneum and remains as a testimonial to this unusual man's advanced taste and forward thinking.

The War Years
1940–45

"Don't You Know There's a War On!"

It's 1943. George Platt Lynes has a new apartment on Park Avenue. Everyone is talking about it. Certain kinds of everyone, at any rate. And you've been invited to the housewarming.

You are working at Vogue *now. It's fun, but you're wondering if you shouldn't join the navy—if they'll have you. Navy blue has always been one of your best colors. Your mother occasionally mentions that she thinks it's time for you to think about getting married. You're wondering about it yourself. You tell her you're not in love with anyone. Which isn't entirely true, but certainly no one to whom you could ever introduce your mother.*

George, who is definitely Platt Lynes now, has done an elaborate decoration of a largish apartment, or flat as he calls it, at Park and Fifty-fifth Street, just catty-corner from where he formerly lived with Monroe Wheeler and Glenway Westcott, after they moved down from upper Madison Avenue. You once asked a painter friend of theirs if their ménage *had ever really been* à trois, *and he said, "Oh, I suppose George let Glenway suck his cock once in a while." You thought this was unnecessarily crude. You were just asking.*

George has fallen in love with Jonathan Tichenor. You've never met him. You know he was John *when he first arrived in New York. George upgraded it. Jonathan is the second Tichenor with whom George has been enamored. The first was Jonathan's older brother, George Tichenor. He had been a studio assistant for George and was killed in the war. No one thinks George Tichenor was ever really Platt Lynes's lover, but he was surely guilty of leading him on, posing for nude photographs and allowing himself to be a love object.*

One of Platt Lynes's writer friends told you that the photographer told him, "If I can't get the Tichenor I want, I'll take the Tichenor I can get." That sounds unnaturally harsh and not much like the George Platt Lynes you know. And by now you know him pretty well.

George has done a startling job on the new apartment. He has a taste for Victorian mixed in with unusual colors and modern paintings. He has some inherited family furniture he likes to make a fuss over. He often tells friends that his ancestor George Platt was a decorator who furnished homes in the mid-nineteenth century.

He also loves those old Axminster carpets. His are fragments from the grand old Saratoga Springs Hotel in upper New York State. Evidently they stretched for miles in the endless salons of that monster watering place.

He also has a beautiful Marsden Hartley painting over the couch and a large Tchelitchev. As you enter the party, you look around to see if Tchelitchev is here. You'd love to call him Pavlik, but you don't know him that well. Will you ever? You were present when he was the set designer for a Cecil Beaton shooting of Marlene Dietrich at Vogue. *You saw Miss Dietrich brush Pavlik's hand aside as he was adjusting the front of her dress for the camera. And heard him say repeatedly for the rest of the afternoon, "But she does not understand. She does not understand." Poor guy, he was really embarrassed. You've worked with Miss Dietrich a couple of times and she can be quite a bitch.*

Tchelitchev is across the room talking to someone who looks like Somerset Maugham. It is Somerset Maugham, looking like an aging turtle whose shell is a well-tailored pinstripe suit. Tchelitchev is looking horsey. Like a horse, that is. It's the nostrils, they flair when he talks. He also bridles and tosses his head when he's deep in conversation. Whoa, dobbin, you think. Most likely he'd only laugh if you said that to him.

That little gent looking at the Hartley painting must be Christopher Isherwood. He looks about twelve. There was lots of talk a few years ago, when the English came over, about their skipping out on the war. It does look bad what with London getting the hell bombed out of it. You decide that if his friend W. H. Auden and he can live with their defection, so can you. Auden never comes to these parties. Probably not serious enough for him. More likely he thinks he's too unattractive to snag any boys. He does look as if his skin is getting too loose for him. You went to one of his poetry readings last month and his jowls were getting jowls.

George rushes by with those damnable hard-boiled eggs, as ever. "Hi, Sandusky," he says. (He's always called you Sandusky since that incident in his kitchen years ago.) "This is Bridget Bate Chisholm," he adds with a toss of his head toward a beautiful young woman with dark hair and large eyes. As she turns, you can see that she has a perfect profile. You know about her. Young, wealthy husband off in the service somewhere, apartment at the Plaza Hotel. Many parties. You've never been invited. "What should I do with this coat?" she says to you helplessly. "Let's look for a bedroom," you suggest, and together you find a large bedroom done in dark green and purple. It sounds terrible but actually it's quite dashing. Medieval but dashing. A young man is sitting on the side of the bed looking at his clasped hands. Sort of blond. Sort of handsome. Nice clothes. Bridget breezes in. "Can I drop this off here?" she asks, throwing about two tons of mink on the bed beside him. He doesn't answer. Bridget goes to a mirror and talks to him over her shoulder as she inspects her perfect face and hair carefully. "What's your name?" she asks. For twenty-two or twenty-three she is very much in command.

"John . . . Jonathan," he says. It is obviously Jonathan Tichenor.

"Come with us," she says, turning toward the noise in the living room. Her husband must be rich. That dress has to be Hattie Carnegie. And we walk out, one of us on each side of John. Jonathan. "I'll introduce you to all these people." Bridget waves her arm grandly. "Just a bunch of old poofs, really."

Monroe and Glenway are not at the party. They disapprove of George keeping house with Jonathan Tichenor. "Everyone will know," they said. You think they're probably more distressed at being left by themselves as an obvious male couple, instead of an enigmatic threesome with George. You wonder who they think doesn't know they're fairies. At least they haven't gotten all involved with cover-up marriages like Lincoln Kirstein, Carl Van Vechten, Kirk Askew, and lots of other people. You're still something of an idealist, even if you have been in New York for six years.

You go over to talk to Paul Cadmus, who looks younger every time you see him. He still has a lot of summer tan left, and when he turns to look at you with those sweet blue eyes, you feel that perhaps he actually *is* glad to see you. Whether he is or not, he is the warmest and the most human of the whole lot here tonight, you decide. He has his new romantic interest, George Tooker, in tow. They say that he's a wonderful painter, too. Quite small with round, startled blue eyes. You can see why Paul adores him. He's like a wonderful *poupée* you might find under the Christmas tree—a smart, talented, wonderful doll as you'll come to find out.

Fidelma Cadmus Kirstein joins you, looking very smart. She's wearing a turban. You are reminded how unusually beautiful she is. No wonder everyone wants to paint her. Like her brother's, her beauty is very human. "Oh, good, there are some women here," she says. "Lincoln is always giving these parties where I'm the only woman. I call them the Lost Boys parties." She laughs. Whatever goes on between her and Lincoln they seem to like each other a lot. Except that they call each other Goosey. You could live without that.

There is a couple with Fidelma whom she introduces as Mr. and Mrs. Jared French. Mrs. French is quite beautiful, too, in a curious way. It's as though she is in a glass bubble looking out at the world, a world she doesn't quite *understand and doesn't seem to have any real wish to understand. She smiles, nods, murmurs, but is she really there? you wonder. Perhaps she's deaf. She shares with Fidelma Kirstein a kind of beauty that seems to be looking out at the world in a bit of wonderment, not at all aware of the uses this beauty could be put to. You like them both enormously for that.*

On the other hand, Mr. French seems to understand the uses of beauty completely. He is quite dashing; a small mustache. Jared French is a painter also, and he tells you he shares a studio with Paul Cadmus somewhere down in the Village.

He's sexy, Jared French. You can tell he has a good body just from the way he stands. He's wearing a tweed jacket and bow tie, which maximizes his handsomeness. You wonder how it happens that you haven't met him before. You think he hasn't really noticed you until you feel his hand on your behind as he passes in back of you. You take it and place it firmly on his own buttock. You say nothing. You just don't want to be known as a slut.

Paul invites you to come next summer to Fire Island where he goes with the Frenches to paint. "Half the houses were blown away in the last hurricane," he says. "It really is surreal." You've seen his painting of George Tichenor holding a kite, which is one of your favorites. You like Paul's painting as much as you like him. Brilliant and vivid, yet so measured and precise. And very still at the same time. You're saving up your money to buy one of his paintings—which will take quite some time on your pathetic Vogue *salary.*

You wander off to look at the apartment. It really is beautiful, with purple and red and a strange green used together, a very Platt Lynes kind of taste at work here. A number of his needlepoint cushions are strewn about. He does a lot of needlepoint. He probably doesn't read much. He can needlepoint while he's talking to people and he probably isn't alone very often. He doesn't seem to be the kind of person who would want to be alone for any length of time.

You see a cushion in the master bedroom that must be a view of Stoneblossom, the country house he used to share with Monroe and Glenway. He won't be going there much anymore.

You suddenly realize that you have completely forgotten to ask Fidelma Kirstein about Lincoln and hurry back into the party to find her. She tells you that she hears from him regularly. He's in the army as a private and actually likes it. It sounds like fun. Lots of men. Fidelma spends a lot of time taking care of Lincoln's mother. She doesn't say that the elder Mrs. Kirstein is demanding, but you're sure it's not easy for Fidelma. You wonder if she ever ponders what she has gotten herself into. While you're talking to Fidelma, a couple comes up; they are Glenway Wescott's brother Lloyd and his wife, Barbara. You've met them several times before. At least they're not abandoning George because of his relationship with Jonathan Tichenor. You vaguely remember hearing that George Tichenor was from New Jersey, where their showplace farm is located. So they may know Jonathan as a neighbor already.

Lloyd Wescott is a sort of handsome Abraham Lincoln. His wife is one of those elegantly groomed, beautiful women, with great posture, large, clear eyes, a great profile. Warm. They're handsome together.

She's happy, you think. A large farm in New Jersey, a good-looking husband, beautiful paintings, you've heard. And you saw the mountain of chinchilla she left on the bed when she arrived. And she's supporting the arts, you think. Giving her brother-in-law and his boyfriend a home.

You're laughing at your own joke when you bump into good-looking Bob Bishop coming out of the bathroom. He's in uniform, which makes him even handsomer. Blonds always look superb in uniform. He had his retouching studio next door to George's studio over on Madison Avenue and then joined the . . . what is it?. . . the ski corps or something like that. You drag him into a corner and he tells you about the training out in the Rockies. It sounds like absolute hell. He says he doesn't think they are ever actually going to do anything with the ski troops, and he plans to try to resign and join the Canadian Air Force. He has a Canadian passport since he was born there. He asks you if you are there by yourself. You say yes. He doesn't follow up on it. Maybe you should have.

You get your coat and drift toward the door. There aren't as many good-looking young men here tonight as is usual at George's parties. You smile at the Fabulous Sergeant, a young man stationed at Governors Island who comes to many of these events. You go up to him and say, "What's your name?"

"Dick Sisson."

"You're so handsome you have to be an actor once this whole thing is over."

This is probably what half the people here tonight have told him, but he's a nice guy and says sincerely, "I'd like to."

Lincoln Kirstein is one of the few old guard in the military. Paul told you that when he went to see the draft board, he took some of his work and they got the idea right away. They were kind to him, he said, and told him he could be rejected on several grounds. One of them was "insanity." He enjoyed that. George Tooker has just gotten out of the marines. Years later Lincoln tells you that George killed Japanese with his bare hands. That's just Lincoln's sense of humor. Still, even though George looks like a china doll, you imagine he could be rather tough.

Pete Martinez is off somewhere in the navy. Whether you like boys or not doesn't seem to matter to the military if you don't make a big fuss about it. Of course, George Platt Lynes—with his white hair and perennial tan—wouldn't have slipped in so easily. He looks wonderfully young tonight. You wonder how the army could have resisted him. He would have looked fantastic in uniform, as a military photographer. Cecil Beaton did it, and no one could be swishier. Perhaps George really didn't want to do it. Across the room, laughing, he is so youthful that you can't help thinking that perhaps he has had his face done. He now looks younger than when you first met him. If anyone would have had a face-lift, it would have been him.

You leave, thanking George and telling him his new apartment is beautiful, which it is. He seems pleased to hear it.

You're still living in Grove Court in Greenwich Village, and lucky to be there. With the war, apartments are impossible to find. You walk over to Seventh Avenue to take the local train to Sheridan Square. With the brownout, it's dark in the streets, but you can see clearly, and there is no danger—except for all those cute soldiers and sailors raging through the streets. Someone says, "Hey, beautiful," as you go down the subway stairs, but that's as far as anything goes for you these days, unfortunately.

The War Years

With the coming of the war, the struggle to survive the Depression ended suddenly, not so much with affluence as with the country's need for everyone to take part in the war effort. For many Americans the war came as something of a surprise. Although there had been every indication for almost a decade that Nazism in Germany would lead to a worldwide war, most of the people in the United States had been able to ignore it.

Caught up in building their careers in the world of the arts, George Platt Lynes, Lincoln Kirstein, Paul Cadmus, and the group who surrounded them had not paid much attention to events in Europe. Even annual trips abroad did not suggest the catastrophe that was to come. When friends had to flee France in 1939, cutting short their holidays as the Nazis threatened to invade, Americans still paid little attention, and even the subsequent bombing of London did not distract them in any real way from their pursuits.

George Platt Lynes continued his photographing of fashion and the famous, distracting himself with an ever-increasing interest in male nudes. Paul Cadmus remained immersed in his painting, but it began to undergo a sea change. From acid critiques of those people the journalist

H. L. Mencken called "the booboisie," his work took a turn toward the magical and sensuous. It was certainly very much affected by his long summers on nearly deserted Fire Island in the company of Jared French and his wife. Lincoln Kirstein was deeply involved in building a national ballet company. The School of American Ballet he had founded with George Balanchine was producing more and more well-trained dancers for his company.

When the Japanese attacked Pearl Harbor in December 1941, Americans stopped ignoring the war overnight. The men in the Lynes-Cadmus-Kirstein group, many of them homosexual, now had to face their futures in a nation at war and decide what their role in it would be.

George Platt Lynes continued on in his professional life almost as though the war did not exist, though he was to be greatly affected by it. Paul Cadmus moved his art even further into a world set magically apart from the war. Lincoln Kirstein, however, entered the military. He wasn't offered a commission and spent the war as an enlisted man in Europe.

George Platt Lynes

George was devilish and devil-may-care.

—Bernard Perlin, painter

In the period immediately before the war, George Platt Lynes lost his studio assistant James Ogle. Ogle, who had married Jane Kemper—an earlier assistant—had set up on his own as a photographer. Some of his first work as an independent photographer included photographing Platt Lynes in his studio with his new assistant, George Tichenor. Another addition to the staff was Dora Maxwell, a sturdy, steady young woman from Oklahoma. Her title was studio manager, and she handled all the Platt Lynes photo sessions, booking the models, organizing studio equipment, and answering and making phone calls. Platt Lynes, himself an expert typist, handled the billing. Dora Maxwell also became proficient in the dark room while working at the studio and gradually took on the bulk of this work. She worked long hours and was not well paid, but she loved her work and was compatible with her boss. George was now definitely Platt Lynes. He began using his middle name professionally just before the war, probably because his fortunes were running high and he wanted a fancier name to go with his fancy new life. And perhaps he suspected his name would live on, and he wanted it to have a distinguished sound.

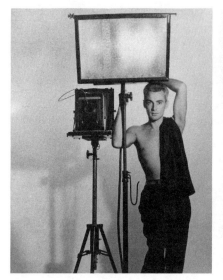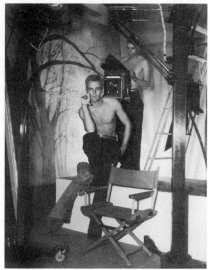

George Platt Lynes in his studio, by James Ogle, 1940. (Courtesy of James Ogle. Reprinted by permission)

George Platt Lynes (foreground) with George Tichenor in studio, by James Ogle, 1941. (Courtesy of James Ogle. Reprinted by permission)

Some of Platt Lynes's friends of that period believe that the new assistant, George Tichenor, was from a New Jersey family and had first encountered his new employer on Lloyd and Barbara Wescott's farm. However he came to work in the photographer's studio, Platt Lynes was soon infatuated with him. Muscular, dark, and brooding, Tichenor provoked perhaps the strongest emotions that Platt Lynes felt during his lifetime. The potential for a romantic attachment was probably what prompted Platt Lynes's offer of employment in the first place.

Observers of this relationship believe that Tichenor never returned Platt Lynes's affection, but that he was not reluctant to manipulate his employer to retain the connection. He evidently had no qualms about posing nude for Platt Lynes and enjoyed the photographer's attention. Platt Lynes was then thirty-three and Tichenor twenty. The painter Bernard Perlin, who was in the Platt Lynes circle, has written, "I suspect that there was some intimacy, but Tich was very hard to get . . . for one thing, he kept falling for Ginger Rogers or whoever—in a word, he played GPL like a yo-yo, teasing him, keeping him panting."

With the coming of war, Tichenor was eager to sign up for military service, but a childhood illness had left him deaf in one ear. This made him unacceptable to the military. Determined to serve in some capacity, he joined a civilian ambulance service and prepared to embark for overseas. Platt Lynes did haunting and prophetic photographs of Tichenor, naked in a hammock with bandaged eyes—a kind of helpless, suffering, modern pietà figure. He also did a portrait of Tichenor in his military-style driver's uniform just before his departure.

Tichenor was on a troopship headed for North Africa when it was torpedoed in the Atlantic. The young ambulance driver was among those rescued, and the survivors were disembarked in France and placed in an internment camp on the Spanish border from which Tichenor was repatriated to the United States. Still determined to do his part in the war, he embarked again for North Africa and this time made the passage safely. But soon after, he was killed by a German strafing attack on the ambulance convoy in which he was driving at the battle of El Alamein in Egypt. His death was devastating to George Platt Lynes.

In the short period that he was in Platt Lynes's life, George Tichenor had also posed for Paul Cadmus and was the model for *Aviator*, in which he holds a kite overhead. The original drawing for the painting was given by Cadmus to Platt Lynes.

As soon as war was declared, George Platt Lynes offered his services to the public relations department of the air force at Mitchell Field on Long Island. The major in charge was a friend, and Platt Lynes did photographs of the pilots at the field, which were later published in the magazine *Minicam*. He wrote his mother that he had been offered a first lieutenant's commission to do war photography in early 1942, but decided against it as he was reluctant to close his business. He was called for the draft in April 1942 and was examined at Governors Island. He was rejected and wrote his mother, "Although I am a little disappointed, I am relieved . . . I've a bit of a nervous heart, and a bit of blood-pressure (low, I gather) and chronic sinus; not much of anything, I was not excused altogether." His letter to his mother demonstrates how deft George Platt Lynes could be at concealing the truth from others, but he told his brother some time later what really happened, "that he was excused on his single visit to Governors Island as he was a professed homosexual, information elicited not volunteered."

Platt Lynes was still living with Monroe Wheeler and Glenway Wescott on East Eighty-ninth Street, and the big excitement in their household was a Pavel Tchelitchev exhibit at the Museum of Modern Art in October 1942. Wheeler, who had been supervising publications for the museum, was now also mounting exhibitions and had convinced the trustees that the Tchelitchev show would be worthwhile. A large painting of George Platt Lynes in his working coverall was to be completed by Tchelitchev for inclusion in the show. In fact, it was never entirely completed and is now in the home of Mr. and Mrs. George Platt Lynes II after spending many years at Haymeadows, the second home provided for Wheeler and Wescott by Lloyd and Barbara Wescott.

Young men who were passing through New York or were stationed nearby came to parties at the three men's apartment. Among these servicemen was Richard Sisson; extremely handsome, he was known as "The Fabulous Sergeant." Sisson was stationed on Governors Island in New York Harbor throughout the war, and was a regular at these parties. Platt Lynes photographed Sisson in uniform. After the war he was to reappear in the photographer's life in Hollywood, where Sisson went to pursue a career as an actor. The writer Donald Windham said about the dashing Richard Sisson, "To compare the average person's kiss to Richard Sisson's is to compare a zephyr to a hurricane." He was obviously not just fabulous looking.

Platt Lynes also photographed young Robert Bishop several times in uniform. Bishop was a highly skilled retoucher of photographs who used a small studio attached to the larger Platt Lynes studio on Madison Avenue. He did all the retouching of Platt Lynes's photographs plus work for other clients. Blond, handsome, and well built, he was pressed into service frequently as a model when a photograph required a good-looking young man. Although vigorously heterosexual, he admired George Platt Lynes and the two men became close friends. He never objected to posing for Platt Lynes, and it is he who was photographed, his torso bared, looking up at a disdainful and looming Somerset Maugham, trussed up in a cravat and double-breasted pinstripe suit.

This photograph represents Platt Lynes at his most Machiavellian. He began his portrait of the camera-shy British author in a standard way. Set the lights, did some pictures, and then called Bob Bishop in from his adjoining studio to pose with Maugham. He then asked Bishop to divest himself of some of his clothes, and then more. Neither model had any idea of where the session was heading until it was over and Platt Lynes had his remarkable and revelatory portrait of the famous and circumspect Maugham.

When interviewed by Russell Lynes in the 1980s, Robert Bishop remembered a typical Platt Lynes shoot in this way: "He was almost like a performer onstage, sort of gliding around, floating around, so gracefully. He was charged with nervous energy and seemed to find it difficult to

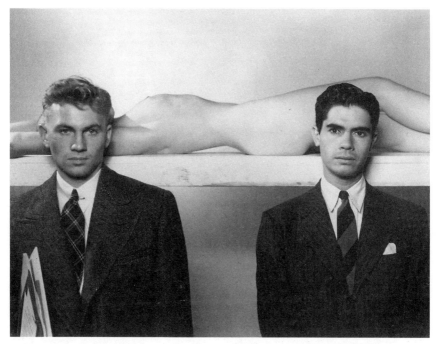

Robert W. Bishop (left) and José Martinez with female nude, by George Platt Lynes, circa 1942. (Private collection. Courtesy of Mr. and Mrs. George Platt Lynes II. Reprinted by permission)

relax. He was quick in his movements and intense. His laugh was a quick, nervous one. His mind worked quickly, and decisions were, it seemed, always the right ones. When shooting in the studio, he had total concentration with peripheral vision. All the elements, the lights here, there the subject's comfort, clothing in place, film in holders, exposure . . . George seemed to do it all himself. He was a perfectionist.

"This was never more so than in his ballet photography where he could gather together as many as eight dancers in controlled motion and come up with a fine photo and beautifully lit. This is a very difficult feat and George did it routinely. I've seen attempts since by photographers but never a success. When shooting a picture George was never still. He almost went into a trance. He smoked those little brown cheroots, always had one in his hand. When he contracted cancer, he blamed it on New York pollution." ("They weren't cheroots," Russell Lynes noted. "They were cigarettes in dark brown paper. Ordinary white cigarettes would not have suited George's eccentric posture.")

Laurie Douglas by George Platt Lynes, circa 1940 (solarized photograph). (Collection of the Beinecke Rare Book and Manuscript Library, Yale University. Courtesy of Mr. and Mrs. George Platt Lynes II. Reprinted by permission)

Although Platt Lynes was attractive to the female models who posed for him, they all understood and accepted that he preferred men, yet as early as 1938 George Platt Lynes, in a very uncharacteristic moment, had become attracted to a young female model. Laurie Douglas was launched in her modeling career by Platt Lynes when she visited his studio shortly after arriving in New York from California.

When interviewed later by Russell Lynes, she said, "I had no intention then of modeling, but curiosity took me to the studio at 640 Madison, where I gave some pictures to Dora, who took them in to George, who said, 'This I've got to see!' He came out and took one look, asked me to pull my hair on top of my head, and said, 'How would you like to go to work tomorrow at nine?' I started work as a top model—there was no 'apprenticeship.'. . . When I went to Powers [model agency] and they asked for pictures and said they would start me at the bottom price, I showed them George's pics and told them I could already ask for top price. They were flabbergasted.

"Of course I knew George was gay," she later wrote to Russell Lynes from her home in Tangiers when he was preparing to write about his brother. "I suppose that's why he was so much fun for girls to work with—they felt so easy. Then there were those who were going to make a pass at him anyway. I could never conceive of making a pass at a homosexual. Maybe that was one of my attractions for George.

"In 1938 and '39 I was in a Noël Coward show on Broadway for about six months and modeling, too. Helen Bennett and Tony Sorel were also in the show. George came to see us often and was proud that Noël had chosen three of 'his' girls to be in the show. At this time George told me to get rid of my first husband as he hated him—which I later did."

But when George made romantic overtures, Laurie Douglas was surprised. "In 1941 George and I went to Chicago to photograph a line of clothes that Pauline Fairfax Potter had done for Marshall Field department store. From Chicago I was on my way to join my husband in California for another try, and it was at this time that George made his first pass. He had to go out to dinner (with the fashion consultant on the job) but came to tuck me in bed . . . he said he hated to go to the damn dinner and would much rather stay with me, whereupon he sat on the bed, took me in his arms, and kissed me not at all like a friend or a father! (Leaving me, I might add, in a state of shock.)

"Well, after I got to California, George sent me a photo of his reception room covered with my photos, saying he had given a cocktail party there and invited all my friends and . . . 'we all cried copiously.' (I still have the photo. I was back in N.Y. by the end of '42 to take up modeling again, and somewhat later George got his apartment at Fifty-fifth and Park. I was living at some dump over near Eighth Avenue as it was the only place that would take my two Siamese cats. George called me one evening around nine P.M. asking me to come over to see the apartment. I said I was tired and had to work in the morning. He said he would get a cab and come get me just for a little while and I could help him hang window shades. I said alright, but just for a little while.

"When we arrived he made us a drink—I admired the apartment—we sat on the sofa and talked until finally I said, 'Well, we better hang those shades because I have to go soon,' He said, 'Well, you see it's like this!' I said, 'What's like this?' He said, 'I didn't really ask you here to hang window shades.' I said, 'What did you ask me for?' He said, 'This!' Whereupon he pushed me over on the sofa and we never looked back. That has to be one for the books!

"A model friend of ours tried to make George one afternoon and he told her he *had* a girlfriend. She asked him, 'Who?' and when he said, 'Laurie,' she said, 'Aren't you the sly ones!' She was a good friend of mine, too—so then it was all over town. George gave me a Cartier ring—the gold earrings made by Fulco [Fulco di Verdura, the fashionable jeweler of the time]—bought an East Indian nose ring with sapphires and rubies, which I refused to wear—and some other things I can't remember. All have since been lost.

"Adelaide [George's mother] came to visit one afternoon when I was at the apartment, and she was looking at George's book of nudes when George pulled me down on his lap and sat with his arms around me. Adelaide came across the nude of me, looked up through her lorgnette, and said, 'Charming, my dear, charming.' She really was unflappable. (I wasn't!)"

George was not pleased when she went dancing at the Stork Club and El Morocco and she began to feel resentful since George "was acting like he owned me." She told Russell Lynes, "On the nights George had business dinners he made sure he knew where I was—like the night he called Monroe [Wheeler] and made him ask me to dinner with Cecil Beaton so he would know where I was till he got back. As you can understand, this began to pall after a while."

"Jonathan came into the scene about this time," Laurie Douglas continued, "which was lucky for everyone. . . . George started to make remarks in front of his male friends (and me) that he had Jonathan, and I was so much gravy . . . that he didn't want his boyfriend making passes at his girlfriend."

Laurie Douglas was referring to Jonathan Tichenor, who had replaced his brother George as Platt Lynes's studio assistant. More compliant than his brother—or perhaps simply more impressionable be-

Jonathan Tichenor *by Paul Cadmus, 1944 (pencil on paper, 8¹/₄" x 7¹/₂"). (Collection of Mr. and Mrs. George Platt Lynes II. Courtesy of D. C. Moore Gallery, N.Y.C. Reprinted by permission)*

cause he was younger—Jonathan was drawn into a relationship with the photographer.

Jonathan Tichenor soon left the studio to join the ski troop division of the U.S. Army. He enlisted with Robert Bishop, the young retoucher who used the small studio next to Platt Lynes's. Bishop was an expert skier, and perhaps his enthusiasm for the glamorous ski corps aroused Tichenor's interest. After Bob Bishop left for the army ski corps, his little studio was used by the American painter Marsden Hartley. How Platt Lynes came to meet Hartley isn't known, but they became friends. Platt Lynes had a number of Hartley paintings, which can be seen in photographs on the walls of a number of his apartments. He also used Hartley as a model in a series of haunting photographs, in which Platt Lynes used low strip lighting along the back of the studio to get the effect of light at the end of the day. In one photograph, a shadowy young man stands at the horizon line. This was probably Jonathan Tichenor. Hartley, who had recently lost a young man he loved through drowning, has an air of great mourning. In another photograph, the painter wears a heavy overcoat and seems about to depart for somewhere. Again, there is a feeling of deep mourning.

In September 1943, Platt Lynes wrote his mother, "Did I write you, or did you see in the papers, that Marsden Hartley died? The painter to whom I loaned a little room all last winter. He was sixty-six but he was at the top of his form and we were very devoted to him; it was a shock."

Without Tichenor and Bishop, Platt Lynes had to lean heavily upon Dora Maxwell to help him with shootings and darkroom work. Fortunately, she was very capable in both of these areas.

Dora had her own wartime drama. Francis "Kiko" Harrison, the handsome younger half brother of Barbara Harrison Wescott, had entered Dora's life. Kiko's early life had been spent in Scotland, and his fresh good looks and British manner made him instantly popular in the Wescott circle. He posed a number of times for Platt Lynes, both clothed and nude, and while at the studio met Dora Maxwell. Dora, while large and plain, had enormous zest and confidence, and the two became attracted to each other. Kiko was commissioned as a naval officer in the submarine force, and in January 1944, on the spur of the moment, he and Dora decided to get married before he shipped out the following day.

George Platt Lynes, Monroe Wheeler, and Glenway Wescott threw themselves into this project. The group took the train to Elkton, Maryland, the nearest state where there was no waiting period for a wedding license. They arrived there in the dead of night, roused a justice of the peace, and witnessed the wedding. A ring of Platt Lynes's was used as a temporary wedding band. The entire wedding party then sat in the local train station until dawn and the first train. Back in New York, they had a wedding breakfast at the Plaza Hotel before seeing Kiko off to the plane that was taking him to the West Coast to join his ship.

Dora Maxwell remained as studio manager for Platt Lynes until the

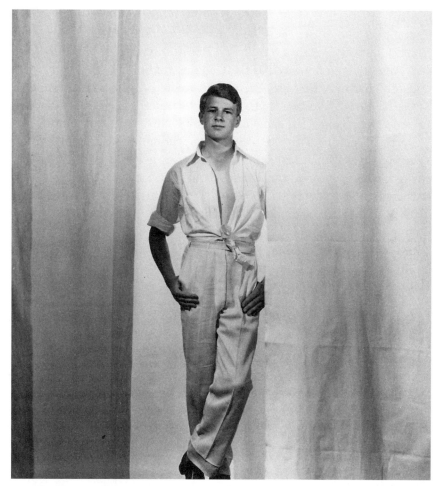

Francis Burton "Kiko" Harrison by George Platt Lynes, circa 1938. (Collection of Anatole Pohorilenko. Courtesy of Mr. and Mrs. George Platt Lynes II. Reprinted by permission)

war was over, when she left to join her husband. Kiko, after advanced studies, was employed as a physicist by the Atomic Energy Commission. With Dora he moved to Los Alamos, New Mexico, where they remained for many years.

A new entrant into the Platt Lynes circle in this wartime period was the young painter Bernard Perlin. Perlin was one among any number of new friends at this time, but later he became a much closer friend and confidant to the photographer. Originally from Richmond, Virginia, Bernard Perlin had come to New York in his early teens to study art. In the early 1940s he was taken by a friend to visit Paul Cadmus at his studio on St. Luke's Place, and the older painter immediately thought his friend Glenway Wescott would find Perlin interesting. He called him and Wescott soon appeared at the Cadmus studio. He directed his formidable charm at Bernard Perlin and invited him for a weekend at Stone-blossom. Wescott and Perlin became lovers, and through Wescott the young artist came to know the entire circle of friends.

Perlin remembers that visitors to the home of Barbara Harrison Wescott always remarked upon a large Courbet of a cow, framed in cowhide, that decorated the dining-room wall. He also remembers that Barbara Wescott wandered about her farm wearing a necklace of large black pearls. She lived glamorously wherever she found herself.

Summertime visitors to the Wescott farm took part in nude bathing. There was a water hole on the nearby Mulhocaway River, and if the weather was warm, family and friends went for a dip in the altogether. George Platt Lynes enjoyed displaying his shapely body and often photographed male nudes sprawled in the water and the nearby woods, but some visitors were dismayed to find a Wescott sister and her brood removing all their clothes a few feet down the riverbank.

Lincoln Kirstein found Perlin's work promising, and they too became friendly. With the coming of war, Bernard Perlin found employment in Washington as a poster designer in the department of propaganda. Lincoln Kirstein's sister, Mina Kirstein Curtiss, was an executive with the Office of Wartime Information (OWI) and helped Perlin get his position. His unit was disbanded in less than a year, and he was then attached to a group of *Life* magazine artists working near the front lines to record images of the war. Perlin was posted to Cairo to record the North African and eastern-Mediterranean fronts.

Unlikely as such assignments might be in later wars, in World War II there was a great interest in communicating to the public the reality and danger of the war. This was before television, and in certain fields of battle, photographs would not be feasible, although photographers were also covering war zones all over the world. This is how Bernard Perlin found himself accompanying commando raids out of Cairo. While the raids were dangerous, Perlin was evidently no hindrance to the highly trained commando units he accompanied. He brought back powerful impressions of a night raid on Cyprus that made dramatic viewing for the readers of *Life*.

According to Perlin, Cairo was teeming with handsome young men from a myriad of military services, and as in any wartime environment, a

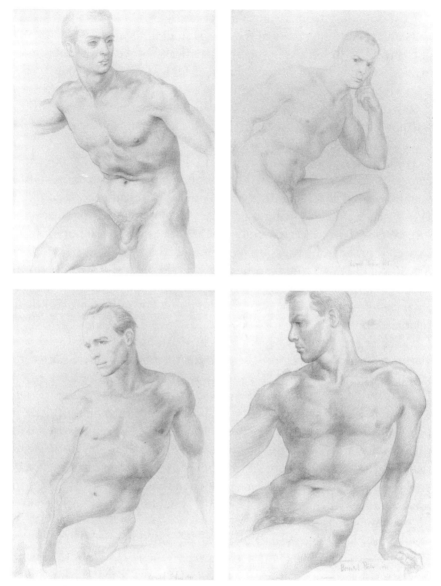

George Platt Lynes, Lincoln Kirstein, Glenway Wescott, *and* Monroe Wheeler *(clockwise from upper left), as mythological figures by Bernard Perlin, circa 1941 (silverpoint, 7" x 6" each). (Collection of John Connolly and Ivan Ashby. Courtesy of Bernard Perlin. Reprinted by permission)*

lot of frantic sexual activity took place. For a young man from the largely covert homosexual world of the puritanical United States, Cairo was an eye-opener and an opportunity to live out one's most lavish fantasies.

Corresponding with friends like Bernard Perlin, George Platt Lynes had contact with the reality of the war, although his own life was largely unchanged. In 1943 the photographer radically broke up the rhythm of his life. He moved out of the apartment he had shared for many years with Monroe Wheeler and Glenway Wescott and took an apartment of his own at 421 Park Avenue on the northeast corner of 55th Street. This was done to provide a home for himself and Jonathan Tichenor, who was away in military training.

His setting up his own apartment at the age of thirty-six stunned his friends Wheeler and Wescott. Their friend George was planning to live openly with his lover, and they considered this in bad taste. It also left Wescott and Wheeler living together as lovers, not "sharing digs" in a threesome. Glenway Wescott didn't like it because he felt it put Monroe Wheeler in an embarrassing position at the Museum of Modern Art. Russell Lynes wrote that they were afraid of "malicious gossip," of which there must have been plenty. Certainly there couldn't have been anyone among their acquaintances who didn't know the nature of their relationship.

Wheeler also visited Russell Lynes in Washington, where Lynes was working during the war, to discuss the situation. Wheeler wanted to know why Platt Lynes was "turning away from his two most concerned friends who had so assiduously guided and promoted his career, one of whom was his intellectual lode star and the other his longest, dearest love?" Russell Lynes had no answers but suspected his brother wanted to shed his dependency on these two men. A friend of the 1930s has said that Monroe taught George Platt Lynes everything, remarking, "He couldn't even carry on a conversation when they first met." It is easy to understand why Platt Lynes felt a need to establish his own identity, and his own home.

George Platt Lynes took the apartment on the fourth floor of the small, five-story building, above the jeweler Fulco di Verdura. The once well-known actress Fanny Ward, whose stage career dated back to before the turn of the century, lived on the second floor above a fashionable florist shop, The Rosary. She was discovered by Platt Lynes one day sitting on the staircase, ordering her money into little piles of bills. She had been a famous beauty and had held on to her looks far longer than her peers. Fortunately, she had also held on to her money.

In describing the apartment, Russell Lynes wrote, "The furniture that gave the flat, as George always called it, a quiet, comforting, somewhat Victorian air came partly from the rectory in Englewood: 'George Platt' chairs and an oval, inlaid 'American Rococo' table made by Platt, lamps that would have been at home at the 1875 Centennial Exhibition, a chaise lounge upholstered in tufted velvet, an Empire black bookcase with brass beading around its glass doors. On either side of the fireplace were large red Chinese tea boxes with sloping lids, in one of which was firewood. Over the mantel was a pair of white oval plaster plaques of heads in the neo-classical manner. George had bought them in a New Jersey junk shop for $5 apiece. There were green leafy plants on a paneled desk with a white marble top and wherever else there was room for pots, for George was 'good with plants.' He had contrived a rather formal and at the same time relaxed room that invited conversation and music and intimacy, one where it was as natural and discreet to sit on the green carpeted floor as on the furniture upholstered in velvet. (The carpet had been rescued from Stone-blossom, where it had been on loan in a bedroom.)"

Many were the friends who came to visit the photographer in his new apartment. Not only did he mix with many socialites, but his friends included the poet Marianne Moore, who had originally come to be photographed and stayed to know and like him. Paul Cadmus and Jared French were close to him in the 1930s and remained friends, and his school acquaintance Lincoln Kirstein came with his wife, Fidelma Cadmus, until the army sent him overseas.

Platt Lynes invited the writer Katherine Anne Porter to "come and dine off my purple-and-black table in my green and white room to view my artworks, many of which are borrowed, and my handiwork, much of which isn't mine at all. It all adds up to a fine effect." Porter was a lifelong friend, and he wrote her frequently about his concerns for Jonathan Tichenor in the military. In May 1944, he wrote to her and reported, "And now he has had himself discharged and will be back this week." How Jonathan got discharged in the middle of the war seems never to have been clarified or discussed, but once back he decided he wished to have a career as a photographer. Platt Lynes, who loved a project, threw himself into his lover's new vocation wholeheartedly. In two months he was able to tell Porter, "Jonathan is doing well. He got himself the job of taking the photos for the Souvenir Program of the Ballet Russe de Monte Carlo (the Danilova–Freddie Franklin lot) and took them very well. He has had a couple of paying portrait jobs, a fashion sitting and a Life Goes To a Party sort of job, as well as all the experiments and things for free. It's a good beginning, and I'm pleased with his progress."

By the end of 1944, George Platt Lynes's life had an appearance of

Russell Lynes *by Bernard Perlin, 1945 (silverpoint on paper, 10³/₄" x 7³/₄"). (Collection of Mr. and Mrs. George Platt Lynes II. Courtesy of Bernard Perlin. Reprinted by permission)*

Mildred Akin (Mrs. Russell) Lynes *by Bernard Perlin, 1945 (silverpoint on paper, 9³/₄" x 9¹/₂"). (Collection of Mr. and Mrs. George Platt Lynes II. Courtesy of Bernard Perlin. Reprinted by permission)*

stability. Jonathan Tichenor had returned to New York and was living with him. His friend and retoucher Bob Bishop had also returned and had again taken a studio adjoining the photographer's. Because of his Canadian birth, Bishop had been allowed to leave the ski corps to join the Canadian air force, but had subsequently been discharged from the RCAF because the war was winding down. His presence was always much needed by Platt Lynes.

Platt Lynes had a large exhibition of photographs at the Wadsworth Atheneum, among them a selection of his neglected mythology pictures. There had been another exhibition at the Art Alliance in Philadelphia, and the December 1944 issue of the magazine *Dance Index* had been devoted to his ballet photography. However, in the middle of the year he had written to Dora Maxwell, "Big economy campaign here. Added up yesterday, found I owed in the vicinity of $10,000. Christ!" (This would be about $100,000 in today's dollars.) Even in the midst of success, he was sowing the seeds for further trouble.

Despite his enormous debts, George Platt Lynes was determined to find a country home for Jonathan Tichenor and himself. He no longer visited Stone-blossom and missed going to the country. After much searching, he finally settled on renting a house in East Hampton in 1945. Russell Lynes wrote that this house was to become "the eye of an emotional hurricane or, as some of his friends saw it, a teapot in which there was a tempest."

Russell and his wife, on the other hand, had returned to New York and bought a small house on the Upper East Side for $21,000. They also bought the North Egremont house from Russell's mother. Both of these houses were to be temporary havens for George Platt Lynes in the future. Russell Lynes was soon employed by *Harper's* magazine, where he rose to become managing editor. In the years ahead, his wife and he were to be sources of security for his ever more erratic brother.

Paul Cadmus

Memories of summer past in the long winter to come will survive as faded magic.

—*Lincoln Kirstein*

Paul Cadmus spent the early 1940s painting subjects that had little to do with the battles and bombings of World War II. When he was called up by his draft board, he had to decide whether or not to tell the truth about his sexuality. Most homosexual men did not, and they served in the armed forces throughout the war, but Cadmus was truthful and received a deferment. The artist said, "I took my artwork with me when I was called, and it was pretty clear where I stood. They were actually very nice and offered me several choices as to the type of rejection I could have. One of these, as I remember, was 'insanity.'"

Cadmus did not return to the violence and sacrifice of his 1940 painting *Herrin Massacre*. Instead, the human body in the sun, at the seashore, and in ballet rehearsal studios occupied his thoughts and work. Yet the war influenced his paintings *Survivor* and the later *What I Believe*, just as it affected everyone on the home front.

Immediately before the war and during its first year, he did portraits of his friends who lived and weekended in New Jersey. In 1940, he did a triple portrait of Monroe Wheeler, Glenway Wescott, and George Platt Lynes in front of Stone-blossom. Bare-chested, Wheeler wears a little embroidered Moroccan cap he frequently wore when relaxing (perhaps

Paul Cadmus by George Platt Lynes, 1941 (gelatin silver print, 7¹/₂" x 9¹/₂"). (Hallmark Photographic Collection. Courtesy of Mr. & Mrs. George Platt Lynes II. Reprinted by permission)

to conceal a bald spot) and looks serious and aloof. Wescott kneels in the center against a large tree that stands behind the trio. He is wearing some kind of mysterious black satin or oilcloth lounging suit. Strangely wrapped at the waist, it seems to be a vaguely oriental outfit of his own invention. He appears youthful and handsome as he looks down on the reclining Platt Lynes. The photographer wears only a kind of twisted and rolled loincloth, identical to the one he wore when photographed by Man Ray in Paris. One arm supports his head, the other circles it. Like Wheeler, he seems withdrawn, and also somewhat bored. Behind them in the distance stands the handsome house they occupied on weekends, the house that was doomed by flooding when the state government decided to form a reservoir some years later. Every detail of this painting is realistic, yet the mood of the three men is clearly captured: Their world is perfect but emotionally empty. Only Wescott yearns slightly for Platt

Conversation Piece *by Paul Cadmus, 1940: triple portrait of Monroe Wheeler, Glenway Wescott, and George Platt Lynes (left to right), with Stone-blossom in background (mixed technique: oil and tempera on linen on pressed wood panel, 22^1/$_8$" x 33^1/$_2$").(Collection of Mr. and Mrs. George Platt Lynes II. Courtesy of D. C. Moore Gallery, N.Y.C. Reprinted by permission)*

Lynes, who doesn't care. Although Cadmus never had a disparaging word to say of anyone, he clearly had an opinion of these men and their lives. There is no hostile criticism in the painting, only an accurate rendition of their lives together.

Meticulous rendering of detail also characterizes Cadmus's 1941 portrait of Mrs. Joseph Russell Lynes, the photographer's much-adored mother. Paul Cadmus did not know Mrs. Lynes well, and this painting was almost certainly commissioned by her son. But here again there is a perfection in the painting of Mrs. Lynes's white and beautifully arranged hair, of which she was proud. Her triple-strand pearls, gold bracelet, and black lace shawl suggest an affluence she did not have. Seated leaning against the back of an elegant chair in a standard pose, she seems to be looking back at a life already lived, and her face has a slightly bitter expression. Her husband's photograph, by their son, hangs on the wall, and in its glass are reflected church spires, recalling her husband's life as a pastor. He, too, is leaning upon his supportive hand, in the same pose as his wife uses here and as his son assumed in the previous year's painting of the three friends: perhaps a comment by Cadmus that the pretense of social standing is a fatiguing one and requires all the support it can get. Again in this portrait of Mrs. Lynes, her world is quite a perfect one, but empty, with little to look forward to. Mrs. Lynes was an extremely self-contained woman who did not even attend her son's funeral—nor did anyone realize until her own death that she, through canny investments, actually had quite a lot of money, none of which she ever offered to her hard-pressed son in his final, desperate years. Cadmus captures this enigmatic quality of someone who has endured much and has become reserved and formal in self-defense.

The third of these portraits is titled *Lloyd and Barbara Wescott with Eclipse of Morston, Mulhocaway Butterfat Favorite and Heartsease Butterfat Heather* (1942). Blond Lloyd Wescott looms large in the center, the pitchfork held across his shoulders, making them seem even larger. Eclipse of Morston is a giant Percheron horse. The two Butterfats are massive prize cows. Gigantic barns stand behind and a sky reaches off endlessly. At the heart of the painting stands crop-haired Barbara Harrison Wescott. She seems tiny and fragile in the midst of all this healthy, hearty hugeness. Yet her money has provided it all; she created this model farm for her model husband and provided model circumstances for his relatives, the friends of his relatives, and even the friends of the friends. As with Mrs. Lynes's portrait, she is unsmiling and seems to be looking far off into the distance. She, too, is a woman who has had to keep her own counsel. In her world there is no one like herself: She is alone and it shows. For the third time, Paul Cadmus has depicted a beautiful and perfect world, but even the animals cannot keep it from seeming empty.

These portraits contrast sharply with the world Cadmus captures in his beach scenes, which are truly vast and yet do not seem empty at all. In 1941 he painted *Aviator* using George Tichenor as a model. The sculpted body of Tichenor wears rolled-up blue pants and an open blue shirt; his equally sculpted face looks up at a box kite, held aloft against a darkening blue sunset sky streaked with pink cirrus clouds. Daylight is still on the sand and dunes. Here there is perfection, too, in the young man's body, but grace and hope and energy are also embodied, even against the coming of night. The eternal qualities of beauty represented by Tichenor seem to hold all of the painter's interest.

In the companion piece, painted in 1944 and entitled *Survivor*, George Tichenor's younger brother, Jonathan, lifts the remnants of a wire fence to continue his passage down a beach. The dark sky beyond seems to be the last evidence of a passing storm. On the beach, where the receding waters have left it, are the remains of the kite his brother lifted in the earlier painting. The delicate, elongated, almost angelic blond Jonathan inhabits a wrecked world. Acid-green brief trunks seem to have been added later to his naked form, as though Cadmus had changed his mind about allowing his model to wander naked in this ravaged landscape. And empty as the landscape is, a subtle, emotional quality permeates it: A ruined world is about to be rebuilt by fragile humans.

This same empty landscape that is somehow full of emotion and promise was captured in *The Shower* of 1943, *Point o' View* of 1945, and *Fences* of 1946. Of the three, all taking place on the beaches of Fire Island, *The Shower* probably best exemplifies why the work of Paul Cadmus is frequently defined as Magic Realism. The naked man in the outdoor shower, the second male resting tan and warm beside the shower stall, the enigmatic woman wrapped in a beach towel in the middle distance, inhabit a sunset moment that most of us have experienced. A moment when light and nature conspire to create a kind of perfection.

Lincoln Kirstein writes of this painting, "Clouded skies imply late daylight, or even a season's ending. Soon the beach will be bare of bathers. Memories of summer past in the long winter to come will survive as faded magic. When such were actual moments in place and time, reality was even more magical. This picture is a portrait of such ambiguity made specific."

The war years were made supportable for Paul Cadmus by his capturing of these moments when reality *is* magical. If reality can be magical, then horror and cruelty are made bearable.

The same beach scenes filled with magic were subjects that fascinated both of the Frenches also. As early as 1940, Jared French had painted *Figures on a Beach*. A woman lies sleeping draped in towels; a deeply tanned young man kneels beside her, winding a large towel about himself, and behind them, another young man is coiling rope against the far-reaching sky filled with the same streaks of cirrus clouds as in the Cadmus paintings. This young man is wearing a white T-shirt, a garment recently appearing in American men's wardrobes as government-issue underwear. He is also wearing white cotton briefs, another new addition to men's underwear at this time. Even more than in Cadmus's *Shower* painting, the relationship of the three people is highly charged but enigmatic.

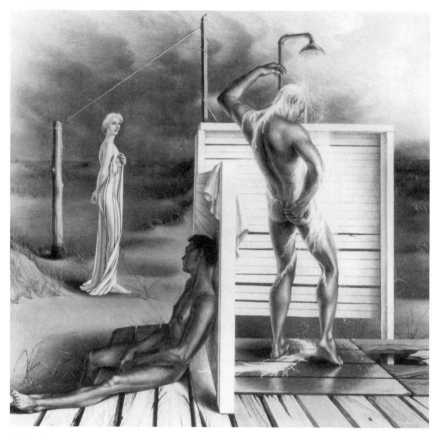

The Shower *by Paul Cadmus, 1943 (egg tempera on pressed wood panel, 15¹/₄" x 15¹/₂"). (Collection of John P. Axelrod. Courtesy of D. C. Moore Gallery, N.Y.C. Reprinted by permission)*

Immediately after this painting, Jared French began peopling his paintings with men who looked like the early Greek kouros statues. Wide-staring eyes and pointed profiles removed their perfect selves from reality. He deviated from this style in 1942 to paint *Homesickness*, in which a crop-headed blond young man stands on a dark shore, opening his arms to a distant view of pyramids floating in the sky. This strong statement of the eternal quality of male beauty is modernized with rolled-up and rolled-down trousers exposing untanned flesh. This garment is similar to the rolled pants worn by the Tichenor figure in Cadmus's *Aviator.*

Jared French's use of figures hearkening to an ancient Greek past increased from this time on. His portrait of his wife, Margaret Hoening

French, done in 1944, shows intimations of this future style. Her serene face and large, staring eyes have a "not of this world" quality that was very much her own and might well have prompted her husband to inhabit his paintings with more of the same types of being. Above her head in her portrait are the same streaks of cirrus clouds that suggest impending change.

Her own painting of this period, *The Moon by Day*, done in 1940, has a scattering of distant male nudes near an apparently deserted wooden island building, perhaps a coast guard station. A moon hovers faintly in the great stretch of sky across the water behind the building. Something less magical but perhaps even more eternal is in this painting in tempera on a gesso panel that could easily have been done in the Renaissance.

Fidelma Cadmus Kirstein's portrait of her husband, done at this time, has nothing reminiscent of the beach. But the clear light across Lincoln Kirstein's face and the pale blue sky behind him has everything in common with her brother's work in the early 1940s and that of the Frenches. She captures perfectly the lurking suspiciousness in her husband's handsome face, an expression that was to become more pronounced as the years passed. For many, this is the best portrait of Kirstein, a man who loved to have himself portrayed.

In addition to the portraiture and the magical scenes of beach life he painted during the war years, Paul Cadmus also recorded scenes at the School of American Ballet. This school, founded in 1933 by Kirstein and Balanchine, had studios in a building on Madison Avenue between Fifty-ninth and Sixtieth Streets in New York. The studio of George Platt Lynes was in a building across the street on the uptown side, making it convenient for the many dancers he photographed during this time.

Cadmus's painting *Arabesque* (1941) is painted from the point of view of someone seated on the floor in a ballet studio, looking up at the back of a male dancer and a young woman in black leotard, in a high second-arabesque position. In the background another young woman in the short rehearsal tunic of the period does a *passé* to the knee on pointe in a not very precise manner, which was probably also typical of the period.

In the 1944 painting *Reflection*, a mirrored wall forms the background in which a black-tighted dancer stands, her leg raised. In front of the mirror, three dancers lounge. The male dancer sprawled full length displaying his handsome buttocks and legs has the head of Sandy Campbell. Not a dancer, he was a Princeton freshman at the time he met Paul Cadmus at a party in 1943. Campbell, who was about to be drafted,

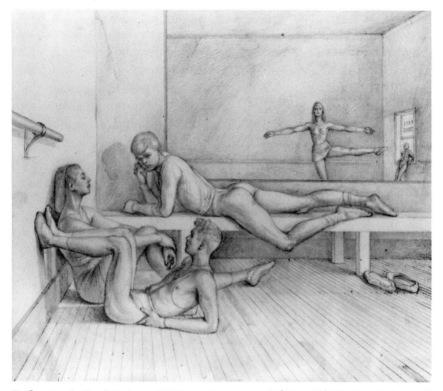

Reflection by Paul Cadmus, 1944 (pencil on paper, 16³/₄" x 19¹/₈"). Sandy Campbell posed for dancer on bench, Fidelma Cadmus for woman against the wall, Donald Windham for dancer in foreground. (Private collection. Courtesy of D. C. Moore Gallery, N.Y.C. Reprinted by permission)

asked the artist to do a pencil portrait of him for his mother. Cadmus, quite taken with the young man, suggested that he do a portrait for himself as well, and this led to his incorporating Campbell in his painting. Some photographs were also done, and Cadmus was soon enamored of his good-looking model.

The second figure, a woman seated with her back to the wall in a red top and snood, has the regal profile of Cadmus's sister. Although thirty-seven years old at this time, she still had youthful allure. The third figure, a young man supporting himself on his elbows and with his feet placed against the wall, was originally drawn with the face of the young writer Donald Windham.

Windham had come to New York with his lover, Fred Melton, in 1939. After several years Melton left him to marry a young woman in

Georgia, and Windham survived by working for *Dance Index*, a magazine supported by Lincoln Kirstein. He lived in the Cadmus/French studio when they were on Fire Island in the summer, and Fidelma Cadmus Kirstein, who at times painted in this studio, often took Windham home to feed him a solid meal. He also visited the artists at their island summer rental and was frequently photographed alone and in groups with them. Donald Windham's distinctive profile did not survive in the finished painting of *Reflection* because, before it was completed, Sandy Campbell and Windham had fallen in love. This was not a happy event for Paul Cadmus, and he subsequently changed the features of Windham in his painting to those of someone anonymous.

A third painting, *Dancer* (1945), is a strongly foreshortened view of a male dancer lounging on a studio floor reading a book. The sinuous poses of dancers' bodies appealed strongly to Cadmus, as did their world of bare wooden floors and light-filled space. Here, too, the work has the "waiting for something to happen" quality that suffuses his beach-oriented work. Cadmus said of this tiny, $1^1/2$ x $1^1/4$-inch painting, "I think I was trying to disappear because of this war."

The many photographs taken by Paul Cadmus and Jared and Margaret French during their summer vacations of this period testify that reality *was* magical for them. They were often joined in Saltaire, the Fire Island community where they rented a summer house, by Fidelma Kirstein. Her husband was overseas in the army, and she had remained in New York to care for his ailing mother. The painter Bernard Perlin also joined them there, before leaving for duty in the Near East as a war artist.

Perlin and Paul Cadmus were companions for a short time during these early years of the war. A number of pictures show them sunning nude in the dunes with a clothed Margaret French seated nearby. The pictures were taken by Jared French.

All these pictures, taken with Margaret French's Leica camera, later came to be called PaJaMa photographs. There were any number of pictures of Jared French's handsome body, as well as disembodied heads and hands peering over crests of sand or clinging to driftwood. Glenway Wescott, who usually remained clothed, was photographed when he visited, as was George Platt Lynes, who was emphatically unclothed. These photographs show people inhabiting an empty but somehow symbolic and meaningful beach world, the same that Paul Cadmus painted during this wartime period. At the end of these seasons in the sun, the young George Tooker appears in the PaJaMa photographs.

Recently discharged from the Marine Corps, George Tooker resumed his studies at the Art Students League, where he met Paul Cadmus. The two men became lovers, and Tooker rented a studio near the
St. Luke's Place studio that Cadmus and French shared. Cadmus's statement on this arrangement was: "I had Jerry in the daytime and George
at night." Tooker's large, clear eyes and expressionless face add their own
magic to the PaJaMa photo collection. His image was the inspiration for
one of the most beautiful Cadmus paintings, *Inventor* (1946). The young
man's figure holds a delicately balanced mobile made of fragments of
driftwood, shells, feathers, and a crab carapace. Behind him, a door
opens onto a glittering sea and drifting clouds. This is the last of Cadmus's beach-inspired paintings that hold out hope in the form of a beautiful body in a beautiful place in a beautiful moment.

Lincoln Kirstein

"Am I not really dead, mate?"
Then shitless scared I am.
Another buzz bomb cruising
Claims I'm not worth a damn.

—*Lincoln Kirstein*

On the brink of the United States' entry into World War II, Lincoln Kirstein was leading his ballet company on a tour of South America. The war in Europe had already been going on for two years, and the Western Hemisphere was on its own for cultural exchange. Movies such as *Flying Down to Rio* and the importation of the Brazilian bombshell, Carmen Miranda, had awakened North Americans to the fact that there *was* a culture south of the border.

Kirstein's friend Nelson Rockefeller, whom he knew from the Museum of Modern Art, was President Roosevelt's coordinator of Inter-American Affairs at this time, and Rockefeller had underwritten this tour of the American Ballet through South America.

Starting on June 25, 1941, in Rio de Janeiro, the company, comprised of fifty-one people and sixty-eight large trunks of costumes and other theatrical effects, gave more than one hundred performances in seven South American countries. The tour had its hair-raising moments, especially when the plane carrying the company flew low through the valleys of the Andes to reach Chile. For most of the dancers, this was their first airplane flight. After the performances in Chile, Kirstein flew back to Washington, ostensibly to make sure that the male dancers would not be

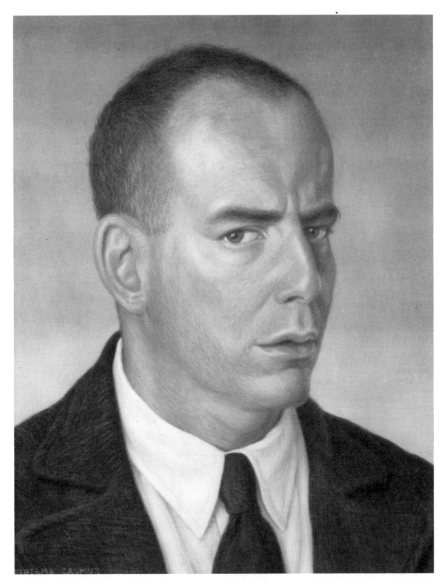

Lincoln Kirstein *by Fidelma Cadmus Kirstein, 1941 (egg tempera on masonite board, size unknown). (Collection of the Estate of Lincoln Kirstein. Reprinted by permission)*

drafted before the tour ended. In reality, the problem was money: The reviews had been good, but box office receipts were meager since the company lacked the glamorous Russian ballerinas necessary to attract audiences. Kirstein secured additional government funds, and the tour continued up the west coast of South America. After giving its final performances in Caracas, the company sailed back to New York on November 6.

Lincoln Kirstein with ballerina Gisella Caccialanza in Buenos Aires on tour with the American Ballet Caravan, 1941. (Courtesy of San Francisco Performing Arts Library and Museum. Reprinted by permission)

Fidelma Cadmus Kirstein by George Platt Lynes, 1941. (Collection of Paul Cadmus and Jon Andersson. Courtesy of Mr. and Mrs. George Platt Lynes II. Reprinted by permission)

This was a dangerous journey, as German submarines were already torpedoing American ships in the Atlantic.

The company made its way back, on a long, slow voyage, without mishap, but returned to a New York that had become very different for young men. José Martinez found that his friends in the ballet company were, for the most part, signing up. At first, Martinez was in a conscientious objectors' organization in Philadelphia, joining the English writer Christopher Isherwood, who was already there. In his diaries, Isherwood records how glad he was to welcome Martinez, with his ready wit and high spirits. Later, even though he was a Mexican citizen, Martinez joined the U.S. Navy, where he spent the remainder of the war.

After the ballet tour ended, Kirstein was sent back to South America in

1942, to buy paintings and sculptures for the Museum of Modern Art. (When the museum exhibited its Latin American collection in 1943, Kirstein wrote the catalog.) In fact, there was another reason for the trip: he had been sent by Nelson Rockefeller to report on how well the U.S. diplomatic corps was functioning in the countries he visited. His letters to Rockefeller somehow got into the hands of the State Department, which objected strenuously to this extracurricular spying. Kirstein received the lion's share of the criticism, probably because his reports were accurate and unflattering. As a result of this imbroglio, he was not offered a commission in any branch of the armed forces, although many of his friends from Harvard were.

Perhaps anticipating the war that lay ahead, Lincoln Kirstein had married Fidelma Cadmus in April 1941. He also managed to find time to found the magazine *Dance Index*, whose first issue appeared in January 1942. Throughout the war Kirstein remained an editor and a major contributor—in November 1944 Platt Lynes sent him photographs for the current issue, calling them "not too tiny representations of the girls and boys you left behind"—but the young writer Donald Windham took over the editorial chores while Kirstein was in the army. The final issue of this important scholarly magazine was published in 1948.

Even though draft boards rejected anyone they could identify as homosexual, large numbers of gay men and women served in the armed forces during World War II (estimates range from 650,000 to 1.6 million). Kirstein became one of that number in 1942 when he was drafted into the U.S. Army and sent to Fort Belvoir in Virginia for basic training. He trained with the Corps of Engineers, graduating in January, 1943. In his graduation picture, his overseas cap sits high on his large head, his arms are folded awkwardly over his lap, and he seems a good deal larger than the rest of his classmates.

At one point, Kirstein obtained "compassionate leave" to return home because his widowed mother was thought to be dying. Mrs. Kirstein, who enjoyed poor health, lived with Kirstein's brother, George, on the Upper East Side of Manhattan. She did not die then, however, and in fact lived on for another fifteen years.

While on leave in New York, Kirstein was photographed in his private's uniform by George Platt Lynes, and in the picture he has removed all insignia or rank. He was perhaps inspired in this by Jean Cocteau, who had done the same thing while serving as an ambulance driver in the French army in World War I. Obviously if Kirstein could not be an officer like his friends, he was going to be a special case unto himself.

Lincoln Kirstein also published, in 1943, a book called *For My Brother*, based on a true story told to him by José Martinez, whom he refers to as Jose Martinez-Berlanga, carefully following the Hispanic custom of combining the father's and mother's family names. (The dancer never used the compound name in his stage credits.) In his later years, Martinez said that he often tried to find a copy of this book, printed in London, but the entire stock had been destroyed in a warehouse fire during the wartime bombing.

In 1944 Kirstein attended a party given by Katherine Anne Porter in wartime Washington. Russell Lynes, who was working in the capital as a speechwriter, observed that Kirstein spent the evening in deep conversation with General Lucius Clay, whose wife was a poet and a friend of Porter's. Lynes assumed they weren't discussing military matters, as Kirstein was a private first class. However, this acquaintance may have come in handy at the end of the war when the general was the U.S. military governor of Germany. Kirstein was soon attached to the military government's division of Monuments, Fine Arts, and Archives, recovering looted artworks.

Whether Kirstein actually spent his time in uniform wearing insignia or not is impossible to verify, but he was certainly granted privileges not available to the average Pfc. In his book of poems based on his war experiences, *Rhymes of a Pfc*, published in 1964 and in an expanded version in 1966, he writes of living with an English family while awaiting orders (he was shipped to France twenty days after D Day). He also describes slipping out of his encampment to see John Gielgud on tour in *Hamlet*, "the best night of my life (in a theater)," but certainly not the ordinary GI's idea of a night on the town. He also writes admiringly of General Patton, for whom he was a driver in France. In another poem, he recounts experiences from the time when he was attached to the Third Army's Monuments, Fine Arts, and Archives Division. He was part of the team that recovered art stolen from occupied countries, primarily France. In one town in Germany they came upon a former SS officer who had headed the pillaging of Paris. The officer wanted safe-conduct passes for his French wife and small child and himself to leave the area in exchange for revealing the hiding place of the looted art. Though his request was refused, the German told them where the art was anyway. Later Kirstein heard that the officer had killed his family and himself, fearing retribution from the Germans. Kirstein's verses on this incident don't indicate much regret, not even for the wife and child; instead, he meditates on art's ability to survive war and its destructive forces.

A striking thing about these poems is how openly the poet displays his

Military unit in which Lincoln Kirstein served in World War II. Kirstein is third from the right, second row, partially hidden. (Courtesy of James Radich. Reprinted by permission)

physical interest in other men. In "Gloria" a drag queen tells the story of a sailor who is booted out of the navy for homosexual carryings-on. "Fixer" is about a young enlisted man who runs out on a sexual assignation with a male friend of his father's who can help him get a better military assignment and spends the night with the fixer's hunky marine sidekick. In *"Das Schloss,"* which takes place at the war's end in occupied Germany, a countess is trying to prevent her castle from being used as a U.S. Army headquarters; her son plays the *Goldberg Variations* for the American soldier who is sent to inspect the castle. As the American departs,

> *I thank this young man. In some happier dispensation*
> *He'd have been a close friend; nay, even a lover.*
> *Impulse shoves me to the brink of intense declaration.*
> *Music undoes me. I'll help him, forgive him, restore him,*
> *Unite what is left of our lives, slave for and adore him—*
> *But conscience or caution warns of possible bother.*

A young man playing Bach on a harpsichord in a castle ballroom: These lines reveal a great deal about the essentially romantic nature of Lincoln Kirstein.

The toughness and terror he saw in his wartime experiences were things that he rarely discussed outside his poetry, but those experiences may well have had much to do with his later casual dismissal of friends. In the violence of the world as he had seen it, social rudeness probably seemed like a small matter.

James Radich served with Lincoln Kirstein in the same military government detachment that was sent to France immediately after the invasion army. He remembers Kirstein as being self-effacing and low-profile, and even in the company photograph one sees Kirstein slightly averting his face, almost as though he was slightly ashamed of being there. This unit was being trained as military police. Radich, who had followed the world of ballet from his hometown of Sacramento, California, recognized Kirstein's name stenciled on a duffel bag and introduced himself. He remembers his fellow Pfc typing in front of his tent every day and saying to him once, as he came out of the showers, "Did'ja get blowed?"

Radich is referred to in the poem "Boy Scout":

Our Sacramento soldier leans on a nubile tree,
Extracts an ancient Scout knife to carve initials three. . . .

In a collection of Kirstein's writings, *By With To & From*, the editor, Nicholas Jenkins, notes, "Making use of his dignified Harvard-polished bearing and his familiarity with French and German, Kirstein roved through Europe unfettered by the Army's rigid hierarchy, working as courier, chauffeur and interpreter. (When the war ended, he was one of the very few foot soldiers able to claim that he had his own jeep.)"

Whatever or whoever the power sources were that allowed Lincoln Kirstein his unusual freedom while serving in the U.S. Army (certainly his sister serving in important civilian posts in Washington didn't hurt), he made excellent use of it and served his country well. Learning that the Nazis had hidden much of their looted art in a salt mine in Austria was a stroke of luck for Kirstein but also a major contribution to undoing the war's damage. He is quoted by Nicholas Jenkins as saying that the war was "the key experience of my time." In his own immediate group, Kirstein had the most direct experience with the war, and it taught him how to reach goals by going outside the usual chains of command. He was to put that skill to good use upon his honorable discharge in 1946 as he worked to establish an important, nationally known ballet company.

Fidelma Cadmus Kirstein

There was always something enigmatic about Fidelma Cadmus Kirstein. Even in early portraits of her she gazes forth at the world in a way that suggests she knows something others don't.

She was well trained in art and was working as a designer of wallpaper when she was still young. She left her parents' home and for a time lived with her two aunts in Greenwich Village. Like her brother, Paul, she continued to paint seriously while doing commercial work, studying at the Art Students League in the evening and on weekends. After meeting and eventually marrying Lincoln Kirstein, she continued to go occasionally to work at her brother's studio on St. Luke's Place.

Her husband asked Pavel Tchelitchev if she had talent, and Tchelitchev, who liked no painting other than his own, said no. From then on Fidelma Kirstein received no encouragement at home, and gradually with the responsibilities of her husband's social life and of caring for his perennially ailing mother, she spent less and less time painting.

And yet, as with Jared French's wife, Margaret, the quality and skill of her work is undeniable. Certainly both women suffered from the attitude of the period that women painted decoratively and were not to be taken seriously.

But her portrait of her husband is one of the best of the many he posed for. And her other paintings show a gentleness and kindness not seen in her brother's work, whatever other resemblances there may be.

That erratic and brilliant Lincoln Kirstein loved Fidelma is beyond question. He was deeply appreciative of her understanding of the workload he burdened himself with and also of his emotional instability, which was aggravated by that pressure. They both struggled with shaky emotions from time to time, and his wife's experience and support of his recurring moods was a strong bond between them.

That her husband often fell in love with young men must have been distressing, but she accepted the situation and was usually understanding. On one occasion she asked her brother to speak to her husband after Kirstein insisted upon holding artist Jensen Yow's hand while they were with a group of friends. She accepted Lincoln Kirstein's homosexuality, but she preferred that demonstrations of his affection for other men not take place in her presence.

However, longtime friends such as Bernard Perlin do not think that Fidelma Cadmus Kirstein regretted her marriage. She seemed to enjoy the life she led as the wife of a patron of the arts.

Fidelma Cadmus Kirstein was a beautiful woman who posed often for her brother and Jared French, as well as for Pavel Tchelitchev. She was photographed by George Platt Lynes on several occasions, once in a velvet evening gown that had been designed by Charles "Chuck" Howard at the beginning of his career in dress design. In the photograph she wears the dress with style and aplomb.

She was not a vivid or dominating presence in the glittering world of creators, talkers, and celebrities in which she lived. But she played an important role by being calm and understanding and accepting both their talents and their faults with grace.

Like her friend Margaret French, she may have been an observer and a supporter, but the men who surrounded her very much needed just such a reassuring presence.

Fidelma spent her last years in a nursing home, where Kirstein visited her each week. When she died in 1991 at eighty-five, her artistic abilities had not been fulfilled, but she had lived through most of a century deeply involved with many people who had made it fascinating, and she kept her own counsel well through those many years.

The Postwar Years
1945–50

Going Hollywood

It's 1947 and George answers the phone when you call. He's living in Holly-wood now. It's something of a comedown for the great George Platt Lynes to be running the Vogue *studio in Los Angeles, but it's a living. And he needs a liv-ing right now. With the war over, he's gone out of style in the flood of new young photographers. "Come on over," he says, "and meet Greta Garbo. She's coming to my party tonight."*

She was there, Greta, but she didn't stay long. Not very tall, and her head seemed too large for her body. Her face, anyway. Like Gloria Swanson, the only other movie star you've ever met. But beautiful. Not much hair, though. Maybe she just needed to wash it.

You are in Hollywood on a fashion shoot. You're a full editor at Vogue *now. You'd like to leave, but where is there to go except to* Harper's Bazaar? *And that's hardly a step up. Maybe* Vogue Paris. *That could be fun.*

A lot of good-looking young men are at George's party. One of the best is George's new boyfriend, Randy Jack. Randy is shortish and dark and cute, but a far cry from Monroe Wheeler. Poor George. Randy tells you he was a sailor during the war. He must have been extremely cute in uniform with that trim little body and American-boy features. Every girl's dream.

He tells you that George wants him to become a dancer and that he's study-ing every day with Nijinska here in Hollywood. Nijinsky's sister, who evidently is tough as an old boot. You know George must be planning to use his contacts with Balanchine and Lincoln Kirstein in New York to advance Randy's career later.

Randy introduces you to Katherine Anne Porter, the writer who is staying with George right now. Katherine Anne isn't particularly interested in talking to you. She has white hair, is quite patrician-looking and haughty. She keeps looking over your shoulder as she talks about how much she hates working for the movie studios. You excuse yourself so she will be free to talk to someone more famous than you are.

White seems to be the theme this year. George has his usual tan and is all in white. He looks trim. He must be going to the gymnasium regularly. Katherine Anne is also in white—a linen dress. And Randy is in a white shirt and shorts. All to fit into George's all-white house, which is sparsely furnished and fitted with wooden blinds.

He tells you he plans to completely redo the house, but he has run out of funds temporarily. What a fool he is, really. A house he couldn't afford. A career in a nosedive. He's something like a Russian prince, you think. He knows what he must have and thinks little about who is going to pay for it. What furniture he has is that canvas folding type of thing, what Vogue *would call safari furniture. There are many paintings to compensate, however. All on loan from Edward James, the English millionaire, Randy tells you. Edward James has established himself in Mexico and left all his paintings in George's care. George is going to be quite miffed when Edward wants them back.*

You see Burt Lancaster across the room. So handsome. You wonder if it's true what they say about him and his passion for getting blow jobs. He's going to have to pass, as far as you're concerned.

You talk to one of the models for the bathing-suit shoot you're doing with George. Her name is Laurie Douglas. She tells you that George did her first pictures as a model and that she started off immediately as a $300-a-day girl. Top fee. She's a Conover girl. Or is it John Roberts Powers? She must have been drinking too much because she also tells you that she had an affair with George. You look into her glass. An olive looks back at you. You wonder how many she's had. "Oh, yes," she says, "he was crazy about me. He even told his mother." She asks if you'll get her another drink. When you bring her another Martini, she tells you that she did nude pictures for George last week. You are glad to hear that and think how dear it is that people out here feel no need to keep anything to themselves. It's sort of like the radio. You turn it on, you hear everything, you turn it off, and there's no one there.

You go and get yourself a Martini and discover the Fabulous Sergeant is standing by the bar. He's not a sergeant anymore. "Dick, Dick, Dick . . . ," you say. "Sisson," he says, "but I'm calling myself Richard Shaw these days. I'm an actor now." Charmingly, he pretends to remember you from New York, which couldn't possibly be the case. You wonder why anyone so impossibly handsome isn't already a star. You feel a little bit like becoming a fan yourself. He introduces you to his friend, Peter Hanson. Not an actor, but handsome, too. Blond. Peter asks you how you like it here in the Swish Alps. You don't get it. He points out that you're in the Hollywood Hills. Swish. Swiss. You're still not sure you get it.

You look about. Many of the men here are blond. Tan, of course. And everyone is good-looking. Since you're in the Hollywood Hills, you act like a Californian and introduce yourself to a beautiful blond young man who has just arrived. The young man's name is Carlos, strangely enough. You say, "You must be an actor." He says that in fact he isn't, but that he's working at a studio in the art department. He's quite a lot of fun, this Carlos. You point out that the model across the room was photographed nude last week in this house. Carlos tells you that he was, too, adding, "George must have had nothing to do at the studio." He says that probably everyone in the room has been photographed by George with his or her clothes off. You say, "I haven't. Should I be insulted?" Carlos says, "I would be." "Do you think Thomas Mann has?" you ask. Thomas Mann, the famous German writer, has just entered, wearing a white linen suit that is miraculously not very wrinkled. Maybe he walked across town and hasn't sat down in it yet. Carlos says he thinks it's entirely possible, as George can get practically anyone out of his knickers. Mr. Mann is accompanied by a gaggle of European creative types who descend on the hors d'oeuvres trays like locusts. God knows what they do. Compose, write, direct, act? Whatever they do, you can tell it is very serious, very artistic. Carlos changes his mind about Thomas Mann posing nude and tells you that he probably wears a double-breasted suit at all times. Even to bed. "He probably just lowers his tie," he says.

You go to the bathroom and notice that George's bedroom has that tortoise-shell wallpaper that he uses everywhere he lives. And his mother's portrait by Paul Cadmus is on the wall. As you come back down the stairs, George seizes you and introduces you to his brother and sister-in-law. They seem happy to meet someone from New York. Russell is fair-haired and doesn't resemble George very much. He's pleasant in a formal way. Obviously, he's been well brought up. His wife is equally aristocratic but a lot more fun. Handsome, dark, and a great figure. Her name is Mildred. She says, "George insists on calling me Akin. It was my maiden name. My name was Mildred Akin and they called me Mildewed Acorn at school. Naturally, I've always detested Mildred."

The martini seems to have taken over your personality and you tell the Lyneses that George seems to have photographed most of the people in the room nude. "Me, too," says Akin, pointing out that it was some time ago. "Where did that picture go?" she asks her husband. He looks at her as though they only recently met.

Charming Carlos McLendon comes up to you, and Akin and he get along *like a house on fire. Two charmers outcharming each other. Katherine Anne Porter is sitting by herself in a corner, looking glum. You couldn't be happier.*

You promised Mrs. Vreeland, the fashion editor, that you'd have all the clothes organized for the shooting tonight, so it's time to go back to your hotel. You're trying to find a telephone to call a cab when Richard Sisson offers to drop you off. They live in that direction. He and Peter Hanson are obviously a couple. You feel a little pang. He really is handsome.

In the car they tell you that they met on the corner of Hollywood and Vine. Truly. And they've been photographed nude by George in his house, too. Several times. But always together. Really more mood stuff than full frontals, they assure you. No full frontals? Well, almost no full frontals. They're a really nice couple of guys. Too nice for Hollywood, you think.

In your room, as you sort out the gingham rompers and the new Lastex strapless one-piecers that are now all the rage, you think that George seemed distracted and not very happy, somehow running through his paces in a mechanical way. This whole Hollywood thing must not be working out very well for him. How could it? There really isn't any life out here in the bleaching sun. There's just the activity of creating pictures and films that resemble life, so as to entertain people in the rest of the country. And when they come out to enjoy that life for themselves, they discover there's nothing to enjoy.

You're glad you are going back to New York Saturday on the 20th Century Limited. Maybe you'll sleep with someone on the train.

George Platt Lynes

Has anyone seen my rat?

—Bridget Bate Chisholm

When the war in Europe ended in May 1945, George Platt Lynes had already weekended in the new home he had rented in East Hampton a number of times. He had celebrated his thirty-eighth birthday there on April 15 with Russell and Mildred Lynes and Paul Cadmus, who stayed nearby with his friend Bridget Bate Chisholm.

During that summer of 1945 Platt Lynes makes no mention in his letters of the human and economic devastation in Europe. His concerns focused on the absence of a cook and the noisiness of his nephew and niece when they visited. The atomic bombing of Japan in August and the end of the war there goes unmentioned, too, submerged in the explosive news that Jonathan Tichenor has left him for Bridget Chisholm.

Bridget Chisholm was married at the time, but her husband, Hugh Chisholm, a discreet homosexual, was in Rome working for the U.S. government's information bureau. She had taken a major fancy to Jonathan Tichenor during the summer. She had interested the young man in pursuing a career as a painter as well as a photographer, and Tichenor had enrolled at the Art Students League at her urging. Paul Cadmus remembered traveling by train to Long Island with her and her white rat, Ratrick. The rat escaped from time to time, and Bridget would pass through the railroad car, asking, "Has anyone seen my rat?" Platt Lynes wrote Dora Maxwell in August, "Bridget's in the same class. . . . She has a few new young men, J. for one. . . . I'm a bit bored by her these days but she's beautiful still and amiable." Platt Lynes could be somewhat naïve, and at the time suspected nothing, but his sister-in-law was more perceptive. Mildred Lynes remembered being at George's country house "sitting on a sofa with Bridget and Jonathan while Bridget was painting her toenails bright red and was busy weaving a flirtatious web around Jonathan. It was obvious what was going on—spider and fly. Women are quick to notice such things."

Despite Bridget and Jonathan's flirting right under his nose, George Platt Lynes was taken completely unawares. According to one friend, he realized he was losing Jonathan Tichenor when the young man "came home one night smelling of pussy, and I knew that was it." The same friend remembers that Jonathan Tichenor, despite his romance with Bridget Chisholm, was the epitome of the haughty, well-dressed, cuff-linked, young gay man of the period. Platt Lynes was determined to forget his unfaithful lover, and he had the *J* that was tattooed on his arm removed, leaving a large scar.

He distracted himself with a handsome new lover, William Christian Miller. In October 1945 they attended a Halloween party given by Alice Delamar, an important benefactress of the arts, at her country home in Weston, Connecticut. For the party, Platt Lynes and Miller dressed in tight-fitting costumes, reminiscent of the commedia dell'arte, with Fulco di Verdura jewels pinned on them. (Platt Lynes favored Verdura jewelry and often gave pieces as gifts.) He did a series of photographs of Miller and himself in these costumes. The party was held in a barn on the Delamar estate, decorated fancifully with autumn leaves by Pavel Tchelitchev. Miss Delamar provided a studio home for Tchelitchev on her estate and was a patron for many years. Those who attended the party remember the handsome young-man-about-town Bill Harris arriving with a friend, both dressed as nuns, on roller skates. Many flirtations and sexual high jinks occurred that evening, according to the guests.

A curious side of George Platt Lynes's personality began to emerge at this time, as evidenced by the scrapbooks he kept. These large scrapbooks were filled with pictures of Edwardian beauties and American actresses in elaborate dresses, pictures of athletes and handsome college rowing teams, drawings by Pavel Tchelitchev of society personalities, all of which were cut from magazines. Unnervingly, there would also be an occasional picture of a lynching or something similarly brutal. At the

Self-portrait by George Platt Lynes, 1945, with William Christian Miller (left) and George Platt Lynes in costume for a Halloween party given by Pavel Tchelitchev on the Weston, Connecticut, estate of Alice Delamar. (Collection of Peter Hiler. Courtesy of Mr. and Mrs. George Platt Lynes II. Reprinted by permission)

end of the war he began gluing in *Life* magazine photographs of Nazi atrocities: heaps of emaciated corpses, a well-fed and warmly dressed child from a guard's family glancing at a stack of dead bodies as he walks past, and sequential photos of members of the French underground being executed by firing squads. There are many, many pictures of this kind, interspersed with shots of half-dressed American servicemen with strong bodies, servicing airplanes and occupied with duties behind the lines. This abstract interest in cruelty would flicker up again and again later in life.

In January 1946 Platt Lynes decided to take a vacation and wound up in Hollywood visiting Katherine Anne Porter, as he was unable to get a flight to visit friends in Mexico or the Caribbean. Once there, he not only visited but worked. Besides Porter, he also knew the English writer Christopher Isherwood and Bernardine Szold Fritz, an old friend from Paris. There was also MaiMai Sze, a beautiful Asian friend who was living with Irene Sharaff, the famous costume designer. While in Los Angeles, he did portraits of Thomas Mann and Aldous Huxley. Bernardine Szold Fritz introduced him to the designer Adrian, who was married to the former film star Janet Gaynor. Platt Lynes quickly wove a network

Living room of George Platt Lynes's home at Sunset Plaza Place, West Hollywood, California, 1947. (Private collection. Reprinted by permission)

of friends, old and new. After three weeks of partying, sunshine, and many new acquaintances, he returned to New York, determined to relocate on the West Coast.

His decision to leave New York was strengthened by frequently seeing Jonathan Tichenor and Bridget Chisholm, by now married, moving in the same social circles as he did. To Katherine Anne Porter he wrote, "The Tichenors are all over the place, playing poor." Though his career had been flourishing in New York, he left.

He traveled to Los Angeles in May with his brother and sister-in-law and Laurie Douglas in a big, blue secondhand Buick convertible. The Grand Canyon didn't interest Platt Lynes. "It's totally without human scale," he told his brother. Once in Hollywood, he planted his relatives in a dingy hotel and went to the Beverly Hills Hotel for his "image." Soon he had found a large house on Sunset Plaza Place, borrowed the $12,000 necessary for a down payment, and spent months "doing it up." Fortunately, commercial work was very available, and soon he was making jaunts to Mexico, San Francisco, and Honolulu.

Platt Lynes wrote to his friend Diana Sheean, wife of the foreign correspondent and author Vincent Sheean, in July, "Fancy, after all these years, coming face to face with Theda Bara; she still has extraordinary eyes. But Janet Gaynor is my pet. Where do the young ones hide? . . . Are they worth looking for?" Hollywood never got really interested in him, which was a disappointment for someone who thrived on being the center of attention.

To keep himself amused, he gave many parties, which added to the pressure upon his budget, pressure that was compounded by the extravagant decoration of his new home. His inability to comprehend a relationship between his income and his "outgo" became increasingly evident.

A new lover was to add even more to the financial pressure. Randolph Omar Jack, known as Randy, had come to the West Coast in the U.S. Navy. Randy met George Platt Lynes through mutual friends shortly after discharge from the Navy, and the photographer encouraged him to embark upon a career as a dancer. Jack came to live with Platt Lynes and studied ballet daily. Randy Jack remembers that the interior decoration of Platt Lynes's new home was done with the help of Kate Drain Lawson, a New York friend then doing set design for the Pasadena Playhouse.

Some of the paintings in his home were on loan from Edward James, the English millionaire who had financed Ballets 1933. James was busy establishing a ranch in Mexico and was looking for storage for his art. Randy Jack recalls Edward James as "a strange little guy who said, 'I've got some stuff. I'll send it over.'" The "stuff" included a gigantic Dalí painting, *Impressions of Africa*, which leaned against the wall in Randy Jack's bedroom. (The next time he saw the painting, it was installed at the National Gallery in London.) Platt Lynes was quite unhappy when Edward James asked for his paintings to be returned. They had been in his possession long enough for him to have begun thinking that they were his.

In addition to redoing his home, Platt Lynes also redid Randy Jack. Jack's slightly bat ears were pulled into line at Platt Lynes's suggestion. Photographs were done of the plastic surgeon's glamorous wife in exchange for the operation. Platt Lynes wrote to his mother about the operation: "And you know me, I can't leave things alone but redecorate or remodel anything I can lay my hands on, people as well as houses."

Randy Jack also remembers the day Greta Garbo came to call with Cecil Beaton. To amuse her, Platt Lynes showed her his albums of nudes. She preferred the male nudes to the females. The photographer wrote of her, "She was easy and amiable and surprisingly well-dressed (in corduroy pedal-pushers, etc. to be sure, but really well done). And there were surprises for me, too, in the familiar face and voice, still unbeaten, perhaps unbeatable. We all fancied her to no end."

His portraiture met with great enthusiasm from the subjects, who in addition to Aldous Huxley and Thomas Mann soon included the composer Arnold Schoenberg and Lotte Lehmann, the famous soprano. Lehmann wrote him he was "a miracle man!!! You succeeded in making me rather young and lovely!"

However, *Vogue*'s art director, Alex Liberman, was much less pleased and throughout Platt Lynes's residency in Hollywood was unappreciative of his work. But *Vogue* editor Liz Gibbons, who had been a favorite Platt Lynes model, remembers Liberman as being unreasonable and not exhibiting great judgment with Platt Lynes's photographs. She also remembered a shooting that ended with a model washing her muddy son in the bathtub at Platt Lynes's home. The child was complaining that there were no sailboats in the bathtub when the photographer passed the open door. Platt Lynes glared into the messy bathroom and said, "You can be glad there are no *sailors* in there for you to play with!"

One of the more fascinating men Platt Lynes reacquainted himself with in Hollywood was Denham Fouts. He had photographed Fouts in New York in the 1930s, and they met again in Hollywood. Denham Fouts's life was fictionalized by Gore Vidal in "Pages from an Abandoned Journal," by Christopher Isherwood in the novella "Paul" in *Down There on a Visit*, and by Truman Capote in *Answered Prayers*. Legend has it that he was discovered as a teenager working in his father's bakery in Florida and was spirited off to Europe by a wealthy tourist. There he was claimed as a lover by aristocrats and celebrities, both men and women. Among them were Crown Prince Paul of Greece and the French actor Jean Marais. In this pre-war period Peter Watson, heir to an English margarine fortune, became enamored of Denham Fouts. The story is told that they were to meet in Shanghai and catch ship together, but when Watson arrived, Fouts had already departed with a caravan for Tibet. In the early days of World War II, Fouts had been sent

George Platt Lynes's study at Sunset Plaza Place, West Hollywood, California, 1947, by George Platt Lynes. Peter Hanson's head appears behind the desk. (Collection of Anatole Pohorilenko. Courtesy of Mr. and Mrs. George Platt Lynes II. Reprinted by permission)

back to the United States by Peter Watson, with a large Picasso painting, *Girl Reading*, as his "severance pay." Fouts died in Rome in 1948 of drug addiction. The painter Bernard Perlin remembers seeing him there: Denham Fouts in bed like a corpse, sheet to his chin, a cigarette between his lips turning to ash. His lover would remove the cigarette just before it burned his lips. At night Fouts took out his cigar box of drugs, injected himself, and, like Coppélia, came to sparkling life for the evening.

While in Hollywood, Platt Lynes not only did fashion work and portraits, but added to his collection of male nudes. Many handsome young men were available to strip and photograph—and often to take to bed. Randy Jack was, of course, photographed, as were the Fabulous Sergeant, Richard Sisson, and his lover, Peter Hanson. Both Sisson and Hanson were ex-servicemen who had come to Hollywood to pursue careers and met there, amazingly enough, at Hollywood and Vine. Blond Carlos McLendon also posed nude, and he remembers the George Platt Lynes recipe for Martinis: gin, vermouth, and a touch of olive juice. Laurie Douglas was also photographed nude in a number of locations in the sparsely furnished house in Hollywood.

But before the end of 1947 George Platt Lynes was already planning to move back to New York. In August, he wrote to Lincoln Kirstein, "Kassandra A. Porter predicts we'll both be out of here by May. I'm sold down the river (to *Vogue* magazine) until then anyway." "Kassandra" hit it on the nose.

Katherine Anne Porter was ending her stint working for the movie studios, but remained in Hollywood. She had moved in with Randy Jack and Platt Lynes. Porter had written an article about Gertrude Stein that Russell Lynes had published in *Harper's* magazine in December 1946, and its criticisms of Miss Stein had caused a furor and a wave of hate mail descended on Porter. After reading her negative fan mail, George Platt Lynes said to the writer, "I had never realized what a heel you are!"

Porter was soon to learn what a heel George Platt Lynes was. Her good-looking nephew Paul Porter had come to Hollywood and met the photographer, and he, too, was treated to having his ears pinned back by a cosmetic surgeon in exchange for Platt Lynes's photographs. In his new persona, he became an integral part of Platt Lynes's circle for a brief time. Katherine Anne Porter was taken aback by their association, and she broke off with the photographer just before he left for New York, but this rift was not to last.

Platt Lynes wrote to Paul Cadmus in February 1948, "It seems now that I'll be here another year anyway, but not all the time. If I stay, I'll come and go and see you all more often." But in a few weeks Cadmus heard that his friend was heading back to New York to resume his place in his circle of friends.

Platt Lynes's contract with *Vogue* terminated in May 1948, and he departed with Randy and their poodle, Bozo, in tow. His plan to bring his Finnish cook, Taime, back east did not work out. Having made no other plans for the return to New York, the two men moved in with Russell and Mildred Lynes and their two children in their small town house.

Katherine Anne Porter, Randy Jack, and George Platt Lynes (left to right) in the garden of Lynes's Hollywood home, 1947. (Collection of Randy Jack. Reprinted by permission)

Crammed with paintings and household effects, the dwelling had a hard time holding everything, and in two weeks Platt Lynes and Randy Jack had moved to 145 East Fifty-second Street. Randy Jack pursued his ballet studies for a while, but soon began a career as a model that proved to be far more successful. Two and a half months later, he left Platt Lynes, his finances secure and a new career launched.

Within ten days Randy Jack was replaced by Charles "Chuck" Howard. While serving in the U.S. Navy, Chuck Howard had met the painter Bernard Perlin in Miami Beach. Howard had come to New York after the

Charles "Chuck" Howard by George Platt Lynes, circa 1949. (Private collection. Courtesy of Mr. and Mrs. George Platt Lynes II. Reprinted by permission)

war and met Platt Lynes there at a farewell party for Perlin, who had received a grant to study in Rome. Shortly thereafter Howard moved into Platt Lynes's apartment. Platt Lynes now found himself with plenty of work and plenty of people to see. His old coterie of Monroe Wheeler, Glenway Wescott, Paul Cadmus, Jared and Margaret French, and Lincoln and Fidelma Kirstein welcomed Chuck Howard, in part because he had a beneficial and organizing influence upon the photographer.

Platt Lynes was making other new friends. The dancer Francisco "Frank" Moncion posed for him and became a friend, as did Jensen Yow, a young artist Lincoln Kirstein had discovered. There were also Wilbur Pippin and Fred Melton, who ran the Pippin Press, a company underwritten by Lincoln Kirstein that did fine silk-screen print reproductions.

Platt Lynes had now returned to favor with Glenway Wescott and Monroe Wheeler and was a guest at their new country house, Haymeadows. When there, he and friends would dine at the nearby Lloyd Wescott home, where guests were served by recently released inmates of a New Jersey women's prison. One man remembers being seated next to

George Platt Lynes at dinner, and Lynes remarking, not too loudly one hopes, "Our maid who is serving us is a murderess." The household staff came from the penal institution because Lloyd Wescott was intimate with the directress of the prison, a Miss Mann, who often sent parolees to the Westcotts for their first job out of prison.

An unusual member of the Platt Lynes circle of friends was Lucia Davidova, the subject of a fine Pavel Tchelitchev portrait. Jensen Yow remembers her as having been known as a "pearl feeder." Her luxurious skin contributed gleam to pearls, and she was hired by wealthy women to wear their pearls to maintain their luster and glow. She would go to bank vaults and sit there reading for hours at a time, "feeding" other women's pearls.

Although Platt Lynes was busy with work and socially occupied, his finances were in no better shape than ever. To understand himself, he resumed seeing the psychiatrist he had consulted before leaving New York. Of this he wrote to the again friendly Katherine Anne Porter, "No analysis for me, not this time, but a sorting out, making the accumulated muddle make some sense, putting the past in its place . . . our contretemps of just before your departure, for example. I wish, too, I could ask you to elaborate on your 'the first good [is] to know yourself a little better than you do, perhaps.' What need I know?" His inability to understand himself created havoc with his finances, and in desperation he asked his brother to help him. A business manager was hired, but there was no constraining or explaining to the impetuous George Platt Lynes. His need to be the giver, the controller, the star of the movie of his life, was far more urgent than any considerations of thrift or prudence. The manager soon abandoned the project and left.

As the decade ended, Dr. Alfred Kinsey, whose *Sexual Behavior in the Human Male* and its statistics on homosexual activity had caused enormous controversy when published in 1948, entered the lives of the Platt Lynes circle. He had first met Wheeler and Wescott, and although his book on male sexuality was completed, he wanted to interview and record information on the sex lives of this exotic coterie of friends. When interviewing George Platt Lynes, Kinsey discussed the erotic in art and the role it played in the artists' lives. Financially, Kinsey was a great help to Platt Lynes as he commissioned over one hundred prints to be made for the Kinsey Institute at the University of Indiana in Bloomington. And purchased many more.

In addition to interviews, Dr. Kinsey was interested in observing sexual intercourse. Glenway Wescott, an avid voyeur, arranged a number of homosexual couplings for him to observe. Large orgies were also arranged by Wescott at which the doctor was present. A number of men traveled to Bloomington, where they performed sexually for the institute's film camera. Among them were Charles "Chuck" Howard and William Christian Miller. Miller, who had been a lover of Monroe Wheeler's, was favored by Wheeler, and Howard was the preferred candidate of Glenway Wescott. There was little chemistry between the two men, and Howard has said, "It wasn't Hollywood." When Dr. Kinsey published his book on female sexuality, he included a lot of this new information pertaining to males. This sexual research in the Wescott circle was to continue well into the 1950s.

From recent biographies, we now know more about Dr. Kinsey, and that he enjoyed sexual exploits with his male staff, who were also required to sleep with Mrs. Kinsey. He evidently became enamored of Bill Miller, and they had a brief relationship.

As his finances declined, Platt Lynes seemed to become increasingly experimental sexually, perhaps due to his contact with Dr. Kinsey. Richard Sisson remembers being at a party at George Platt Lynes's after all the California contingent had moved back to New York. The guest of honor was someone with a penis so large that he had never been able to have intercourse. The celebration was because he had finally managed with Platt Lynes himself. Sisson believes that Platt Lynes photographed this phenomenal part for Dr. Kinsey. Eventually, however, Platt Lynes became disappointed in Dr. Kinsey, believing that his interest in sexual behavior was not clinical but veiled voyeurism.

By the end of the forties George Platt Lynes was drinking more than was good for him (as his letters indicate), his career was spinning downward, and instead of trying to deal seriously with his financial problems, he was increasingly involved in sex.

Katherine Anne Porter

Katherine Anne Porter is among the most esteemed women writers of the twentieth century in America. Beautiful, white-haired, elegant, a lady. When she made some money late in her career with her novel, *Ship of Fools*, she bought an emerald as big as the Ritz (twenty-one carats).

Born on May 15, 1890 in Texas, she had already written her first collection of stories, *Flowering Judas*, when she entered the lives of George Platt Lynes and Lincoln Kirstein in the early 1930s. Her relationship with Lincoln Kirstein was professional. He liked the prestige of knowing her, and she liked the possibility that he could help her get published or bail her out financially if she needed it. Neither eventuality ever occurred. She knew Paul Cadmus in New York later in the decade but their contact was slight.

In her youth and through the 1930s, Katherine Anne Porter lived a hand-to-mouth existence, surviving on little money and working slowly. She was helped financially by Barbara Harrison, who sent her to a mountain sanitarium in Switzerland when she was threatened with tuberculosis.

Porter's literary output was small, but her reputation was a solid and important one. The critic Edmund Wilson declared that Porter wrote "English of a purity and precision almost unique in contemporary American fiction," and discriminating readers recognized the quality of her work. This recognition came in part because of her association with Platt Lynes (his glamorous photographs of her appeared in *Vogue* and other smart magazines) and with Wheeler, Wescott, and the other culture brokers and taste makers in their circle. Yet, through all the years of her wary friendship with these men, she never lost her negative feelings about homosexuality, and she peppered her correspondence with references to "dumb Lesbians," E. M. Forster's "Afflicted Brotherhood," André Gide's "evil malodorous life," and a New York City that "simply swarms with every little pervert from every little town from every point of the compass in this land. . . . I find myself sharing a house with the most depraved and tiresome set of half-humans I ever saw."

She was married four or five times (one marriage was annulled) and had many affairs, mostly with younger men. As she aged, Porter remained beautiful, wore white a great deal, and seemed ever more icy and sharp-etched in her growing fame. She went to Hollywood in the late 1940s to work for the movie studios, where she was decently paid for producing virtually nothing. Her life in Hollywood was eased somewhat by sharing the home of George Platt Lynes after he arrived there in 1946. Platt Lynes did some lightly surreal photographs of them together at the house: Katherine Anne posing on an upper balcony, Platt Lynes in the garden below, shirtless, each ignoring the other. Some snapshots also taken in the garden show Platt Lynes and his lover Randy Jack barechested and sporting brief white shorts, Katherine Anne in a white dress, and their white poodle, Bozo.

Katherine Anne Porter had a handsome nephew who came to Hollywood when she was living with Platt Lynes. Paul Porter probably had some unclear ideas of becoming a movie actor. As people remember him, he had much of his aunt's beauty and also her arrogance. During his sojourn in the movie capital he was photographed by Platt Lynes and, for a time, became part of his circle.

Katherine Anne saw this as a betrayal of their friendship and may also have been offended by Platt Lynes's choice of her nephew rather than herself as a sexual partner. She did not sever her relationship with Platt Lynes because of this incident, but it clearly told her that his pleasure-seeking had become more important to him than any considerations about jeopardizing a longtime friendship.

Of the two, Katherine Anne Porter was more of a survivor than

Katherine Anne Porter by George Platt Lynes, circa 1942. (Courtesy of Mr. and Mrs. George Platt Lynes II. Reprinted by permission)

George Platt Lynes. She went to the University of Michigan to teach in 1953 and became a highly esteemed professor of English. From there she counseled the drifting and floundering Platt Lynes, and during his final illness she was as supportive as possible in her letters. She was dismayed at Platt Lynes's death, but of all his friends she must have sensed most keenly the inevitability of his decline. Her warnings and attempts to be a stabilizing force in his life had been of little use, and as a writer she surely knew that his story, once begun, would work itself out in a tragic way. Bitterness was no stranger to her, and given her emotional isolation, she could perhaps accept his life and view it in its wholeness better than someone more hopeful and romantic.

In the 1960s she was to know an ever-increasing renown. Her one full-length novel, *Ship of Fools* (1962), dedicated to Barbara Harrison Wescott, was a resounding success, and for the first time she had some financial independence. The book was made into a film, and the role that most closely resembled the writer herself was played by Vivien Leigh, whose beauty and tragedy mirrored the author's. In 1966, a year after the film's release, Porter's *Collected Stories* won the Pulitzer Prize in Fiction and the National Book Award.

In her later years, Porter became a sort of itinerant writer-in-residence, teaching at the University of Virginia, Washington and Lee University, and other colleges. Eventually she retired to the University of Maryland, which accommodated her in style, and she left her papers to the university when she died on September 18, 1980. She remained close friends with Wescott and Wheeler and Anatole Pohorilenko, who was Wheeler's companion, and Pohorilenko remembers visiting her large, top-floor apartment, which had been formed by putting two smaller apartments together. It included a large dining room, and all the rooms were beautifully furnished.

The ring with the square-cut emerald surrounded by diamonds that she had purchased with her earnings from her novel she had no real occasion to wear, but they were the jewels she had dreamed of having. At the end of a long life of struggling in poverty, Katherine Anne Porter had made it through: famed, secure, bejeweled.

———⟨ఄఄ⟩———

Paul Cadmus

I am all of the Seven Deadly Sins in a way, as you all are, too. As Flaubert said about Madame Bovary, "Madame Bovary, c'est moi."

—*Paul Cadmus*

In the year the war ended, Paul Cadmus was still living on St. Luke's Place in New York, still vacationing with Jared and Margaret French, and still with no major love interest after the Sandy Campbell disappointment. He started work on a sequence of egg tempera paintings called *The Seven Deadly Sins*, beginning with *Lust* (1945) and concluding with *Gluttony* (1949). A new panel, *Jealousy*, was added to the original seven sins in 1983. Lincoln Kirstein writes that one of the painter's definitions of evil is "the incapacity to love beyond the limits of the self." This would seem to be a key in all of his depictions of the sins, which are "riveting in their diabolical repulsiveness," according to Kirstein, but Cadmus himself said of the seven deadly sins, "They are not deadly in moderation."

With *Lust*, Cadmus created a sad, grinning figure with both male and female characteristics that resembled a huge penis encased in an oversize condom. As he was entering his middle years, this figure undoubtedly embodied his feelings of the emptiness and waste of sexuality unlinked to any specific person. *Pride*, puffed up in the stance of a society woman, has everything to do with self-concern. Thick-legged *Sloth*, head in the clouds and sticky integuments dripping down to the ground, is sightless, lost in its inability to act. *Gluttony*, like an overstuffed pigskin football, is lost in stuffing its gullet while bursting at the seams, with no concern for anyone else in its intake. Dragging a long train like a shed snakeskin, *Envy* minces across a spike-studded landscape. A venomous cobra is its headgear; snakes burst from its heart. This creature can never care for another. Nor can *Avarice*, a skull-headed spider grasping everything with its clawlike hands, pulling everything into the gorged treasure sack of its body. *Anger* bursts bloodily through the glass in which it has been reflected. This is perhaps the only sin concerned with others, but only to destroy them—muscled, red machismo, its only intention is to destroy.

For Cadmus, this must have been a period of intense consideration of the human condition. His conclusion, as reflected in *The Seven Deadly Sins*, was that self-absorption leads to self-destruction. Kirstein judged that this sequence is "in concept and achievement a capstone in Cadmus's career."

In this same period, Paul Cadmus developed an interest in the English writer E. M. Forster. Shortly before the war, Forster had written an essay on his personal philosophy, which resonated with Paul Cadmus. In this essay, Forster had written, "If I had to choose between betraying my country and betraying my friends, I hope I should have the guts to betray my country." About 1943, Cadmus had done a small painting called *To E. M. Forster* of a couple on a beach, the man sleeping nude, the woman reading a book whose cover carries the dedication "To E. M. Forster." Cadmus shared with Forster the belief that love was not something extended toward a distant deity, but, as Lincoln Kirstein has written, "was rather the brave, simple, questioning affection and/or understanding of ordinary men and women by other women and men."

In 1947 Paul Cadmus met E. M. Forster in New York, and their long conversations led to Cadmus's painting *What I Believe*. In strong counterpoint to his *Sins* paintings of this period, *What I Believe*, painted in 1947 and 1948, is a kind of paradise. In it, many of Cadmus's friends are assembled naked. He is seated amid them with a drawing pad and pencil, staring fixedly forward. Beside him is a man placing his arm protectively across Cadmus's shoulders, and behind them a woman leans tenderly forward to place her hand also on his shoulder. This couple could well be Jared and Margaret French, his former lover and his wife showing how much they cared for the painter. Just beyond stands E. M. Forster, hand extended in an explanatory gesture.

The painting shows this "brave, simple . . . affection" in many permutations. In the foreground, a young man reads Forster's "What I Be-

To E. M. Forster *by Paul Cadmus, circa 1946 (black and white egg tempera on trac-*
ing paper toned on back with pigment, 4" x 6¹/₂"). (Private collection. Courtesy of
D. C. Moore Gallery, N.Y.C. Reprinted by permission)

lieve," the booklet propped against a naked figure that might well be
Jensen Yow, the handsome young art student who posed for both Cadmus and Platt Lynes and became a permanent part of this group of
friends. In the middle background are Lincoln and Fidelma Kirstein,
surrounded by pet animals. Lincoln is playing the pipes like a mature
Pan while a young man relaxes against him. Elsewhere a male couple
embraces tenderly, and a trio of naked young men build a house, and a
satyr and an earth mother and their progeny rest quietly.

Overhead are the streaky, cirrus skies of earlier Cadmus works on Fire
Island, but at lower right a deathly gravedigger expresses horror. In the
distance, humanity in its racial and religious diversity moves endlessly
along, ignoring the three demagogues who harangue them. In this
painting, beauty, art, and affection form the beacon of light against the
dark cloud of war and hate, and all three depend on "the sensitive,
the considerate and plucky," as Forster defines the people who make the
world worth living in.

Paul Cadmus painted *Playground* in 1948. It depicts tenement
teenagers, with their briefly beautiful bodies, "hanging out" and is cen-
tered around an angelic blond boy. The yearning in this boy's eyes can
never be fulfilled in this harsh environment. Above him, hanging from a

Architect by Paul Cadmus, 1950 (egg tempera on pressed wood panel, 16" x 16").
Charles "Chuck" Howard was the model for the foreground figure. (Collection of the
Wadsworth Atheneum, Hartford, Connecticut. Courtesy of D. C. Moore Gallery,
N.Y.C. Reprinted by permission)

fence, one of his friends apes a pose of flying to heaven. This painting is
about the waste of youth and beauty in an uncaring, unseeing world. Despite its bright colors, there is much sadness, which echoes the artist's
feeling that beauty should not be ignored, should not be forgotten,
should exist for some reason.

In 1950, Cadmus painted *Architect*, a kind of companion piece to his
Aviator of 1941 and *Inventor* of 1946. George Tichenor, who died in the
war, had posed for *Aviator*, and the painter George Tooker, with his mysterious gravity, had inspired *Inventor*. The enigmatic gaze of Chuck
Howard centers *Architect*. A glittering cube sits in front of him, represent-

Paul Cadmus (left) and George Tooker, Palisades Interstate Park, circa 1947. PaJaMa photograph taken by Jared French. (Private collection. Courtesy of D. C. Moore Gallery, N.Y.C. Reprinted by permission)

ing the glowing living spaces he creates. Behind him, floating in the space enclosed by the buildings is a male nude, which is contemplative in a Renaissance pose. The model for this body was George Tooker: Cadmus said, "I wasn't forgetting George while I was painting Chuck." A ruby glow emanating from the area of his heart suggests the richness of humanity, for which there is no place in these buildings, and Howard's stare suggests that the architect knows nothing of this humanity. The painting isn't cruel, but says much about modern emptiness of space and spirit, an elegant evolution from Cadmus's almost cartoonlike criticism of the 1930s.

Chuck Howard was a favorite model for the artists he met in the postwar years as his unusual sculpted features and beautiful body appealed to many in this group. In addition to Paul Cadmus, he posed for Jared French, Bernard Perlin, and George Tooker and was sculpted by John LaFarge, the son and namesake of the well-known nineteenth-century painter. Howard was also photographed by his lover George Platt Lynes and the PaJaMa group.

Throughout this postwar period Paul Cadmus shared his life with the painter George Tooker. In 1945, Tooker vacationed on Fire Island with Paul Cadmus and the Frenches; in 1946, they were in Nantucket; and in 1947 and 1948, the group was in Provincetown, Massachusetts. For the artists to whom he was introduced by Cadmus, George Tooker's well-knit body and guileless face made him an interesting model. He was photographed by George Platt Lynes in 1945, and in the PaJaMa pictures of this period Tooker appears frequently.

In 1947 Paul Cadmus and George Tooker were photographed together in the Palisades, the tall stone cliffs that overlook the Hudson River. The two men are on a promontory of rock, with Tooker jutting forth like the figurehead of a ship bearing Cadmus's body. On this expedition Tooker agreed to pose nude upon the great rocks of the Palisades, and he and Cadmus came close to being arrested.

Although these photographs were never meant to serve as reference materials for the artists who took them, something in the paintings of this group in the early 1950s suggests the atmosphere left an impression. Tooker's *Bathers* of 1950 and *Acrobats* (1950–52) and *Divers* (1952) have the luminosity, distance, and clouds that are also seen in the paintings of Paul Cadmus and the Frenches.

In 1949, Paul Cadmus and George Tooker, again with the Frenches, made a six-month visit to Europe together. Soon after, they were no longer a couple.

Jared French

Jerry painted a picture called Evasion.
Jerry was very good at that.

—*Paul Cadmus*

The gifted painter Jared French was born in 1905 in Ossining, New York, and grew up in New Jersey. After graduating from Amherst College, he continued his studies at the Art Students League, where he met his longtime lover, Paul Cadmus. Cadmus credits Jared French with steering him away from his early career as a commercial artist and into serious art. The two men bicycled through Europe and lived in Mallorca in the early 1930s. In 1937 French married Margaret Hoening, and soon after his marriage Glenway Wescott described French as "a commonly handsome man of my age, with a small eye and a tough little blond mustache; with a certain stolidity that highly sexed men often have. . . ." Cadmus's friend James Hunt Barker remembers that Jared French, despite his marriage, did not like Paul's involvement with other men and was jealous and possessive. French continued to share an art studio with Cadmus for many years, and the two men and Margaret French formed a trio of photographers later known as PaJaMa.

The art of Jared French was always finely wrought, and the egg tempera medium he favored resulted in many exquisite paintings. But, with the exception of *Mealtime: The Early Coal Miners* (1936) and some other murals executed for the Works Progress Administration in the 1930s, they have a marked formality and stillness.

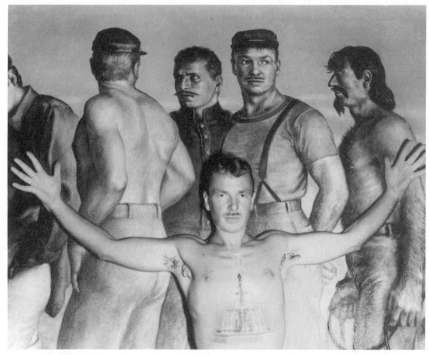

Jared French in front of his own portrait in his mural for the Parcel Post Building, Richmond, Virginia, 1936 (vintage silver print). Note the fountain painted on his chest. (Collection of Anatole Pohorilenko. Courtesy of D. C. Moore Gallery, N.Y.C. Reprinted by permission)

In 1938 French designed the sets for Ballet Caravan's *Billy the Kid*, and the following year he began painting a nude triptych of Wescott, Wheeler, and Lynes. Other paintings such as *Rope* and *Crew* show French's interest in muscular young men and in (often ambiguous) relationships between males.

In the 1940s he favored creating likenesses that were strongly reminiscent of Etruscan figures, often in multiples. These figures, which could also be compared to Attic statues, had inscrutable smiles and staring eyes, and despite their beautiful physiques they never came alive. Later paintings, such as *Business* (1959–61), were also formal, still, inscrutable, and their dreamlike quality reflects the artist's interest in the writings of Carl Jung.

George Tooker recounts that when Jared French had his first major show in the Robert Isaacson gallery in the early 1940s, the artist came to the gallery the day before the opening and announced that nothing would be for sale. His excuse was that his wife did not wish him to sell

Margaret French *by Jared French, 1950 (ink on paper, 11¹/₂" x 8³/₄"). (Collection of Mr. and Mrs. George Platt Lynes II. Courtesy of D. C. Moore Gallery, N.Y.C. Reprinted by permission)*

anything. Could it have been he didn't want to run the risk that none of his paintings would be bought?

His wife was always protective of him and seems never to have taken offense at his many affairs and sleep-overs with other men. These included a brief fling with Chuck Howard in 1949. While spending time in Florence in 1951 with Paul Cadmus and Margaret, French became involved, more seriously than was his custom, with a young Italian. Later this man was replaced by another young Italian. Because of this relationship, French decided to make his permanent residence in Rome. Margaret gamely moved to Rome herself to be near him. Her life seemed to revolve about him, whatever he did and wherever he was.

To some degree, this was equally true of Paul Cadmus. When the Frenches bought a summer residence in Hartland, Vermont, Cadmus was given a house of his own on the property. This house was then taken back to be given to Jared French's Italian lover, who still lives there during the summer. Paul Cadmus never took umbrage at this. Only after Jared French moved to Italy did Cadmus truly separate himself from his early lover.

French never received the recognition or success of Paul Cadmus or George Tooker. His prickly personality and his feeling that more was due him than he received no doubt had something to do with this.

French died in 1988 in Rome, where many of his paintings remain in the custody of his close friend Roberto Gianatta. Margaret French died in 1998.

Lincoln Kirstein

I've had more trouble over money than I've had over sex.

—Lincoln Kirstein

Lincoln Kirstein returned to New York from war-ravaged Europe in 1946 and immediately hurled himself into his project of building a national ballet company. With George Balanchine, he organized Ballet Society in the latter part of 1946, a membership organization that presented ballets at the Central High School of Needle Trades and other venues, and then in the fall of 1947 at the New York City Center for Music and Drama. Maria Tallchief, who was Balanchine's wife at the time, was the prima ballerina of the company, and many dancers who had formerly been associated with Ballet Caravan and the American Ballet were reassembled for this company. A new crop of dancers from the School of American Ballet was also to be shown off to New York. Tanaquil LeClercq, a graduate of the school who was later to become Balanchine's fourth wife, was the young revelation of the premiere season. The important new ballet was *Symphonie Concertante*, choreographed by Balanchine for Tallchief and LeClercq.

To support the fledgling ballet company, Kirstein used his boundless energy to raise funds among his rich friends and art patrons and other contacts, and he himself often donated the necessary funds from his private assets. Commenting on Kirstein's openhandedness, Balanchine

Lincoln Kirstein by George Platt Lynes, 1946. (Collection of the Art Institute of Chicago. Courtesy of Mr. and Mrs. George Platt Lynes II. Reprinted by permission)

once told an interviewer, "He gives you money and runs away before you can thank him."

Kirstein asked Stravinsky to compose the score for *Orpheus*, paying the $5,000 commission, a very substantial fee at the time, out of his own pocket. And it was Kirstein's "happy idea," according to Stravinsky, to invite Isamu Noguchi to design the sets and costumes. In the spring of 1948 Ballet Society returned to the City Center and presented this new work. A major collaboration of the Russian composer, the Japanese-American sculptor, and Balanchine, *Orpheus* brought Ballet Society to a

Nicholas Magallanes (foreground) and Francisco Moncion in pose from ballet Or-
pheus, 1948. Photo by George Platt Lynes. The two men repeated their pas de deux
from the ballet nude for the photographer. (Collection of Bernard Perlin. Courtesy of
Mr. and Mrs. George Platt Lynes II. Reprinted by permission)

new level of importance and prestige. With it came the opportunity to
become the resident ballet company at the City Center under the name
the New York City Ballet. The company appeared under this new name
for the first time in October 1948.

For the 1949 season, the company presented Balanchine's new stag-

Maria Tallchief in the title role of The Firebird, *by George Platt Lynes, 1949. (Collection of Bernard Perlin. Courtesy of Mr. and Mrs. George Platt Lynes II. Reprinted by permission)*

Jensen Yow by George Platt Lynes, 1949. (Collection of Jensen Yow. Courtesy of Mr. and Mrs. George Platt Lynes II. Reprinted by permission)

ing of *The Firebird* with the aid of the impresario Sol Hurok. Hurok owned the Marc Chagall sets and costumes from a 1945 production done for Ballet Theater and was prepared to loan them to the new company. Starring Maria Tallchief in what was to be her most famous role, this production made a popular addition to the repertoire and further enhanced the New York City Ballet's prestige.

Lincoln Kirstein's dream of a national ballet company was approaching reality, and rapidly. He had only returned from the war three years previously, and already a major dance company had been established. The company's success was confirmed in 1950 by a European tour. England was impressed by *Orpheus, Firebird,* and the Balanchine classic *Serenade.*

Kirstein engaged his longtime friend George Platt Lynes to record the company in photographs for the ballet programs and also for posters for the front of the theater. When interviewed by Russell Lynes for his brother's biography, the former model and fashion editor Liz Gibbons commented on the ballet photo shoots: "I never could understand the homosexual attraction for male ballet dancers (GPL told me they *all* 'screwed like minks'). I'd drop by GPL's Madison Avenue studio frequently and find photo sessions of male ballet dancers in frenzied sessions. Lincoln Kirstein . . . often standing by." For both Platt Lynes and Kirstein, male dancers played important roles in their lives, often being lovers or bed partners.

Friends who visited the School of American Ballet to watch classes with Lincoln Kirstein reported that he would say, "Let's go visit the boys' class. After all, they're so much more complete."

Kirstein established a pattern then for brief sexual flings and longer liaisons with other men. Wilbur Pippin, a one-time bed partner of Lincoln Kirstein's, says of this brief encounter, "I guess I was the last one left at the party." Donald Windham remembers that Kirstein called his Afghan dog his "cruising machine."

But more important than his fleeting interest in this male dancer or that one was Lincoln Kirstein's interest in the art student Jensen Yow. Robert Chapman, then a professor at Harvard University, remembers visiting his friend Kirstein in the late 1940s and being told, "I want you to meet Billy Budd." Kirstein drove him to the West Village, near the docks. In a small rooming house he was introduced to the blond and open-faced Jensen Yow and was as smitten with him as Lincoln Kirstein.

Yow worked for Kirstein's fine-arts and wallpaper-printing companies, Pippin Press and Pippin Papers, for a time. Urged to pursue a career restoring fine art on paper, he went on to become head of the restoration department at the Morgan Library and subsequently had his own company, working out of a third-floor studio in Kirstein's home. He remained in propinquity all of Kirstein's life.

In the immediate postwar period, Lincoln Kirstein not only found time to build a ballet company, he also became fascinated with the work of the sculptor Elie Nadelman. Nadelman was recently deceased and his widow's home, Alderbrook, on the Hudson River in Riverdale in the Bronx, was crammed with his art. Kirstein visited her there, they became friends, and for a time Lincoln and Fidelma Kirstein lived with Mrs. Nadelman. Later, in their Manhattan town house, the Kirsteins had several fine Nadelman sculptures. In 1948 Lincoln Kirstein published a monograph about the artist, and in the sixties he suggested using two Nadelman figures as models for the enormous white statues, sculpted from the largest blocks of marble ever cut in Carrara, Italy, that dominate the Grand Promenade of Lincoln Center's New York State Theater.

In the next decade, with the economy booming in the postwar United States, Kirstein was to find funds and interest to make the New York City Ballet a more and more important company and to establish it on the international scene.

The Fifties
1950–55

Is This Hell's Kitchen?

It's 1951 and everyone is saying, "Hasn't he done wonders with it?" when you enter George Platt Lynes's new flat on West 55th Street. You're not so sure. The whole point of renting a cold-water flat is to save money, not to spend money. You know that George's fortunes are at a low ebb, and he has obviously spent a lot of money redoing this little four-room railroad apartment. Walls have been torn down. The omnipresent tortoiseshell wallpaper and the wooden shutters are in place. Perhaps he brought the shutters with him from California. You doubt it. Once again, he has spent a lot of his own money (or somebody's) on a home that belongs to someone else. Being from Sandusky, you think this is not wise. You've known George for almost fifteen years now. Things don't look good.

You look around and think that some of George's guests have not been a wise choice either. His parties these days have no women, only young men on their way up or older men looking for love. Or lust. Or something. For a moment you wonder if men come to George's parties mostly to avoid police raids on the bars. Of course, it's still chic to go to a party at George Platt Lynes's. But what used to be the sexy undercurrent has surfaced as the sole purpose of the event. You think sadly that in some ways George has become a kind of madam. Or pimp. For himself or others.

George looks good, more mature but still strikingly handsome. There are no real hors d'oeuvres anymore. And some young men are drinking beer, which they undoubtedly brought with them. George's circumstances have reduced him to making his parties BYOL—bring your own liquor. Or pretty much. Cecil Beaton is here. He remembers you from the Vogue *days. Now you're photo editor at* Harper's Bazaar, *clawing your way to the bottom, as you call it. Cecil is concerned about George's career and urges you to put some work his way. You tell him you do regularly, but that he often turns it down as being beneath him, which is irritating, as you've had a hard time convincing your bosses that you should offer it to him in the first place. To his credit, Cecil does not suggest that you send some work his way. He's a terrible social climber but a gentleman, say what you may. He leaves your side, saying he's looking for the young man "who is built like a beer can." You wonder if he's talking about Mel Fillini. You tell him you can't help him, you haven't seen any beer cans lately except in the kitchen.*

Both Paul Cadmus and Lincoln Kirstein are here tonight, too. Paul isn't with George Tooker anymore, you understand, but he doesn't appear to be particularly lonely or subdued. You and Paul talk mostly about his work. He's working on a painting of Jensen Yow and Jack Fontan in a bathroom. One kneeling in the tub, the other combing his hair in the mirror over the sink. Paul said it's a challenge for him because the light is from an overhead skylight, but he's happy with how it's going. You admire Paul, even envy him a bit. He really is an artist in the tradition of the Renaissance. His work holds his attention completely, but he isn't all wild-eyed and ranting about it. And if his heart is broken, you aren't going to hear about it from him.

You say hello to Lincoln, who stares at you and turns away. Just then the painter Bernard Perlin passes. Bernard is tall and sardonic with a rollicking sense of humor. You tell him that Lincoln Kirstein doesn't seem to remember you although you've met repeatedly for almost fifteen years. Bernard says, "Lucky you," and tells you about a wild party he had been to recently in a town house in the far West Twenties. A new neighborhood, evidently, for good-looking guys without much money. He said a line formed to descend into the basement where some guests were giving blow jobs to the other guests. "What hospitality," you say. Bernard says he noticed Lincoln standing patiently in the line. "Maybe he thinks it's better to just forget everything," Bernard says, and goes laughing off toward the kitchen for another drink.

A lot of dancers are here tonight. The usual bunch from the New York City Ballet: Nicky Magellanes, Frank Moncion, Billy Weslow. Pete Martinez is no longer around; he's gone somewhere like Norfolk to teach. And some new faces like Ralph McWilliams. George may be losing interest in his fashion work, but he's still doing wonderful pictures for the New York City Ballet. His portrait of Maria Tallchief in Firebird *is a stunner. They're using it as a poster outside the City Center. Interesting how they say she sued Balanchine for divorce on the grounds that he never intended to consummate their marriage. No one ever discusses this subject. It's something like war crimes. No one knows where the whole subject will lead and how he will be implicated himself.*

You go to the kitchen to see if you can be of any help and talk a little with Ralph McWilliams, who is both extremely sexy and rather intelligent. He was at Juilliard studying piano, started studying a little dance and voilà. George comes by and says, "Want to see some new pictures?"

You go into his tiny bedroom and he pulls out a scrapbook with some of his latest additions to his photographs of men with their clothes off. You have to hand it to George. He has taste. This is nothing like the Athletic Models Guild. You recognize that extremely handsome guy Jack Fontan. He has been the boyfriend of Jensen Yow, Chuck Howard, and Bill Harris. All the beauties.

There was that new redheaded guy, Mel Fillini, too. Wow, what a winkie. And George's new studio assistant, Umberto Visbal. What a good-looking brute. George can get anybody out of their clothes. And here's the handsomest man in New York, Bob Bishop. The dark-haired one. What a face. What a body. George gets them all. But when is he going to get his life in order?

Paul Cadmus

Despite the fact that [Bar Italia's] *color is literal and descriptive, the work must still be recognized as a tour de force of draftsmanship, and a complex and well-integrated composition. I still think it's the most repulsive painting I've seen in years.*

—*Emily Genauer,* New York Herald Tribune *art critic*

In the 1950s Paul Cadmus was again alone. His relationship with George Tooker had gone aground as the previous decade closed. Tooker has said, "I was looking for a relationship, and my relationship with Paul always included Jared and Margaret French." Cadmus and Tooker had spent one vacation after another with the Frenches, on Fire Island and Nantucket and in Provincetown. Their 1949 vacation was taken in Europe, from which Tooker returned ahead of the other three. He wanted to share his life with Paul Cadmus, but not with the Frenches. In addition, he states that Jared French was never very friendly to him. When they met, Margaret French would embrace him, but Jared French would never even shake his hand. Cadmus's comment is, "George wanted me all to himself, but that was not possible. I was not going to give up Jerry in any case."

Jared French was a very self-centered person and did not want to share Paul Cadmus's attention. So George Tooker dropped out of their foursome and shortly thereafter began a relationship with the painter Bill Christopher, with whom he remained until the end of Christopher's life in 1973.

When Paul Cadmus returned to Europe in 1952, he was alone with

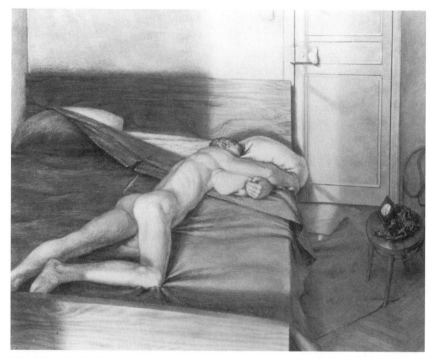

The Nap *by Paul Cadmus, 1952 (egg tempera on pressed wood panel, 13" x 16"). (Collection of Robert L. B. Tobin. Courtesy of D. C. Moore Gallery, N.Y.C. Reprinted by permission)*

Jared and Margaret French again. This summer was spent in Finistère on the northern Atlantic coast of Brittany. His harbor painting, *Finistère* (1952), shows two strong-bodied, bikini-clad young cyclists and hearkens back to his bicycle painting of the early 1930s and also to *The Bath*, his 1951 painting of Jack Fontan and Jensen Yow. Even more, however, both paintings have a strong relationship to Renaissance paintings, where figures, finely realized in almost fresco manner, are stopped in time in the midst of their activities so that viewers may realize their beauty.

The painting *The Nap*, inspired by a trip to Beaulieu-sur-Mer on the French Riviera, has an entirely different quality. The naked male figure embracing a pillow, in what is obviously an inexpensive hotel room, has not only beauty but the pathos of being alone in a third-rate hotel. The sunlight falling through the window makes it beautiful, but a great sadness is here, too. Cadmus's pictures are not usually this emotional. The gray-haired model could have been Jared French . . . or someone met and left behind. When asked about the model during a telephone conversation a few weeks before his death, Cadmus said, "It was a time when I was all alone and very lonely, and the model was more likely based on George Platt Lynes or myself."

In 1953 another trip to Europe with the Frenches was spent mostly in Italy. This trip inspired a more typical Cadmus work, *Bar Italia*, with its biting, sardonic view of humans. In this painting jammed with characters, a few are beautiful but none are appealing. Here there is no tolerance for mankind's foolishness and general ugliness. Italians are preying upon tourists, and tourists are bored or uncomprehending. A quartet of homosexuals at an outdoor café is shown as affected and unattractive, and the faux baroque sculpture in the background is ridiculous. Even Cadmus's portrait of himself in a graying brush cut has an expression that is critical and displeased.

On this trip to Italy, Jared French may have met Roberto Gianatta, with whom he formed a close, lifelong friendship. The Frenches and Cadmus were staying together and separately at various times during the trip between Florence and Rome. Jared French spent time in Rome in a rented apartment in the same building as Bernard Perlin, who was living in Rome in this period and who saw something of Cadmus and the Frenches there at parties and dinners. Perlin remembers being berated in an outdoor restaurant by Margaret French for spreading tales about her husband's activities. Embarrassing as they may have been for her, they were undoubtedly true.

The handsome William Christian Miller was also in Italy that summer, traveling with his patron, Dr. Cary Walker. Miller spent time with Paul Cadmus, and among Miller's photographs were a number of the artist, hair neatly combed with a side part and looking handsome and distinguished. Miller had abandoned his education and any plans for a profession for a life of being kept by older wealthy men. He had been a favorite model for Cadmus in earlier years, and undoubtedly the painter must have felt some pangs over Miller's lifestyle.

Bernard Perlin, who was traveling about Italy, met Walker and Miller in Venice. Of their young and handsome traveling companion Ed Torgeson, Perlin wrote to George Platt Lynes, "Ed is *really* THE GOLDEN BOY of all time. I've never known anybody to radiate such happiness, good cheer, etc., etc. (He really is the walking-talking Xmas card) as that angel. And one of the most glorious, awesome cruisers I've ever observed—not speaking a word of any known language, he just devastates the toughest most desirables. Divine is the word for him."

The Bath *by Paul Cadmus, 1951 (egg tempera on pressed wood panel, 14" x 16"). The models were Jack Fontan (left) and Jensen Yow. (Courtesy of the Whitney Museum of American Art and D. C. Moore Gallery, N.Y.C. Reprinted by permission)*

This trip may also have been the inspiration for one of Cadmus's most important works, *Night in Bologna*, completed in 1958. In this highly architectural work, a handsome Italian soldier stares at a passing prostitute, who is trying to catch the attention of a pale traveler with a childish face seated at a table with his suitcase. The pale traveler, in turn, only has eyes for the muscular soldier, bursting out of his uniform. No one else is in this long, receding arcade of arches. Through an opening a tall brick tower rises phallically into the night sky. This is another Cadmus painting in which beautiful execution is coupled with a strong emotion—in this case, the emptiness of the night is equated with the emptiness of yearning for what one is not going to get. Despite its architectural complexity, *Night in Bologna* is far simpler than many Cadmus paintings, and far more emotional in its haunting nighttime loneliness.

Ted Starkowski (right) and Chuck Howard on Fire Island, New York (silver print). PaJaMa photograph taken by Paul Cadmus. (Author's collection. Courtesy of D. C. Moore Gallery, N.Y.C. Reprinted by permission)

Paul Cadmus has been quoted as saying this is his own favorite among his paintings. "If I had to save one of my pictures, it would be that one. And yet it's not typical of my work. . . . I was very pleased by a review in

The New Republic by Frank Getlein, who discussed the painting under the heading 'Some Quieter Americans.' And 'quiet' I've never been called before . . . for some reason that pleased me."

Cadmus had begun painting "quiet" works some years earlier, however. One called *Manikins*, done in 1951, has two wooden puppet figures—the kind used by artists—lying together in the "spoon" position. A much larger articulated hand stands by in an attitude of blessing. The mannequins' heads are pillowed on a paper bound copy of André Gide's homosexual manifesto, *Corydon*. This painting was done the same year as *The Bath*, and E. M. Forster, now a close friend, wrote the artist, referring to the two paintings, "Enjoyed your two wooden puppets and still more your two human ones. Rather wish the two compositions could have been reversed—the wooden puppets showing [illegible word], and the . . . But it wouldn't have done." The demure English author, whose lifelong relationship with a married policeman was only revealed after his death, evidently hankered for more graphic renderings of male nudes embracing.

From this still life of the mannequins, Cadmus proceeded to more still lifes of tendrils of outdoor grasses: *Curlicues* (1955), *Studio Stuff* (1958), *Apple Peeler* (1959), *Family Group*, represented by boxes of facial tissue (1964), and *Glitters*, using glass and silvery papers (1966). These beautifully rendered still lifes were indeed very quiet and were perhaps what Paul Cadmus was projecting for his life to come.

Through the 1950s Paul Cadmus continued to live in the St. Luke's Place apartment he had shared with Jared French. He was there alone now. The rhythm of his life seems to have been long winters of painting intensely, alternating with trips to Europe and vacations on Fire Island in the summers. The nature of his painting made it a slow and dedicated process, and very time-consuming. Cadmus was surrounded by a close-knit circle of friends who filled what social time he wished to spare from his painting, but there were no long-term liaisons.

Lincoln Kirstein

There was cruelty in Lincoln.

—William Weslow

Lincoln Kirstein's life in the early 1950s was largely taken up with the success of the New York City Ballet. Once permanently at home at the New York City Center, the ballet company quickly became a civic institution. New Yorkers, proud of their ballet, attended it regularly. The streamlined, fleet-of-foot dancers executing George Balanchine's abstract and geometrical choreography in classical ballet's vocabulary of steps expressed something New Yorkers felt about themselves. They liked all these slim, long-legged ladies darting about and felt no desire to see a full-length *Sleeping Beauty* or *Swan Lake* in the Russian Imperial manner, although a full-length *Nutcracker* at Christmastime was to save the company financially.

In 1950 the New York City Ballet made its first overseas tour, performing at Covent Garden in London for three weeks and also visiting a number of other major cities in the United Kingdom for an additional three weeks. They were greeted with much enthusiasm, although a few critics demurred.

Lincoln Kirstein had mounted an exhibition of modern painting to appear concurrently with the ballet's London season, which had added to the strain of the visit. The critic Richard Buckle remembers the

Kirsteins staying with him and hearing, long into the night, the tap, tap, tap of a portable typewriter. At this time Kirstein was also an art critic for *The New Republic* magazine, and the effort to manage both the new company's debut abroad and his art duties told upon him. He had a nervous collapse in London, which was to be the harbinger of more to come as he grew older.

The company's life at City Center was comfortable and settled. In Lili Cockerille Livingston's *American Indian Ballerinas*, the ballerina Maria Tallchief reminisced, "We were very lucky at City Center. We were like a big family and the theater was our home. The atmosphere was friendly, and the stagehands, ushers, and box office people were very sweet and supportive. It was a wonderful place to build a company."

In 1951 the ballet company was able to expand its schedule of performances at City Center and it made its first American touring debut with a two-week season at the Civic Opera House in Chicago. Maria Tallchief was the undisputed prima ballerina of the company and had a great success with the new one-act *Swan Lake*. The company was adding other stars to its roster, and in 1951 André Eglevsky and Nora Kaye joined the company. With Tallchief, they did *Pas de Trois Classique*, and Kaye joined Nicholas Magallanes in *The Cage*, an erotic dance of death with choreography by Jerome Robbins that caused a sensation. Lincoln Kirstein was seeing his dreams of a major ballet company, created by George Balanchine and himself, coming true.

By the end of the 1951 season, Maria Tallchief's marriage to George Balanchine was coming apart, but that would in no way affect her position in the company. Livingston's book says that she wanted to have children and he did not. She told Livingston, "It didn't have any effect on our relationship to the company. In fact, after the annulment was granted, I went straight from the courthouse to the theater to rehearse *Scotch Symphony*. Balanchine was so innately dignified and gracious, his marriages were always dissolved amicably. I think it was Bernard Taper, in his biography of Balanchine, who first noted that it was not uncommon to see Balanchine's wives, past and present, lined up at the barre in his class."

Nineteen fifty-two was a year of many changes and advances for Kirstein. He became a member of the board of directors of the City Center in May and in October was made the managing director. His new positions involved far more work than just managing the ballet company and organizing its season since the City Center also presented plays and operas and concerts and tried to remain occupied as much of

Lincoln and Fidelma Kirstein in the living room of their home at 128 East 19th Street, N.Y.C., by Cecil Beaton, circa 1954. (Courtesy of the Estate of Cecil Beaton. Reprinted by permission)

the year as possible. Fortunately Kirstein was an impresario with sound business instincts, and he had the social and financial contacts that helped keep the theater booked.

This was also the year that he acquired a permanent home at 128 East 19th Street, near Gramercy Park. His mother made the Kirsteins a gift of their new home shortly before her death. Fidelma and he were still living in the apartment on East 74th Street, where they had moved in 1948, a space that didn't allow entertaining on a large scale. The new home had been a carriage house and the large, open space on the ground floor was renovated to make a drawing room. Its floor was painted black, and the walls were hung in sacking after a design the decorators Percier and Fontaine had done for the studio of Isabey, Napoleon's court painter. Cecil Beaton took photographs of the Kirsteins in this room shortly after it was redone. In 1956, the room was redone again with a teak floor and the walls rehung in cotton velour. It was redone one last time in 1983 with elegant champagne-colored taffeta.

In this house was Kirstein's art collection, later recorded in the Twelvetrees Press book *Quarry* in 1986. The book was to serve in lieu of memoirs by Kirstein, although later on he did write a memoir of his early years. In the *Quarry* photographs, the long drawing room is filled with paintings and statues. The lighting for the room was done under the supervision of Richard Kelly, a lighting engineer for the architect Philip Johnson. Kirstein wanted gas lighting, but this was considered too dangerous and impractical, so rheostat-controlled crystal chandeliers were installed.

Among the artwork was the original scale model for Augustus Saint-Gaudens's *Diana*. The monumental statue, when finished, crowned the first Madison Square Garden as a weather vane. The smaller model was placed near the windows in the Kirsteins' drawing room and was later donated to the Metropolitan Museum. There were also a number of Elie Nadelman's smooth, wooden, painted statues, bought from the sculptor's widow. Through his interest, Kirstein made Nadelman known as one of America's most important twentieth-century artists.

Fidelma Cadmus Kirstein's contribution to the room's decor was a large profile portrait done of her when she was a monitor at the National Academy of Design. This work was the result of a demonstration of portrait painting by an instructor who used Fidelma as a model. She also brought with her a fine portrait of her great-uncle Carlos Valdes, a surgeon who had been decorated by the Infanta Eulalia for his service to Spain. (He maintained a clinic in Switzerland, according to Lincoln Kirstein, for "royal bastards and miscarriages." There was perhaps some connection between this and the Infanta's appreciation.)

A great admirer of bronzes, Kirstein possessed several by Gaston Lachaise, including a torso and a bas-relief of Mme. Lachaise, a very well-rounded American woman. (Lachaise believed that his wife's body had been the inspiration of his art ever since the time he first saw her walking along a quay in Paris. She was already married but left her husband for the young Beaux-Arts student. Paul Cadmus said of this relationship, "Lachaise fell in love with her buttocks.") Kirstein also owned Lachaise's small nude statuette showing Kirstein in a walking pose. The first casting had been bought for the Museum of Modern Art, but the second, which was made with a gold alloy, was claimed by the model. Kirstein believed that the hands were more finely modeled and that the gold flakes speckling its surface made it a more beautiful object than the first casting.

Kirstein also owned a round bronze plaque by Saint-Gaudens of Robert Louis Stevenson. Kirstein was a great admirer of Saint-Gaudens, and particularly of the sculptor's memorial in Boston for Colonel Robert Shaw. Shaw organized the first black regiment in the Civil War and was killed along with most of his regiment at Fort Wagner in 1863.

On the wall of a long hallway that ran beside the drawing room were hung smaller works by Paul Cadmus, Jared French, Margaret French, Pavel Tchelitchev, George Tooker, and some by Fidelma.

Elsewhere in the house hung Tchelitchev's portrait showing three different images of the ballet impresario. This portrait, which Ned Rorem as a young music student in the 1940s found "dismayingly sexual," is now at the School of American Ballet. Lincoln Kirstein loved having his portrait drawn, painted, and sculpted. Commissioning a portrait was also his way of helping artists he favored. His home was full of these portraits, including Isamu Noguchi's bronze head executed when Kirstein was a student at Harvard. Fidelma's own painting of her husband has great sensitivity and reveals a certain wariness in him that the others lack; it is one of the best.

Installing his art collection in his new home, however, had to be done in odd moments, for the New York City Ballet was taking more and more of Kirstein's time. Going from success to success, the company embarked on a second European tour in 1952. This four-and-a-half-month tour included Barcelona, The Hague, London, and Edinburgh. Historically, it is remembered as a success, but some of the dancers claim that audiences were less than thrilled at the cool, abstract Balanchine ballets and the aloofness of the dancers. Maria Tallchief herself was always greatly welcomed as she managed to infuse the difficult and complicated Balanchine choreography with a steely fire all her own. Her face may have been emotionless, but her body wasn't.

The ballet company took another cross-country tour in 1953. In a short time, the New York City Ballet was becoming an American institution and adding luster to the city's reputation as a cultural center, and New Yorkers attended its performances faithfully. Balanchine had pro-

Tanaquil LeClercq and Jerome Robbins in Bourrée Fantasque, *by George Platt Lynes, 1952. (Collection of Bernard Perlin. Courtesy of Mr. and Mrs. George Platt Lynes II. Reprinted by permission)*

vided the dancers and the dancing, but it was Lincoln Kirstein who had found the money and support and promotion that actually created this company and kept it alive.

At Kirstein's insistence, the New York City Ballet instituted a Christmas season exclusively of a full-length *Nutcracker* in 1954. Maria Tallchief said, "Everyone in New York was against it, including the critics. The company was struggling financially and the comment was always, 'How can you spend so much money on a single production?' Well, thank God we did, because it saved the company. Despite the popular success of *Firebird* and other ballets, if we had not done *The Nutcracker* . . . New York City Ballet probably would have gone out of business." The Tchaikovsky ballet became a staple for the company's tours, and because the lavish production filled the theater with happy adults and excited children every time it was performed, *The Nutcracker* has been a great financial asset for the company. In addition to the ballet, Lincoln Kirstein had his opera and drama work at City Center and his plans for the Shakespeare Festival at Stratford, Connecticut, to keep him going at a furious pace, as his letters to Tchelitchev show.

In September 1950 Kirstein wrote to the painter about visiting West Dean, the Edward James home in England where many Tchelitchev paintings were hung. Kirstein was trying to keep this collection intact in the house and avoid its being sent to the Museum of Modern Art as James had planned. Kirstein had been a longtime patron and admirer of Tchelitchev and wrote that he was very unhappy about the demise of the house and the possibility of the collection going to the museum. He was particularly displeased with the involvement of Monroe Wheeler, whom he felt was a "bitch undertaker." It was Wheeler, however, who managed to preserve the home and its contents by having everything given to the nation and supervised as a guest house for the Rockefeller Foundation. Kirstein's old friend Nelson Rockefeller must have figured in this. Lincoln Kirstein's caustic comment about Wheeler, his friend of many years, is an indication of the unreliability of his friendship. He also mentions a lover, Herb, writing that he loved Herb and hoped that Fidelma's reaction didn't frighten the young man, adding that his wife thought it was a great good fortune on his part to have this new lover—a clear indication of his marital arrangement.

In March 1953 he wrote Tchelitchev about the enormous efforts he had made to become an influential board member at the City Center. He manipulated and cowed the board of directors into presenting a season that included Shaw's play *Misalliance*, which went on to Broadway, a *Merchant of Venice* critics hated and audiences loved, and Rossini's *La Cenerentola (Cinderella)*, in a beautiful production with sets by the then-unknown Rouben Ter-Arutunian.

The result of the enormous efforts made by Kirstein in these years was a nervous breakdown. In June 1955, reminding Tchelitchev of a visit the painter had made to his country house, Kirstein confessed that he was "the mad queen shrieking in the road." Fidelma and Jensen Yow were staunch supporters during this terrible period, and although Kirstein expected to be hospitalized for six months, he was out in six weeks.

In later letters he mentioned a 1:15 A.M. visit from a working-class friend who came by for some sex, and then discussed the New York City Ballet's upcoming tour of England, Scandinavia, and Germany.

Because of his success in forming the New York City Ballet and creating its European tours, Lincoln Kirstein was named an adviser to the State Department on American National Theater and Academy (ANTA) foreign tours. This recognition of his capabilities must certainly have led to his being involved in the planning for the new Lincoln Center for the Performing Arts. These new theaters, grouped around a giant plaza, would provide homes for the New York Philharmonic, the New York City Ballet, and the Metropolitan Opera, which Kirstein hoped Tchelitchev would decorate. The ballet company would share its new home with the New York City Opera. This new cultural center was to be located north of Columbus Circle, in a neighborhood where run-down town houses and stores were being razed to accommodate it.

In the summer of 1955 the first season of the American Shakespeare Festival was held at Stratford, Connecticut. Lincoln Kirstein was a founder and an officer and hoped that this project might fulfill his dream of a national theater. For the opening season he produced a notable *A Midsummer Night's Dream* starring the actress June Havoc, the sister of the famed stripper Gypsy Rose Lee. Many were dubious about June Havoc playing the role of Titania, but she turned out to be excellent.

Lincoln Kirstein was always deeply interested in acting, and while helping to manage the Shakespeare Festival, he repeatedly told Robert Chapman, who lectured on modern drama at Harvard, that he was disappointed in the caliber of actors available to the theater. His codirector of the festival was Joseph Vernor Reed, a wealthy man of impeccable social background. John Houseman was also involved with the Shakespeare Festival, an experience that strengthened his credentials as an important stage director, and Katharine Hepburn starred in *The Taming of the Shrew*, the production for which the festival is best remembered by the general public.

The American Shakespeare Festival and the New York City Ballet were to occupy much of Lincoln Kirstein's time in the years ahead. For the moment, despite his emotional and mental difficulties, the ballet company he had founded was extremely successful, his new home was handsome and a center for the wealthy, famous, and beautiful in New York, and his bouts of depression had abated. He had a beautiful and caring wife and had become a well-known and respected civic figure. He must have felt that his dreams for his life when he was at Harvard had miraculously come true.

George Platt Lynes

It was easier to give in at whatever cost to George than to resist him.

—Russell Lynes

George Platt Lynes's career never recovered from his time in Los
Angeles, though he had been gone for little more than a year. In
that year, the New York fashion photography world changed greatly.
Richard Avedon had become a favorite of the fashion magazines. He
took fashion outdoors into real-life glamorous situations, he discovered
interesting new models, and he captured the interest of Carmel Snow,
editor in chief at *Vogue*. Fashion magazine editors were growing old after
the war and felt a great need to revitalize their long terms of tenure with
new talent. The photographer Irving Penn, too, stepped into the picture
at this time. His camera revived the career of model Lisa Fonssagrives,
whom he was to marry. The imaginative Platt Lynes could certainly
have taken steps to energize his career, but something was missing. He
had lost interest. Never motivated by money alone, that he had little did
nothing to prompt him to try to earn more.

Neither Monroe Wheeler nor Glenway Wescott was able to point
him toward new ideas or trends. Older than he, they themselves were no
longer pursuing new directions in the arts. Wheeler was entrenched at
the Museum of Modern Art, and Wescott had become deeply involved
with the work of his new friend, the sex researcher Dr. Alfred Kinsey.

Platt Lynes wrote his mother in January 1950, "Parties, parties, parties!" The Sitwells were in New York, and Platt Lynes knew them well. He had known Osbert Sitwell since 1927 in Paris and had met his sister—the poet Edith Sitwell—in 1937, also in Paris. She was photographed by Platt Lynes later in 1950 in a crown he had constructed for her to wear. It linked her with the Tudor dynasty, whose royal members she thought she resembled. She was in New York to do a reading of *Macbeth* with Glenway Wescott at the Museum of Modern Art. Platt Lynes wrote his mother in September, "The *Macbeth* is quite wonderful, and both Edith and Glenway are extraordinary." Others who attended the evening are less generous and remember "a lot of shouting." However the reading went, this was Platt Lynes's life in the early 1950s. He lived with Chuck Howard, picked up a little uninteresting commercial work here and there, socialized as a celebrity even though his status as a photographer was much diminished, and was photographing more and more male nudes all the time. The male nude photography was both an entrée to making the acquaintance of handsome young men and a genuine artistic interest. Among his models were many veterans attending New York schools, finishing their education. These young men were eligible for the tuition and other benefits of the G.I. Bill of Rights—unless they had been given "blue discharges" for homosexuality. A few of them may even have been members of the Veterans Benevolent Society, one of the homophile organizations being organized in New York and California.

He photographed art student Jensen Yow a number of times, and Jensen was also frequently on hand to help him concoct painted backdrops and build sets for his fashion shoots. Platt Lynes frequently used these sets and props for the male nude sessions he would do in the evening once the fashion shooting was finished. Through Jensen Yow, he met the extremely handsome Jack Fontan and did striking photographs of him. Yow and Fontan, who were then lovers, were also the nude models for a Cadmus painting of this period. Through the writer Christopher Isherwood, Platt Lynes met beautiful Bill Harris, who had recently arrived from California and who posed for a number of Platt Lynes's photographs.

He corresponded regularly with his mother, employed as a social hostess at a hotel in North Carolina in the winter and similarly in Massachusetts in the summer. She was now seventy years old but successful in her career and had no plans to stop. Her charm, bridge-playing, and social skills served her well in a large resort hotel, and she was much liked by her employers. Many of the people she met in her work gave her

Fashion model in Lincoln Kirstein's house, by George Platt Lynes, circa 1952 (vintage silver print, 9¹/₂" x 7¹/₂"). Marilyn Ambrose is the model. (Collection of Peter Hiler. Courtesy of Mr. and Mrs. George Platt Lynes II. Reprinted by permission)

excellent advice on stock investments, and she was actually in much better financial condition than anyone suspected at the time.

In 1951, the photographer's financial situation worsened, as did his personal life. Although he had clients that were loyal to him, such as the stores Saks Fifth Avenue and Bendel's, his income was not enough to sustain his accustomed lifestyle: the lavish entertaining, the gifts of jewelry to favorites, the keeping up with his society friends. At the same time his relationship with Chuck Howard ended, which removed Chuck's steadying effect on his life. In January 1951, his letter to his mother reported, "Late last week, Chuck decided to go off and live by himself. It's a pity, for I shall miss him; but I don't disapprove. . . . I'm afraid that my influence is too often all-pervading, all-inclusive."

In an attempt to economize, he moved to a cold-water flat in the West Fifties in a building where friends lived. He wrote his mother that it was "very cheap (430 against 4300) . . . and very small and shabby. . . . Some friends of mine, Butch [Fred Melton] and Wilbur [Pippin] live in the same building, so I'll not feel quite isolated."

Platt Lynes did not save the money he anticipated, as he converted his little railroad flat, building bookshelves, painting, wallpapering, and spending a great deal of money he didn't have. Again he spent a lot of money improving the value of a home that was not his. The building had no central heating, and he had to carry coal to his fourth-floor apartment. He wrote his mother, "The electric heaters I borrowed from you . . . I cannot use if any lights are turned on. They overload the lines and fuses blow."

Although he read a great deal (to his mother: "Balzac is my new vice. I am rereading him after twenty years and find him so absorbing that I read on far into the night, until two or three or even four"), living on far-flung West Fifty-fifth Street was lonely for him. It was far different from Park and Madison Avenues. To compensate, he gave frequent parties. His older male friends were happy to come to meet the coterie of young men who always surrounded the photographer.

To save money, he also began cooking at home. This George Platt Lynes recipe for preparing liver was remembered by his friend Ray Unger:

Dust ¼-inch-thick slice of liver lightly in flour.
Melt butter in a pan and fry liver in it for one minute on each side. Remove the liver.
Stir a pint of sour cream into the butter and pour over the rare liver.

This example brings George Platt Lynes very much alive. While attempting to economize by not going to restaurants, he cooked from lavish recipes. He could only go first class.

More and more, Platt Lynes's social life was about homosexuals meeting homosexuals. He was not unaware of this, and it added to his depression. However, his great charm remained undiminished. His friends had always had personal nicknames, and now he added more. The Kirsteins had long called each other Goosie. George himself was called Giorgio, a name given to him in the 1920s by Monroe Wheeler, whom he called Monie. Platt Lynes called Jensen Yow "Pooza" because he fancied that Yow resembled a large cat. Their friend Joe Reyes was called the Baby Gangster. Platt Lynes's assistant Umberto Visbal was known as Bolto, and his main assistant, Bill Vasilov, was The Moujik. Despite misfortunes, Platt Lynes maintained a warm personal world about him.

He also continued his needlepoint projects, often pillow covers. Among these was a pillow covered in roses. He requested clippings of pubic hair from each of his male acquaintances and wove the contributions of each into a rose dedicated to him. Friends remember envelopes arriving with the hair to be threaded into the pillow cover.

He also wrote his mother that he was busy photographing the recently organized New York City Ballet. He had photographed twenty-five Balanchine ballets at this point, starting as early as 1933. Although interesting, this commission was not remunerative work and didn't help his financial situation.

He continued to take some portraits of friends, but—again—this paid little or nothing. He did a portrait of Pavel Tchelitchev, who announced as he entered the studio, "Photograph me like a golden egg." This strange command was taken seriously by Platt Lynes, and in the portrait the painter's head does resemble a glowing oval, as though illuminated with a saint's inner light.

As his economic troubles deepened, Platt Lynes depended ever more heavily upon his younger brother and his wife to help him. However, Russell and Mildred had two small children and no great income, so this was not a simple matter for them. In the winter of 1951–52, Platt Lynes was regularly appealing to the Russell Lyneses to rescue him from difficulties with the IRS and many other pressing creditors. The IRS ordered that his personal property be auctioned in January 1952. This consisted of the entire contents of his studio: cameras, lights, negatives and prints, darkroom equipment, and even the furniture. The valuable furnishings of his apartment had already been put under a chattel mortgage to Russell for previous loans. This auction was to pay some $5,000 in taxes owed since 1946.

So that Platt Lynes could continue with his profession, his brother

Bernard Perlin in Rome, circa 1952. (Collection of Bernard Perlin. Reprinted by permission)

agreed to bid on his studio material through a proxy. The cost was $1,145. His brother then loaned everything back to him, but did not give it to him, to avoid having to repeat the entire exercise in the years to come. Just after the IRS auction, Platt Lynes enraged his brother by borrowing $2,000 from Mildred Lynes while her husband was out of town. She was undergoing a severe depression at the time, and Russell Lynes felt his brother had taken advantage of her condition and was angry. After an emotional confrontation, their remarkable solution was that George Platt Lynes would move into the small top floor of his brother's town house on the Upper East Side. Angry or not, Russell Lynes never deserted his beautiful but improvident brother.

George Platt Lynes's social and sexual life continued unabated through his financial trials. To his friend Bernard Perlin, in Rome on an artist's grant, Platt Lynes wrote, "I'm up to my arse in boys. Mac and Michael and J. again. Old stories, all of them, but old stories are the sort I like. Sam S. [Steward] wants me to investigate a Negro named L. [John Leaphart] but so far there has been no room in the schedule for him. Get me. The baby blacksmith [Buddy McCarthy] does me the honor of declared infatuation. And I purr like a tiger puss."

Jared French was in Rome that summer, with his wife and Paul Cadmus, and to him Platt Lynes wrote in June, "I'm in active revolt against my life. My six PM to midnight-and-after life. The days are dandy. Business, even, is good just now. But I'm weary of trying to please young men, darling creatures though they may be; probably because they don't please me enough. There was a time not so long ago when I could put on a glamour act and bedazzle the bejesus out of them. . . . Now, at best I . . . end up being so bored I could shriek. . . . What do you suppose has happened to your old friend? Whom might he like to please? Who might please him? You, maybe. You certainly. But you're not here."

The flirtatious tone of this letter to French suggests George Platt Lynes was willing to consider even one of his oldest friends as a possible romantic direction. Which was to be the case when he considered trying to ally himself once again with Monroe Wheeler. In a long letter to Bernard Perlin regarding Wheeler, the photographer wrote, "To what extent this wistfulness of mine is prompted by loneliness and/or my fear of young men I wouldn't know. Certainly to some, but I can't believe I think of him only as a refuge. Is any of this clear?"

The wistfulness was, of course, for a youth when his beauty could command any situation. Unfortunately, like the Bourbons whose imperiousness he shared, George Platt Lynes forgot nothing and learned nothing. At any rate, Wheeler was not interested. He had a battery of pretty young men of his own to handle.

Katherine Anne Porter was highly critical of the direction Platt Lynes was taking with his life. In a letter of July 1952 she wrote, "The trouble with you who like this kind of *poule* instead of the female sort is, that men who like the female version know what to call them, and where they belong—they aren't allowed to overrun every scene in life."

Dancer William Weslow, who had a transitory but more serious than usual romance with George Platt Lynes in the early 1950s, evidently treated the photographer to the kind of temperament Platt Lynes had displayed to his admirers in the past. Dining at Platt Lynes's apartment before a performance, Weslow had requested steak because of the demanding dancing that was to be done that evening. Instead, Platt Lynes served him an elaborate veal dish, which the young dancer flung against the wall before leaving in search of a steak.

An interesting sidelight on Platt Lynes is reported by Weslow. He remembers visiting Platt Lynes in his studio and seeing him applying makeup to his models. Paulette Goddard was among these sitters, as was the French dancer Renée "Zizi" Jeanmaire. Platt Lynes used many skills in creating outstanding photographs.

Around this time Platt Lynes also dabbled with doing an alphabet of male nudes posed as the letters of the alphabet. He didn't get very far before abandoning the project, although his friend Glenway Wescott had already written a text for the book. Another abandoned project was a book of portraits, whose costs would be borne by the subscribers. This idea never came to fruition, however, and collections of his photographs were not published until the 1980s.

Platt Lynes did complete a vast project of printing fifty-four photographs for Lincoln Kirstein to decorate the hallways of the New York City Ballet's new offices. Taken over two decades, the photographs recapitulated the entire history of Kirstein's and Balanchine's ballet activities. Old negatives had to be dug out of storage, and croppings and enlargings had to be done to give the pictures a coherent look.

Platt Lynes was also working on the sets and costumes for a new production of *The Four Temperaments* for the New York City Ballet. He wrote Bernard Perlin that he had been "semi-commissioned" to draft the designs, which suggests that Lincoln Kirstein was trying to send more work his way. He found it heavy going and this project was ultimately abandoned.

At this time Platt Lynes lived on the top floor of his brother's town house for six months, which was stressful for his brother's family. Russell Lynes was on a leave of absence from *Harper's* magazine to work on his book *The Tastemakers*, which was to bring him much attention and acclaim. Mildred Lynes was not well, so her husband had to work writing magazine articles and anything he could get his hands on to cover bills.

George Platt Lynes had little concern for his brother's problems, as he had just fallen in love with Don Bachardy, the teenage amour of the novelist Christopher Isherwood. Bachardy and Isherwood had come from California to New York on a visit. They met Platt Lynes at a party, and the photographer was immediately besotted by Bachardy, who was eighteen at this time and appeared much younger. In February, Platt Lynes wrote, "I want you. I want you here. I want you now. But what the hell am I to do about it? . . . I can't in good conscience try to seduce you away from Chris . . . but probably conscience has nothing to do with the case—in circumstances like these it has a wonderful way of not asserting itself." In July, as a postscript to a long, chatty letter about Greta Garbo looking at his scrapbooks of nudes ("She looked carefully at the females and the boys with the big you-know-whats, skipped quickly over the others"), Platt Lynes wrote, "Dear Don, I don't know at this point if my heart is still lost to you. It's very, very hard to tell."

George Platt Lynes's views on his family are encapsulated in a letter

Don Bachardy by George Platt Lynes, 1954. (Collection of Don Bachardy. Courtesy of Mr. and Mrs. George Platt Lynes II. Reprinted by permission)

he wrote to Bachardy in February 1954: "My family? Are you interested, really? I've a mother, 74 this year, now in North Carolina; she's remarkable in most ways and a beauty besides. I've a brother, Russell, who is managing editor of *Harper's* Magazine; he writes too, not in any way of interest to us, but with what's considered success. He's four years younger than I, married to Mildred Akin (a divine dame and an art historian—she lectures at the Metropolitan Museum), is the father of George (George Platt Lynes II, aged 16, a beauty too) and of Elizabeth (aged 14, a charm girl when she feels like being one). And that's all. My father died 22 years ago, aunts, uncles, cousins and the like I've lots of but I manage not only to not see them but never even to hear about them. Edified?"

The letter's condescending tone in regard to his brother is unpleasant, particularly when his brother had rescued him financially several times and was the letter writer's host. The cruel side of George Platt Lynes's nature became more pronounced as he struggled with the reality that he was no longer the golden boy. His niece, Elizabeth Lynes Kaestle, remembers that as a teenager she was inordinately proud of a new pair of high-heeled white shoes until her uncle spoiled them for her by telling her never to wear white shoes because she had large feet. Platt Lynes didn't hesitate to hurt other people's feelings, and with age, he seems to have come to relish doing so.

During those final years a number of his male friends remember the photographer ordering them to make love with other friends, both male and female, whether they felt like it or not, while he watched. Voyeurism seemed to be invading his life, as it had completely taken over Glenway Wescott's.

However interested George Platt Lynes was in Don Bachardy, he could not have supported a young lover. Throughout 1954, he was kept afloat financially by friends and family. He borrowed about $3,000 from his friends Alice and Harold Guinzberg, offering as collateral a small Picasso that had been given him by Barbara Harrison Wescott. He ignored the fact that his painting had already been promised to Russell against an earlier loan. This use of one painting to secure two loans was to cause complications later.

Finally, George Platt Lynes was to have one more apartment to decorate, again on a fourth floor, but this time with an elevator, at 157 East Sixty-First Street. He signed the lease in February 1953, with little idea of how he would pay the rent. Again, an enormous amount of redecoration was done to this rented apartment, with much repapering, painting, and hanging of pictures. This went on for several months, and his studio was virtually closed while he used his studio assistant and every young male friend he could gather around to help. In July 1953, he still considered his flat unfinished, although by now it was a largely dark green and purple, elegant hideaway with a violet carpet and mahogany pedestals supporting lamps with purple felt shades. The decor included the usual

*George Platt Lynes on a couch in his living room at 157 East 61st Street, N.Y.C.,
1954. (Collection of Anatole Pohorilenko. Reprinted by permission)*

gilt-framed drawings, important paintings, and tables strewn with valuable bibelots.

He wrote Bernard Perlin in this period, "Yesterday I was awakened at
eight-thirty in the morning by insistent doorbell ringing. Jen was earlier
than I expected to patch wallpaper. . . . He stayed all morning, adorably
puttering. Noonish Mac [the dancer Ralph McWilliams] turned up . . .

and . . . painted the interior of my smut closet (every man should have a closet that locks). . . . Wish I had a car. I'm so broke thanks to the installation of my palace-type apartment, badly timed to coincide with the usual spring slump—by this time I should have learned, shouldn't I?"

In the closet with a lock must have been a pornography collection—his own photographs that were not for casual visitors or maids to see, as well as a set of dildos. A young acquaintance of that period, Dick Sweet, remembers them as being "like a wrench kit" and inlaid with semiprecious stones. Another friend said they were originally for medical use and went well beyond "large" in the range of sizes.

Jensen Yow remained a strong support to Platt Lynes through these difficult years. From his letters to Yow, it is clear that the photographer depends on him for such favors as carrying a green sofa around the corner, and the young man was also the object of his romantic affections.

In 1950 and 1951 Platt Lynes's letters are largely gossip and household matters, with some references to the fashion backdrops that Yow occasionally painted for him—"The background worked beautifully"—and his inability to pay the artist in full for his work. The photographer also refuses a small loan from Yow, himself struggling to stay afloat financially. In one handwritten note he adds, "If tomorrow after your concert your friend proves unrewarding, call me. I expect to be at home alone." In July 1951, Platt Lynes writes, "Bless you, angel. You *are it.* I love you very much." He includes his phone number in the note—Circle 7-3839. In October the romantic edge is sharper: "I've missed you in an acute new sort of way." A brief handwritten note says, "You were so adorable last night. I loved you more than ever. Bless you."

There the correspondence with Yow ends until the latter part of 1955 when Platt Lynes was in France. In September he urges Jensen Yow to join him there. In October, shortly before his return to the United States, he writes, "I WANT YOU HERE. For my sake, for yours too, and not, not merely in the ways of self-indulgence. . . . I've a notion that you and I can make beautiful (photographic) music together. We could, just might, astonish EVERYBODY." Yow did not go to France but to his great credit he never failed his friend, who he knew was fatally ill.

In his new apartment, Platt Lynes continued to surround himself with young men, despite all his protestations that they bored him. In the fall of 1954 he wrote Bernard Perlin, "I'm back at my spider-in-web work. I invited twenty-odd, and Connolly [John Connolly, a young friend of Glenway Wescott's] invited another twenty-odd, and of course there were crashers. There must have been fifty or sixty altogether, at least fifteen of them I had never seen before."

He kept carbon copies of his correspondence with these many young men, and it makes curious reading. Platt Lynes was indeed a web-weaver: His letters are intimate, amusing, and designed to make the reader feel that he alone is the focus of attention. He wrote to Jensen Yow, Ralph McWilliams, Will Chandlee, Ted Armstrong of the Canadian Army, Ed Torgeson, Romain Johnston, Francesco Varcario, Jack Gillum, Michael Maule, Carlos McLendon, and Guy des Rochers, and mentions a number of other young men with whom he is involved. One of his most touching correspondents was Robert "Buddy" McCarthy, a young, well-built man from Boston whom he referred to as the Baby Blacksmith. He was obviously taken with Platt Lynes, and his letters move from being endearing to bragging about the sexual exploits he was newly experiencing. McCarthy was only too successful in trying to copy the Platt Lynes lifestyle, once he realized that he was not to be loved exclusively.

It is possible to chart the volatility of Platt Lynes's emotions during this time by quoting his correspondence:

March 24, 1952, to Michael Maule:
"Ed Torgeson called me on Sunday afternoon and the little [Ralph] McWilliams came to dine."

May 29 to Jack Gillum:
"My favorites are the same—Jen and Mac—bless their hearts—they don't bore me. Also I've become fond of John Connolly, Glenway's friend."

August 21 to Michael Maule:
"Buddy [McCarthy] comes from Boston to spend the weekend with me."

October 24 to Jack Gillum:
"My last harem disbanded itself, went on tour, a nasty habit that dancer types indulge in. So I'm busy making myself a new one. So far: a baby blacksmith (miniature muscleman) and [Bill Blizzard] a brown boy (beautiful in the lean, long, muscular way, chocolate and ashes-of-roses). I recommend both."

October 31 to Carlos McLendon:
"You sound unhappy . . . perhaps you should have married me when you had the chance."

Thanksgiving, 1952, to Ralph McWilliams:
"I thought as I was falling asleep that it might be fatal (for the likes of me) to fall in love with (the likes of) you—but of course that danger point is past—but how wonderful it is to *be* in love with you!"

January 13, 1953, to Francesco Varcario (Joe Frank):
"It's bad luck or bad management—or so I think—that we didn't get to be friends earlier . . . perhaps you'll not stay in Europe forever after all, perhaps I'll have a chance to see something of you."

November 20 to Ted Armstrong of the Canadian Army:
"Maybe—though these things can't be promised so far in advance— I can provide you with bed and shelter, pleasant the last time."

April 7, 1954, to Will H. Chandlee III:
"Sunday luncheon was fun. Too much travel for just a meal, but there were other pleasures, more than adequate."

April 27 to Will H. Chandlee III:
"For me our weekend—in particular the parts of it when were alone—was ideal, fun as I had supposed it would be, more gratifying than I had any reason to expect."

November 4 to Romain Johnston:
"The point, my point, is that I cannot tolerate even the thought of losing you. . . . I do not feel I have lost you, or that I am likely to lose you, soon or for long. And the other things I said—that I adore you— that I want you to be happy—that I will play any game you like . . ."

November 22 to Ben (no last name):
"Sex-for-science is interesting, certainly, and one of these days it might interest you. I'll explain more thoroughly if you like. But until such time, take it easy. Nobody is going to try to twist your arm. . . . I would like to twist your arm, though in the way of persuading you to come see me again. I liked you a lot."

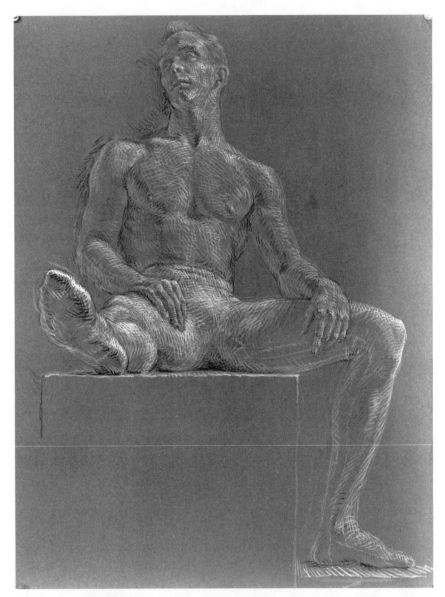

Ralph McWilliams *by Paul Cadmus, circa 1952. (Collection of Gilbert Ireland. Courtesy of D. C. Moore Gallery, N.Y.C. Reprinted by permission)*

There is a kind of emptiness and practiced cruelty in the way George Platt Lynes maintained so many romantic and sexual relationships with so many men at one time. This frenetic weaving of romantic intrigue and sexual activity was to continue until only weeks before his death.

At times, as in the latter part of 1952, commissions came in and business flourished. However, even in the thinnest times Platt Lynes's studio assistant Bill Vasilov remained with him. Vasilov built a circle light for Platt Lynes. Made of a large pipe supporting floodlights, this "ring light" enabled the photographer to create completely shadowless images that in later years were copied by other photographers. (A moody, handsome man prone to depression, Vasilov committed suicide not long after the photographer's death.)

In the early 1950s Platt Lynes gave a new look to his photographs by working with paper negatives. Paper negatives were the earliest material used for creating photographs and gave the images a soft and mottled appearance due to the type of paper used. They were also much less expensive than the standard material used for negatives. Jensen Yow believes that Platt Lynes was inspired to achieve this subtle, atmospheric effect in his work by a painting by Edgar Degas that the photographer saw while shooting the furnishings of Henry McIlhenny's Philadelphia mansion.

At this time, Platt Lynes was also selling photographs to a Swiss homoerotic magazine called *Der Kreis* (The Circle) under the pseudonyms Roberto Rolf and Robert Orville. But when he sent the magazine a series of photographs of male nudes on paper negatives, the editors replied that they did not like the quality of these pictures. Misunderstanding the look produced by the paper negatives, they thought the models' skin looked blotchy and recommended that the photographer study the clear, clean look of George Platt Lynes.

He did more ballet work in this financially pressed period. Ballet Theater commissioned a large number of photos for their New York season program, and for the first time Platt Lynes was well paid for this. He did this entire series, too, in the paper-negative style with which he had been experimenting.

His creative life was full of many special projects, though none of them were very remunerative. He did a book of photographs for Lincoln Kirstein about the New York City Ballet. Platt Lynes's friend Marianne Moore was less than enthusiastic. She wrote him, "I am delighted *to have a picture of you* and the one of Mr. Balanchine," in what she called "an astonishing brochure." The revelatory nature of the ballet costumes probably shocked her retiring nature. George Platt Lynes treasured his friendship with the shy poet, who still lived with her mother in Brooklyn, but he was completely mystified as to why she didn't like his photographs.

George Platt Lynes was not commissioned to do the photographs for the New York City Ballet's new production of *The Nutcracker*, and he feigned ignorance as to the reason. People who knew him at the time say that he had offended Kirstein at a party. When Kirstein asked him about doing the photographs of the full-length Tchaikovsky ballet, Platt Lynes had said, "And this time you're going to pay me something for them, too." Someone else did the pictures, and the difference between them was never made up. His intemperate remark removed another pillar from the photographer's support structure.

In September 1954, his finances spiraled sharply downward. He wrote Perlin, "I've got to raise a hell of a lot of dough, but fast. . . . When (if) I raise this dough, I'm delivering myself, body and soul, into the hands of my lawyer. . . . He'll keep me poor. No more parties (unless somebody else pays for them), no generosities, no luxuries (restaurants and the like); it'll be hell. You'll be coming back to a new me. Can you bear it? Can I?" Platt Lynes had to write to Mina Kirstein Curtiss, Lincoln Kirstein's sister, who had loaned him money, and say that he would not be able to repay the loan, adding, "I do know that I have to reduce my general indebtedness—so perhaps there's hope. Some comfort to me, none, I'm afraid, to you." Despite his casual tone, he must have felt embarrassed and diminished.

In the fall of 1954, his brother wrote him a strong letter about the impossibility of continuing loans: "First, with the Hollywood house, it was a matter of indulging your whims (with, of course, what looked like a perfectly sound guarantee of our investment); then it became a matter of helping you over rough spots with loans that you repaid, then it became loans that you hoped to repay and didn't, and now it has become loans that you are quite frank to say you don't intend to repay. . . . I also know that your income from your business is enough to live on if you are willing to live on it . . . there is no reason why we should have to bail you out again and again and again because you want to lead a kind of life you can't afford. We'd like to lead a kind of life we can't afford too. So does everybody.

"What I'm getting at is simple enough. You can't count on us to get up cash whenever you need it. . . . I'm through, I've had it." In fact, Russell and Mildred were never to stop helping beautiful and improvident George.

Despite his nervousness and emotionality, Platt Lynes's health had been good until the winter of 1953–54, when he had pneumonia twice, an infection he had never had before. He continued smoking heavily.

Then in the spring of 1955 his doctor discovered Platt Lynes had begun coughing up blood. On May 20, he was operated on at New York Hospital. His brother writes, "The operation revealed a cancerous tumor in the right lung; the disease had spread beyond removal or surgical containment. 'They just sewed him back up,' I was told."

Despite the operation, Platt Lynes continued his life much as it had been before, with the exception of stopping smoking. A young black lover of the period, Bill Blizzard, remembers being shown the scar in the shower after they had made love. Bill Blizzard had been introduced to Platt Lynes by John Leaphart, another black model and bedmate of the photographer. Blizzard and Leaphart were photographed together in erotic poses, similar to those Leaphart had earlier posed for with the white Buddy McCarthy.

Platt Lynes's apartment on Sixty-first Street had to be abandoned, as it was not clear when he would work again. He had not been told that his illness was incurable. His great friend, the photo retoucher Bob Bishop, told Russell Lynes, "When George came out of the hospital the first time, he was very sick. He knew he had cancer and he said, 'It's strange, my whole body is practically destroyed but my sex urge is still strong.'" Leaving the hospital, Platt Lynes went to the apartment of a wealthy young man who was a friend of friends and always out of town. From there he moved to the temporarily empty apartment of Moore Crosthwaite, an English diplomat who was secretary to the British ambassador to the United Nations. Crosthwaite and Platt Lynes had cohosted many parties for handsome young men and were longtime friends.

In New York, his many friends rallied about him and were constantly in attendance, preparing meals and keeping him company. A steady stream of beautiful models, society women, and handsome young men in tight blue jeans passed in and out of whatever apartment he occupied. In the summer of 1955, Platt Lynes went to his mother's former home in North Egremont, Massachusetts, now owned by his brother, with the painter Bernard Perlin to care for him. Friends made their way to Massachusetts to be supportive. Bernard Perlin took him to nearby Prospect Lake and rowed while Platt Lynes lounged in the boat sunbathing. He was extremely bad-tempered, but Perlin managed to keep him amused and distracted most of the time.

He visited Paul Cadmus and the Frenches in Hartland, Vermont, where they were spending the summer. He stayed with the artist Ilse Bischoff and wrote to Bernard Perlin, "Paul was SWEET and AFFEC-TIONATE, Margaret was affectionate, even LOVING. Jerry was, or seemed, sort of shitty TRUCULENT at first, but that wore down to what seemed FOND SUSPICION."

News that Platt Lynes was dying reached Tchelitchev in Italy in a letter from Lincoln Kirstein, who mentioned that he as well as other friends had fallen out with the photographer. He felt it was best that George was dying since the photographer would have hated growing old, and Kirstein added that he could not go to see George. Perhaps Kirstein was still angry about *The Nutcracker* photos, or perhaps his life-long antipathy to witnessing the illnesses of friends kept him away.

Katherine Anne Porter also failed to come visit him, which he took badly. Soon thereafter, he decided he would return to New York and then go to Europe. Monroe Wheeler came to Massachusetts to escort him back to New York. On the train they tore up many of Platt Lynes's fashion photographs as being an unworthy testament to his work. This strongly indicated that he knew he was not to live much longer and is also the only verified story of his photographs being destroyed.

His friend François Reichenbach in Paris had extended an open invitation to visit, and Platt Lynes was determined to go. Reichenbach was the nephew of Jacques Guérin, the owner of Dorsay fragrances. As Guérin had been a close friend of Monroe Wheeler and Glenway Wescott in the Paris of the 1920s and early 1930s, his nephew François became their friend as well. He had a luxurious apartment in the Place des États-Unis in the chic Sixteenth Arrondissement, where George was planning to stay. Reichenbach had also offered to pay for the flight to France, and after some vagueness as to when this was to happen, Platt Lynes departed on September 9 for Paris. His former lover and great friend Laurie Douglas was living in Paris then and was there to greet him. A large cocktail party soon followed. Acquaintances like Gloria Swanson and Tennessee Williams were in Paris, and he managed a busy social life. Pain was held in abeyance with drugs, and at dinner with *The New Yorker* correspondent Janet Flanner and a doctor friend, he asked the physician if he could arrange for his dwindling supply to be replenished. The doctor agreed, but when Platt Lynes left early, the doctor said to Janet Flanner, "Your friend, you know, is dying."

On the poor advice of someone, Platt Lynes colored his hair shortly after arriving in Paris. Apologetically he wrote to Bernard Perlin in New York, "It didn't make me LOOK younger, that's for sure. It didn't even make me FEEL younger, as I had hoped it might. So yesterday I . . . had it bleached. . . . It's now what they call Gris Trianon. Grey for sure, but ever so slightly lavender."

After three weeks in Paris, he flew on to Rome, where he again saw Gloria Swanson and Tennessee Williams. His longtime friend Paul Tchelitchev was living in Rome also. Tchelitchev, who was in poor health himself, saw that Platt Lynes was dying and apologized later to Russell Lynes for his lack of hospitality, writing, "I was afraid that George was cross with me as he didn't find that kindness and love he would like to get from me. Besides he wanted a miracle—to be cured—but I knew it was no more possible. He was already gone—awaiting the next train . . . I couldn't do a miracle."

In his letters to the United States, however, Platt Lynes seems not to have given up hope, and he was making plans to remain in Paris. He intended to stay in an apartment offered him by Jacques Guérin, but upon his return to Paris after ten days in Rome, he found a note that read, "You misunderstood me about the Avenue d'Orléans. I don't have this flat anymore!"

However ill Platt Lynes was, his romantic life went on. He wrote Bernard Perlin, "It seems I have a new loverboy, age twenty-five. He's little (almost a midget) and physically perfect, a DOLL." And to Katherine Anne Porter, he wrote that he was returning and would be "accompanied by my latest love, a real live gorilla. You wait. You'll see. He's little and dark and dangerous. He's very strong. He bites. He speaks one known language—French—and that's a help. Sometimes I call him King Kong but in general he's known as Jean-Louis-Roussel-Bossière. He writes music."

Platt Lynes returned to New York at the end of October 1955. When he arrived, he was in fact with a young man, but it was Glen McCourt, a Canadian, who remained in New York for a time to help care for him. But in about ten days Platt Lynes had to reenter the hospital. By then his mother had already departed for Pinehurst, North Carolina, to her work as a hotel social director. He was never to see her again.

At one last dinner party at his brother's home the poet Marianne Moore and other friends were present. Platt Lynes had been barely able to dress and leave the hospital, but he made it through the evening. The cancer had spread to his brain, and he now had severe headaches much of the time. His sister-in-law, Mildred, put ice on his head and wrapped it in a pink towel in a turban shape. On the walls were his paintings, on the floor his carpet. His family had put in place, where they could, his familiar possessions.

He fell into a coma a few days later, but on December 5 the family was called and, arriving at the hospital, found him sitting up in bed reading the newspaper. His brother wrote of this day, "He was cheerful and teasing." His friend Tom Royal also visited him on that day and remembers the snow falling outside as he sat by the photographer's bed.

George Platt Lynes died the next day, December 6, 1955. He was forty-eight.

Afterword

The Funeral Party

It's 1955 and George is dead. I went to his funeral. George Platt Lynes. It was just like one of his parties. Everyone was there and it was sort of wonderful and sort of terrible all at the same time. They had it all the way to hell and gone, down at St. George's Church on Stuyvesant Square, near where the Phoenix Theater was later. A god-awful neighborhood.

I asked his brother afterward on the church steps why they had it there. He said to please their mother, who was Episcopalian. I didn't ask him why, if she was so concerned about the church, she didn't bother to come.

George was always so proud of her for being so aristocratic. I only met her once, but I certainly got the impression that she knew who was number one. Poor George. The last time I saw him at the hospital shortly before he died, he asked, "Where's Adelaide? Why hasn't she come?" Russell said, "She'll be along in a few days. She's coming north for Christmas." George was really just a little boy all his days and he died without his mother. I think she actually had quite a lot of money and never gave him a sou. Who was she saving it for? I think I know the answer to that.

Anyway. The church was jammed with flowers and models and a lot of society people, too. All those beautiful girls who loved to work for him because he was fun and made them look great and wasn't always coming on to them. And all those handsome guys he was *always coming on to. God, there must have been at least a hundred men right there on the premises whom he'd known intimately. Or had known him intimately is probably more accurate. And he'd known some women's bodies, too, to be fair. Which isn't the worst thing in the world at your funeral. It can't be said of many of us that we slept with a hundred people who attended our funeral.*

I have to admit that finally I was among the hundred. He always called me Sandusky, you know. From that first time I met him. In these last years he'd been sleeping with more and more guys all the time. He'd been disappointed in love, but who hasn't? I don't think he wanted a relationship like Monroe Wheeler and Glenway Wescott's. They've been together for umpteen years but sleep with everyone they can get their hands on. I think George had some dreamy idea about eternal love, but then someone new would turn up and he'd get distracted. He was also very much into sex. He was inventive. I did some stuff with him in front of the fireplace at his place on Sixty-first Street with ice cubes that I've never done with anyone else. Or even had suggested. He was a wild and beautiful guy. I don't think he would have liked getting older and uglier all the time. I can't say I like it very much myself.

The family sat in the front row. His brother, Russell (whom I never cottoned to very much; uptight and so concerned about who was who socially. George was never really like that). His wife, Mildred, who seemed to be over having nervous collapses now. And the children. Russell's tiny girlfriend, Kay Somebody-or-other, sat behind them. She may have had something to do with Mildred's nervous collapses. She wears red a lot. It tells you something.

And there were all of George's nearest and dearest. Monroe and Glenway. Paul Cadmus and that arrogant guy he was always linked with, Jared French. And Jared French's wife. You tell me.

And darling Bernard Perlin. The nicest one of them all. Jensen Yow, another sweet guy. Lincoln Kirstein. Looking depressed. But then he always looks depressed.

Ralph McWilliams, Buddy McCarthy, Ed Torgeson, the list goes on forever. It's really strange. I've rarely seen any of those people since. I sat next to Bill Harris. I said, "This is really creepy. He wanted me to sleep with him in the hospital about a week ago." Bill said, "I did. It was like sleeping with the Angel of Death."

The casket was covered in a blanket of white carnations. Bill said, "He hated carnations. It should have been orchids or nothing."

George Platt Lynes

We have lost our dancing master.

—Akin (Mrs. Russell) Lynes

George Platt Lynes was buried in Woodlawn Cemetery in a family plot near many of his relatives. His great-grandfather the decorator George Platt has the largest stone, around which the others are scattered.

In the way of New York, the photographer was rapidly forgotten. Many of the friends who had gathered around him for his frequent parties and dinners left the city, making it clear that he had been the linchpin who had held this social world together. At his parties, careers were launched, liaisons made, and sex lives reinvigorated. Once he was gone, no one else took up the challenge, and an entire style of living pretty much disappeared.

After Platt Lynes's death, his brother, Russell, and Bernard Perlin distributed some of his prints and negatives. His file of prints and negatives had been left to Bernard Perlin to supervise, who gave the ballet photographs to Lincoln Center's Library for the Performing Arts, a branch of the New York Public Library. The negatives and prints of artists were donated to the Archives of American Art, and the other files were retained by Bernard Perlin, who, in time, sold them to Frederick Koch, a collector with a large photography collection.

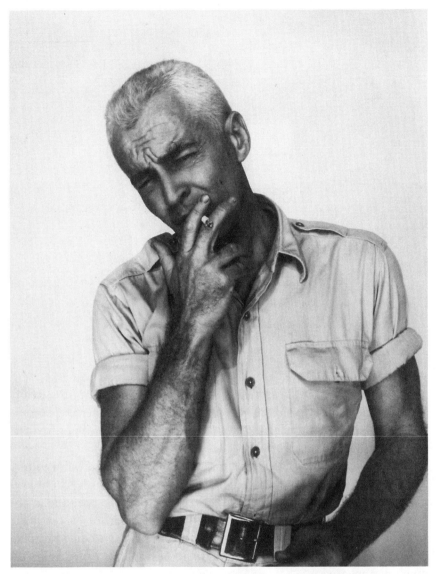

Self-portrait by George Platt Lynes, 1954. (Collection of Robert Miller Gallery. Courtesy of Mr. and Mrs. George Platt Lynes II. Reprinted by permission)

An interesting sidelight concerns a researcher, Arthur Long, who was given access to an additional collection of prints that were in the Russell Lynes home. Ostensibly, Long was researching a book on George Platt Lynes, and his brother was only too happy to cooperate. The book was not forthcoming, and when Long died, his estate was auctioned at

Sotheby's. To the great surprise of Russell Lynes and Bernard Perlin, a great many Platt Lynes photographs were included. Long had been slipping them out a few at a time while doing his research. There was no way to recover them from the auction house, but fortunately these, too, passed into the collection of Frederick Koch, who donated them to the Harvard University Library's Theater Collection.

Platt Lynes collections are also at the Museum of Modern Art, the Metropolitan Museum of Art, and the Art Institute of Chicago. A large collection at the Guggenheim Museum came indirectly from the Monroe Wheeler estate. Another comprehensive collection is at the Kinsey Institute at Indiana University in Bloomington, Indiana. Dr. Alfred Kinsey had made a collection of over five hundred George Platt Lynes prints, many of them nudes, but also celebrities and some fashion material. Kinsey had done this not only in the interest of scientific research but also to help the photographer financially in the years when his career was failing.

The first book on Platt Lynes's work appeared in 1973 when *The New York City Ballet, Photographs by Martha Swope and George Platt Lynes* by Lincoln Kirstein was published by Alfred A. Knopf. The first true retrospective of his work, *George Platt Lynes: Photographs, 1931–1955*, was done by Twelvetrees Press in 1980. *George Platt Lynes—Ballet* followed in 1985, and later, *George Platt Lynes: Portraits, 1927–1955*. Peter Weiermair also edited a catalog for a Platt Lynes exhibition at the Frankfurter Kunstverein in Frankfurt in 1982.

In 1993 the Kinsey Institute had an exhibition of some of its Platt Lynes holdings at the Grey Gallery in New York, accompanied by a catalog edited by James Crump. Although none of the models were identified, the Crump volume was the first to address the graphic sexuality of some of the Platt Lynes photographs, and the historical essay by James Crump was the first George Platt Lynes biography. My own book, *Naked Men: Pioneering Male Nudes*, published in 1997 by Rizzoli/Universe, contained many George Platt Lynes photographs and identified the models.

George Platt Lynes's great legacy, in fact, has been his influence on succeeding generations of photographers of the male nude. Bruce Weber, for example, greatly admires the work of Platt Lynes and has drawn upon it for inspiration, while Herb Ritts has also carried the tradition forward in his own beautiful studio work. Many others have followed upon the path first illuminated by Platt Lynes. His ability to combine sexuality, sensuality, beauty, refinement of lighting, and pose has inspired many photographers, male and female alike. But his love of beauty and gift for lighting and capturing images remains specifically his own and unequaled in his area of work.

A few pertinent statements have been made about him and his work. Russell Lynes wrote an unpublished biography, *The Daring Eye of George Platt Lynes*, in which he wrote, "He was a vain man, vain of his looks with good reason, for he was uncommonly handsome. He understood vanity in others as in himself, and he was sympathetic to it. He both fed vanity in others and was fed by it. . . . George's personal vanity was not the kind that puts people off. It was internal and came out as a kind of charm that many men and women found for different reasons much to their taste."

Long after Platt Lynes's death, Lincoln Kirstein wrote in the 1994 Twin Palms book *George Platt Lynes: Portrait, 1927–1955:* "He wore American work clothes as a working costume and diplomatic uniform also earlier than anyone else. He was a physical, not a social snob. He preferred the looks of fascinating or beautiful faces."

In one of his letters written to Bernard Perlin in Rome in 1954, George Platt Lynes wrote, "I go on taking photographs for my pleasure . . . after all these years I'm just becoming aware of it. I'm the damned soul of my (damned) camera—and God, how it hates me sometimes! And I think I'd be a poor thing without it."

He never played the role of the great artist and was always extremely casual about his gift for photography. But shortly before his death he came to know that it was his work and his creativity that had been the true structure of his life.

Paul Cadmus

Paul and the Frenches were very secretive. They revealed very little about themselves. Yet they were very gregarious.

—*Donald Windham*

Even at ninety-five, Paul Cadmus remained undiminished in appearance, spirit, and creativity. His focus for more than the last thirty years was his relationship with singer/actor Jon Andersson. From 1955 to 1964 Cadmus's work ranged from exquisite still lifes to allegorical paintings. After he encountered Andersson in 1964, the younger man's blond good looks and beautiful body became the primary inspiration for the greater part of Cadmus's drawings and paintings.

Paul Cadmus had moved from Manhattan to a studio in Brooklyn Heights in 1961, and he remained there until 1975, when he moved to Weston, Connecticut. His brother-in-law, Lincoln Kirstein, had a studio/home built for Cadmus on Kirstein's property there. The house, a large studio with reception rooms and bedrooms opening from it, sits beside a rocky brook in deep woods. Jon Andersson, an avid gardener, maintains a greenhouse as well as bushes and flowers surrounding the building. Although Cadmus was ever reluctant to discuss his emotional ties and attitudes, one can draw some conclusions from the work that he did as his life advanced.

He did only one of his biting social-satire paintings in this later period, *Subway Symphony*, 1975–76. His largest painting, forty-six by ninety-two

Paul Cadmus (right) and Jon Andersson by Christopher Winslow, 1997. (Author's collection. Reprinted by permission)

The Paul Cadmus/Jon Andersson home in Weston, Connecticut, by Christopher Winslow, 1997. (Author's collection. Reprinted by permission)

inches, shows a subway station crammed with subway riders of every race, creed, and place of national origin. Most of the crowd is overweight or emaciated, or drugged or dysfunctional in one way or another. These are the same drunken and foolish people as in Cadmus's paintings of the 1930s. But now, added to the squalor and decay, there is the potential for violence, and a mugging has just taken place down an exit passage. A riot of vivid colors—pinks and violets, baby blues and acid greens—evoke a psychedelic culture where drugs play an important role. Amidst all this disorder, there are figures of urban vitality and culture: a self-assured young black woman reads a textbook on drawing, while a bare-chested young man with long blond hair who might be Jon Andersson holds his guitar case on his lap and smiles into the distance. The gray-haired artist himself sits sketching on the subway stairs where, just steps away from him, two young men in jeans are cruising each other.

In 1976, the year Cadmus completed *Subway Symphony*, he gave an interview to *The Advocate* responding to the changes that followed the Stonewall Inn riots and the early years of the gay liberation movement. Like others in the older generation, Cadmus valued his privacy. "Although I have never been in the closet," he said, "I have chosen as much as possible the semi-privacy of my semi-ivory tower rather than calling from rooftops and shouting in parades." His art had never been in the closet, either. Over the decades he included specific incidents of gay life and gay history in his work, such as the red-necktie pickup scenes in *Shore Leave* (1933) and *The Fleet's In!* (1934) and the stack of gay books— Gide's *Corydon* and the sonnets of Shakespeare and Michelangelo—in *Mannikins* (1951).

But *Subway Symphony* and to a lesser degree Cadmus's *See No Evil, Speak No Evil, Etc.* of 1985 are the only criticisms of an American culture going all to hell with itself. In the 1985 painting, the blowsy Reaganesque main figure surrounded with press and makeup artists reveals what Cadmus thought of the leadership of the time. But in other paintings, such as *Rise and Fall* (1989) and *The Lid* (1990), naked lovers float, ignoring the catastrophes of crashing stock markets and fiery infernos. The artist seemed to be saying that love and beauty and sensuality can create a world that blissfully ignores the man-made disasters around them—but the disasters remain. Certainly the majority of Cadmus's work in this latter part of his life indicated a dedication to this credo.

His *Study for a David and Goliath* (1971) is almost shocking in its suggestions that the beautiful Jon Andersson is somehow malevolent, the T square in his hand a weapon. And the painter's head, resting against the

Jon Andersson *by Paul Cadmus, circa 1971 (colored crayon on hand-toned paper,*
19¹/₂" x 16¹/₈"). (Collection of Paul Cadmus and Jon Andersson. Courtesy of D. C.
Moore Gallery, N.Y.C. Reprinted by permission)

edge of the bed, represents a decapitation, the red scarf at his neck looking very much like the edge of a severed body. Was he telling us that
beauty can undo the importance of art in an artist's life? Conversely, in
Artist and Model (1973) Cadmus, still scarcely touched by time, worked
with sober concentration on a full-length sketch of his naked lover. And
in *The Haircut* (1986) the artist seems to be enjoying having his hair cut
into a glowing halo by the angelic presence of the muscular Jon Andersson. A strong feeling of caring warms this painting.

But aside from any biographical inferences drawn from the subject matter of these paintings, the great numbers of classical drawings of the male nude done by Paul Cadmus emphasize his reliance upon the tradition of art-making and its importance in his life.

Introducing "Men Without Women," an art exhibit that he curated at his alma mater, the National Academy of Design, in 1999, Cadmus wrote "the male, especially the male nude, has been somewhat overlooked since the Renaissance in favor of the female nude. I would like to redress the balance. The male nude has been a specialty of my own oeuvre when I am not being concerned with the foibles of people in daily life." In appreciation for his decades of work, SAGE (Senior Action in a Gay Environment) gave Cadmus its Lifetime Achievement Award in November 1999.

When Jared French died in Rome in 1988, a relationship ended that had spanned sixty years. It was French who had insisted that Paul Cadmus pursue the life of an artist and he had shared with Cadmus his great interest in the refined and painstaking technique of egg tempera. French may have been jealous that Cadmus received more attention and appreciation during their lives, but he probably shared the concept of jealousy Cadmus portrayed in his 1983 painting, *The Eighth Sin: Jealousy*. A soul is pierced by a red-hot skewer while the androgynous figure gnaws on its own heart, and its head evaporates into countless eyes going up in smoke. In the distance a floating sun might be the head of a penis. Cadmus saw jealousy as a kind of self-imposed hell. As in all of his depicted sins, it is pain and unhappiness that one has brought on oneself.

A painter friend has said, "When you see *Jealousy*, you know he has suffered a lot." When asked if he felt he was essentially the same person he was as a young man, he replied, "No, now I'm more benign. I wasn't so benign before."

Paul Cadmus died on December 12, 1999, five days before his ninety-fifth birthday. He had lived through most of the twentieth century, recording its people in his work. Which survives him. There was a kind of calmness and innocence in the persona of Paul Cadmus. Whatever exterior tempests raged, whatever personal crises occurred, he was never disappointed by that central point where he placed his interest, trust, and love: his art.

Lincoln Kirstein

"I who am now but a thought,
Once was a fanciful man. . . ."

—*Lincoln Kirstein*

From the death of George Platt Lynes in 1955 to his own death in 1996, Lincoln Kirstein's life was a steady flow of cultural contributions and awards for those contributions. The American Guild of Musical Artists (AGMA) gave Kirstein an award in 1957 for all he had done for American dance, and in the following year he received an award for distinguished service from the National Institute of Arts and Letters. The recognition he had long sought was beginning to accumulate, and the cultural establishment was observing him closely as one of its own. Edmund Wilson, writing in his notebook in 1957, observed that Lincoln Kirstein had all the traditional mannerisms of a Harvard intellectual: "sticking the head forward, gesticulating vaguely with the forefinger, certain intonations and an amusing way of speaking without vehemence."

The New York City Ballet continued to flourish throughout his lifetime. In 1956 the School of American Ballet moved from the space it had occupied at Madison Avenue and Fifty-ninth Street for so many years to much larger studios at 2291 Broadway. That year the New York City Ballet made another European tour. This company, in the eyes of the world, was the national company for the United States and encapsulated the American concept of classical ballet—streamlined, athletic, and unromantic.

In his continuing correspondence with Pavel Tchelitchev, now living in Italy, Kirstein told the painter in November 1956, about plans to commemorate George Platt Lynes as the first anniversary of his death neared. Kirstein had organized an exhibition at the City Center, and poet and writer friends were making contributions to a memorial album. He also mentioned that the Museum of Modern Art had told Monroe Wheeler that there was no chance for an exhibit of the photographer's work there. Did the museum find the fashion shots too commercial or the male nudes too erotic?

In April 1957 he wrote again to Tchelitchev with all the sad details of "Chick" Austin's funeral. The three men had known each other through those many exciting years when they were imposing new ideas about art on unsuspecting Americans. It was his last letter to the painter, who died in Rome in July. Kirstein persuaded Huntington Hartford, the heir to a railroad fortune, to mount a large exhibition of Tchelitchev's work at the Gallery of Modern Art in 1964, and wrote the catalog himself. Kirstein had filled his letters to Tchelitchev with the intimate details reserved for friends, but the painter may have been as inconstant in friendship as Kirstein himself could be. Sometime in the 1950s, Tchelitchev had said to his young friend Brooks Jackson, "Kirstein, that *pizdah*, he is lost in a forest of pricks." (Probably the nicest possible translation of *pizdah* is slut.)

In 1958 a relationship with Japan, both personal and professional, was established when the New York City Ballet toured there and in Australia. "Kirstein had brought along *War and Peace*," the ballerina Allegra Kent writes in her memoir, *Once a Dancer*, "and was going to read it cover to cover on our long nonjet flight to Japan." Kirstein remained in Japan to live for a short period and was to return and repeat this experience a number of times. For him, there was emotional sustenance in the Japanese traditions of meditation and restraint. Through the contacts he made there, he was able to invite the musicians and dancers of the Japanese Imperial Household, known as the Gagaku, to appear in a season with the New York City Ballet, which they did in 1959. Kirstein's interests in the arts of Japan continued, and he arranged an American tour for the Grand Kabuki theater in 1960 and a demonstration of traditional Japanese ritual sports for the 1962 Seattle World's Fair. In recognition of his services, the Japanese government awarded him the Order of the Sacred Treasure, Fourth Class. Kirstein's interest in the arts of Japan, like his trips to acquire Latin American art for the Museum of Modern Art and, most notably, his bringing a Russian choreographer to work in the United States, was part of his long struggle against isolationist trends in American culture.

In the 1960s he became an officer of the American Dressage Institute in Saratoga Springs, New York, a center for racing and the raising of horses. The institute trained horses in the art of moving in dancelike formations and performing dancelike movements. This long tradition, made famous by Austria's Lippizaner horses, began in the Renaissance when horses were trained to prance and kick to help them maneuver on the battlefield. The early ballets had formations similar to the dressage of trained horses, and horse ballets as well as human ballets were performed as court entertainment. Kirstein was a well-trained rider, but dressage appealed to him because it contained the same beauty of precise, trained movement as ballet.

In 1962 he organized the New York City Ballet tour of the Soviet Union, giving Russians their first exposure to ballet as it was developing in the free world. Nureyev had found political asylum in France the year before, but seeing Balanchine's short, plotless, unsentimental ballets may have led to defections by other Russian dancers, who had tired of the full-length romantic story ballets of the Soviet stage and wanted to perform in the West with its individual and artistic freedom—and its power to reward superstars with fame and riches.

As a result of this tour, New York City honored Lincoln Kirstein for distinguished service, and in 1963 he was appointed to the Citizens Advisory Committee to the Office of Cultural Affairs. The ballet company he had done so much to found reflected brilliantly upon our country's most famous and sophisticated city, and was becoming an important goodwill ambassador for the United States abroad, as its 1965 tour of Europe and Israel demonstrated.

By 1964 Lincoln Center for the Performing Arts had the New York State Theater ready for occupancy. Supported by Nelson Rockefeller's political and financial influence, Kirstein arranged for the New York City Ballet to move there and open the theater. Classrooms and rehearsal space had been designed by the architect Philip Johnson with the guidance of Kirstein and Balanchine to precisely serve the company's needs, but not everyone was pleased since the rooms were underground and had no daylight.

In July 1966 the Saratoga Performing Arts Center opened in Saratoga Springs, New York, where Kirstein had been practicing his riding and dressage. Kirstein had been enthusiastic about this project from the start, and for several months he met weekly with the center's architect. As a member of the board of directors, Kirstein made sure that the center had a close relationship with the New York City Ballet, which has performed there every summer. The ballet company also provided many of the center's teachers, while the center served as a summer school for young dancers who later joined the company in New York.

The highlight of 1967 for Lincoln Kirstein was his election as a Benefactor of the Metropolitan Museum of Art. Now entering his sixtieth year, he was truly storming the bastions of New York's most conservative society. And yet homophobic attitudes persisted, even among the most sophisticated members of the cultural elite. Edmund Wilson, writing in his diary in February 1967, notes that he likes Kirstein "better than I had when I first used to see him, when he had just come out of Harvard. He is very much less shy, talks amusingly and with a sense of who he is." And at a dinner party Wilson and Kirstein enjoyed talking about books, including Parker Tyler's recent biography of Tchelitchev. But the dean of American literary critics adds, referring to the biography of the Russian painter, "I did not say in Kirstein's presence that it was a book about a pansy written by a pansy for pansies." New York City was as uncomfortable with homosexuality in the 1960s as suburban Englewood had been when George Platt Lynes lived in the rectory there in the 1920s or as Washington had been when Paul Cadmus's *The Fleet's In!* had flustered Navy brass in the 1930s.

Kirstein had more interest than Platt Lynes in the large issues of history and society, and he did not resort to satire, as Cadmus did in his paintings. Instead, he took the path of someone accustomed to working within the established order and bending it to his will. He served in the army, and turned his experiences in World War II into the poems published as *Rhymes of a Pfc* in 1964 (and republished in an expanded edition in 1966). His elite education and his wealth might have led him in another direction, but his outsider status as a Jew and a homosexual continued to shape his life, and he remained committed to causes of social justice despite his growing fame and importance. In 1965 Kirstein traveled to Alabama and took part in the civil rights marches. He understood the value of a recognized name, and he was more than willing to lend his name as well as his physical presence to the movement for equality. When Martin Luther King, Jr., was murdered in 1968, Kirstein quickly arranged for Balanchine to create a stage version of *Requiem Canticles* as a memorial tribute to the civil rights leader. Performed at the

New York State Theater, this theatrical premiere of Stravinsky's religious cantata featured the dancer Arthur Mitchell.

As the decade drew to a close, Lincoln Kirstein was instrumental in encouraging and supporting the Dance Theater of Harlem. This classical company was founded and directed by Arthur Mitchell, for many years the only black member of the New York City Ballet. A leading dancer with the company, Mitchell felt the black community deserved a school and company for its many fine dancers. Kirstein was extremely helpful, and the company made its performing debut in 1971.

A police raid on a popular gay bar in Greenwich Village energized and redirected the gay movement in 1969, but Kirstein as president of the School of American Ballet had a more immediate concern, for the school was leaving its Broadway studios and moving into the Juilliard School at its new location at Lincoln Center. Now the school and the company created by Kirstein were in proximity and were the closest thing to a national school and company for ballet that this country was ever likely to have. That same year, in another sign of official recognition, Kirstein was elected a Fellow of the American Academy of Arts and Sciences.

In 1972 the New York City Ballet honored the composer Igor Stravinsky, who had died the year before, with a festival devoted entirely to ballets danced to his music. The Russian composer had long been involved with Balanchine and Kirstein and with this company. At the Stravinsky Festival thirty ballets were performed in seven performances, and there were twenty-two premieres by seven choreographers, including Balanchine's *Duo Concertant*. Jerome Robbins joined Balanchine in choreographing *Pulcinella*, a highlight of the festival in which both men appeared. The festival was a great success and led to a similar event featuring the music of Ravel in 1975. Kirstein was prevented from attending the Ravel festival because he had been hospitalized for a cardiac bypass.

The company's twenty-fifth anniversary was celebrated in 1973 with the publication of the lavishly designed album *The New York City Ballet*, which included photographs by George Platt Lynes of the earlier Kirstein/Balanchine companies and of the New York City Ballet up to 1955, with subsequent photos by Martha Swope. In the text Kirstein passed over his differences with Platt Lynes, writing a generous appreciation for the photographer's memorialization of ballets and dancers.

On Saturday, April 30, 1983, George Balanchine died, ending a fifty-year relationship with Kirstein. The great choreographer had been his colleague in the decades-long struggle to establish classical ballet in the United States, and Kirstein's sense of loss must have been profound. But there were matinee and evening performances scheduled for the New York City Ballet, and the School of American Ballet was giving a student performance at Juilliard, and so three times that day Kirstein stepped before the curtain and addressed the audience, saying, "I don't have to tell you that Mr. B. is with Mozart and Tchaikovsky and Stravinsky. . . ."

In 1984 Kirstein's monograph about his brother-in-law, lavishly illustrated with Cadmus's paintings, was published. That same year he received the U.S. Presidential Medal of Freedom in recognition of his services to the arts in America and in promoting American arts throughout the world. But receiving the nation's highest civilian award was soon overshadowed by the troubled situation at the New York City Ballet.

After Balanchine's death, there was increasing stress between Kirstein and other board members as to the direction the company should take now that it could no longer rely on the genius of the great choreographer. The philanthropist Anne Bass gave her support to Peter Martins, the dancer who had been selected to lead the company, and this weakened Kirstein's position. In the end, Mrs. Bass's wealth weighed more heavily with the board than Kirstein's history, and he found himself playing a diminished role in the management of the company that he and Balanchine had founded.

Disputes over conflicting visions of the company's future came to a head at a meeting in 1985. Jensen Yow remembers the impresario returning home that evening in a rage. Kirstein had planned to entertain the board of directors at his East 19th Street house, but after the great falling-out at the meeting he had returned alone. Everyone in the house retired, then at midnight the doorbell rang. The board of the New York City Ballet had arrived for the party—and to mend fences with Kirstein. He and Yow got dressed and set out the food and drink that had been put away, but Kirstein's relationship with the ballet company had suffered an irreparable change, and in his last years he was distanced from the company that he had devoted his life to creating.

The private side of Lincoln Kirstein remained an enigma throughout his life. Although Kirstein never responded in an obvious way to the political and social changes of the gay movement, it certainly affected him. Feeling with age a desire to make the record clear, he published a coming-out essay in the literary magazine *Raritan*. But in a characteristic move, Kirstein chose 1982—a year when fear of AIDS was making mainstream America more than usually skittish about homosexuals—to discuss his relationship with Carl Carlsen. And to make sure that the record was unmistakably clear, he republished this essay in *By With To & From* in 1991 and again in *Mosaic: Memoirs* in 1994.

Lincoln Kirstein had an unusual lifestyle, more like a Medici prince in the Renaissance than a modern millionaire in New York. To a degree, he wanted the appearance of a conventional life with a wife and a home. But he made few pretenses and didn't hide his attraction to men. There is no doubt that his interest in ballet was intellectual and esthetic, but he enjoyed the company of male dancers, and their presence was part and parcel of his love of dance.

As his friend Robert Chapman remembers, Kirstein always required the young men in whom he was interested to have some creative skill. He preferred young men with "digital mastery," by which he meant painters, sculptors, and perhaps musicians and dancers and writers. He could indeed be interested in men for their physical beauty alone, but he had even greater interest if beauty was combined with artistic ability. If they lacked this ability, he would dismiss them as being "replaceable parts."

"He had crushes on people, particularly blonds," according to the writer Donald Windham, who had worked for Kirstein at *Dance Index* in the 1940s. This preference was something that his brother-in-law knew well. When Paul Cadmus recommended Kirstein meet the publisher Jack Woody, the artist told Kirstein, "You'll like him. He's cute and he's blond." Of course, Kirstein also liked dark-haired men like José Martinez.

Kirstein could be casual about sexual adventures. When one of the principal male dancers with the New York City Ballet felt that he was out of favor, an intimate of Kirstein's advised him, "Just jump into bed with him."

On another occasion Kirstein expressed some interest in the dancer William Weslow, who replied, "I don't find you attractive, Mr. Kirstein." "Who asked you to find me attractive?" Kirstein snapped back. "I was just asking you to come over to the house for a few drinks and stay over."

One evening some time later Weslow spotted Kirstein at a gay bathhouse and embarrassed the impresario by saying "Why, Lincoln, hello! Come here often?" Kirstein didn't answer; he fled. Another report mentions seeing Kirstein at the Everard Baths carrying on a formidably erudite conversation with a friend.

The young men in whom Kirstein was interested were sometimes integrated into his home. In *Quarry* he writes, "On the third [floor] is a skylit studio, kept by Alexander Jensen Yow, with his library and electronic microscope. For years conservator at the Pierpont Morgan Library, he has for seven been independent and consultant for the Getty Museum in Malibu. His staff and students repair master drawings, prints, and small paintings. To rear is a smaller studio in which David Langfitt works. Five years ago, he was a guard at the State Theater. A Philadelphian, his teachers were Piero, Eakins, Seurat, and Balthus. His portraits, murals, and street-scenes are known. He has benefited by intimacy with drawings by Dürer, Watteau, Ingres, Degas, and Van Gogh, which have come to Jensen Yow for treatment. A daily presence of a prim conservationist and an efficient painter vivifies a constant re-evaluation of objects two floors below."

Kirstein also took a great interest in the New York City Ballet member Joseph Duell, and he had the English artist Michael Leonard draw the young dancer as a character from an eighteenth-century French novel, wearing the powdered wig of the period, but bare-chested. Duell's mysterious suicide, by hurling himself from a window in 1986, just short of his thirtieth birthday, has never been explained but was a great shock to Kirstein.

Many of the men Kirstein admired did not disappear from his life, and he was able to spend his time in the company of those who cared about him. Jensen Yow was always of great interest to Kirstein and was a source of physical and emotional support to the end.

The man who inherited the greater part of Kirstein's estate upon his death, Fred Maddox, played a more enigmatic role in his life. Of Welsh origin, Maddox appeared in Kirstein's life in 1964. He lived in the Kirstein home, leaving each day to work in an architectual office. None of Kirstein's friends are willing to speculate as to whether they were physical lovers. Trying to explain the relationship, Michael Leonard, who knew Kirstein well, gave a painterly interpretation, saying that Maddox "had the kind of face Lincoln liked. Open and naïve." Jensen Yow took a more pragmatic view. "You know," he said, "Lincoln hated to eat alone."

The article Nicholas Jenkins wrote for *The New Yorker* (April 13, 1998) tells much about Lincoln Kirstein, but still leaves him as a mysterious figure. It does not deal as forthrightly with Kirstein's overt, far-reaching, and bawdy sexuality and outright madness as did Kirstein himself in his conversations and personal communications. Kirstein's quirkly attitude toward himself flickers in the names of his autobiographical books. *Quarry* (1986), a book about his home and his possessions refers to the object of a pursuit and to a stone quarry, echoing the stone (*stein*) in his last name. Stone also plays a role in *Mosaic* (1994), the name he chose for his memoirs.

The painter Bernard Perlin, who knew Kirstein for more than fifty years, has defined him as an *écouteur.* Kirstein loved hearing stories about others, particularly if they were sexual and/or unflattering. Perlin has said, "He just ate it up when there was a story about someone. His eyes would gleam and he would come close to hear better. And he was *so* malicious. He described Cadmus's triple portrait of Platt Lynes, Wheeler, and Wescott to me with extreme malice. Malice wasn't his middle name—it was his first name."

A friend once said that Kirstein could be "diabolical," and he was known for his frank criticism of friends and business associates, yet he seemed to feel he was himself beyond criticism. And perhaps he was. He could be friendly one day and cut a person dead the next. More than social gaffes, these mood swings were the signs of serious illness. Kirstein had a long history of emotional instability. Since his college days he had been prone to overwork, to exhaust himself in projects and then suffer from what was called a nervous breakdown. In the 1950s Kirstein underwent electroshock therapy, but he continued to involve himself in innumerable creative projects and always found time to urge artists forward in their endeavors, helping them in any way he could.

Christopher Isherwood observed one of Kirstein's angry, depressive episodes when he dined with Lincoln and Fidelma and her brother in 1956. "Lincoln got up in the middle of supper and walked out," Isherwood noted in his diary. "Fido didn't seem much surprised. She discussed with Paul Cadmus the question of Lincoln's sleeplessness and overtiredness. 'Or was it just that I got on his nerves by talking too much?' she asked, very objectively: 'No—I don't think so.' Fido does ramble on, in an inconsequential way that sometimes seems silly. She has a sort of compulsion to cross the t's and dot the i's. But on the whole I think she's much saner. Probably Lincoln's breakdowns have compelled her to be."

At times, friends meeting Kirstein in the lobby of a theater or at an art gallery opening would be ignored. The actor Sandy Campbell once thought that perhaps he hadn't been noticed at an art opening. He approached Kirstein, saying, "Lincoln, it's Sandy." Kirstein replied coldly, "I know who you are," spun on his heel, and walked away. Taken aback, Campbell then encountered the painter Bernard Perlin and asked, "Have you spoken to Lincoln?" Perlin replied, "Fortunately not."

Allegra Kent experienced one of Kirstein's volatile outbursts in 1977. She had been one of the New York City Ballet's star ballerinas and was then nearing the end of her dancing career. Kirstein "had liked me at one time and this feeling was mutual," she remembers in *Once a Dancer.* "But now I was no longer a valuable company member. One day, on the street, he suddenly yelled at me, 'Not a fucking penny more!' He was talking about my salary. I was surprised, for just moments before he had greeted me with warmth and interest. . . . Kirstein had reached out to embrace me, and in that movement suddenly his face distorted, and, caught in a charge of emotion, he hurled that phrase at me." It was a painful and unnerving experience for the dancer, especially since she didn't know that Kirstein was about to enter a hospital for treatment of his mental illness.

The artist Dan Maloney, Kirstein's protégé, lived in his home and received much of Kirstein's time and attention. One day Maloney returned home to find himself locked out and his possessions deposited on the sidewalk. There has never been an explanation for this, other than Kirstein's increasingly erratic behavior.

Kirstein didn't hide his interest in men, and yet his marriage to Fidelma Cadmus was deeply affectionate and no one doubted Lincoln's concern for her or Fidelma's concern for him. She pulled her husband through many bouts of depression, and he in turn supported her during her own emotional difficulties.

"When Kirstein was forty-two," Nicholas Jenkins notes, "he wrote to [ballet critic Richard] Buckle shortly before the two balletomanes met, 'God has at a crucial point in my life sent me an angel, whom I married ten years ago and with whom I have always been much too happy for my deserts; you can ask Fred [Ashton] about my wife; she is far nicer than me.' "

Indeed, Lincoln Kirstein was never an easy man to live with, however much affection he had for Fidelma. True, he was always ready to discuss his unconventional sex life and his mental instability, but the situation remained and caused tension in their marriage. Yet when Fidelma Cadmus Kirstein died in 1991, Lincoln Kirstein became, if not reclusive, more withdrawn from his usual round of work and socializing. He had lost interest in making creative wheels turn in New York City.

In his last years his secretary, Alex Scherman, would call for him and they would take a daily walk. But for much of the time Kirstein would lie on his bed reading, attended by a faithful tiger cat. There were often footsteps in the halls and on the staircases, those of clients and friends

Lincoln Kirstein by Jerry Thompson, circa 1995. (Courtesy of Jerry Thompson. Reprinted by permission)

visiting Jensen Yow's studio on the top floor, but Kirstein would not acknowledge them. One could never be sure if he was aware of someone else's presence or not. When asked about Kirstein's lack of sociability in his later years, a man who knew him well said that it began with his loss of influence at the New York City Ballet.

In these later years, Kirstein went occasionally to his country home where his brother-in-law, Paul Cadmus, living nearby, would cook for him. Then these visits ceased. When Cadmus urged him to come to the country, Kirstein asked, "But how will I get there?" His brother-in-law said, "We'll send a car for you." Kirstein replied, "But how will I get back?" He did not go.

He would occasionally descend the steps and pass through the halls of his home, like some great haunted wreck of the formidable presence he once was. He was Lear-like in appearance in his later years, and having been rejected and diminished by the ballet company he had founded and done so much to develop must have made him feel that he had truly been sent onto the blasted heath.

The depressions that swept over him from time to time increased in severity and duration as he grew older and finally took a permanent hold. His habit of not recognizing old friends, sweeping them away into some sort of emotional exile, became his way of being. He no longer acknowledged those around him. His home became layered in dust that no one seemed to want to disturb. There was something tomblike about the house, like a burying place to accompany him to the hereafter. The line between life and death grew blurrier all the time, until he died at the age of eighty-eight on January 5, 1996.

Was he satisfied with his life? His brother-in-law has said that he believed Lincoln Kirstein felt he had lived a full life and did not feel unloved. In Cadmus's view, Kirstein loved power and felt that he had succeeded in gaining it.

A memorial service was held for him, although he hated memorial services. His ballet company danced and his loyal brother-in-law spoke. Kirstein had been an important figure in promoting the arts of America, the greatest in the twentieth century. His interest in sex, sensuality, and romance only adds richness to his accomplishments in the world of art and makes real the larger-than-life figure of Lincoln Kirstein.

Postscript

Donald Windham's novel *Tanaquil*, published in 1977, was a *roman à clef* featuring many of the people Windham had known in New York. A white-haired photographer named Joseph Page is clearly George Platt Lynes. Many of the other characters resemble, to some degree, the people who shared his world. The time is World War II. The central characters are Frankie and Tanaquil, who seem to be a kind of Orpheus and Eurydice, wandering through a New York purgatory. Frankie is quite casually bisexual, sleeping with the photographer Page the day after his wedding to Tanaquil, at which Page has been his best man. By the book's end, Tanaquil and Frankie have managed to achieve some balance in their lives and have escaped the fate of most of the other characters: the fate of being lost to the cult of beauty.

Perhaps the people in *this* book were lost to the cult of beauty, too, but they are not characters in a novel. They were, and are, real people, and each of the three devoted himself to love and beauty in his own unique way.

George Platt Lynes incarnated beauty in his own person, and his life was spent at the center of a group attracted to his beauty. As it faded, he was unable to adjust to the loss of this power and his life spun out of control.

Paul Cadmus was devoted to beauty, but his dedication manifested it-self in creating art. This art covered a wider range of subjects than beauty alone. Perhaps Cadmus suffered because of this dedication, but the act of creation supported and preserved him.

Lincoln Kirstein sought power over beauty. In his long life, he con-tributed more to the advancement of the arts in this country in this cen-tury than any other person. But seeking power led him to a casual disrespect for other people and even to the edge of madness and beyond.

Most people hate history because it has no recognizable relation to their own lives, because historians shy away from the emotional and in-explicable aspects of human lives. In addition to providing the details of time and place, I have tried to make this a real story of real lives, with all the emotions, sensations, and sexuality of real people. Because surely that was how it was. These were sensual people pushing their lives to new limits in a repressive, heterosexual society.

The work of Cadmus, Platt Lynes, and Kirstein is all the more re-markable when we remember that it was accomplished in the face of the homophobia of American society and its cultural elite. Coming of age during the 1920s, the three men experienced that decade's zest for fresh ideas and freedom from stale conventions. In this breezy spirit they set their goals and forged their careers and found beautiful men to love. Working in the arts let them adopt an "everybody knows and nobody cares" attitude, which was true for them, but untrue for many others. The liberation that has been set under way, in some part because of their example, now allows many to live with the freedom they enjoyed.

There are those of us who cherish history . . . cherish it for its "de-lightful undermining of certainty." What was so certain in the days when George Platt Lynes, Paul Cadmus, and Lincoln Kirstein began their lives and careers has now become uncertain, and many new certainties have arisen. Their openly led lives resulted in so much that is free and brave today, and this new century will be much better for the lives they lived. We owe them much.

Sources

In researching *Intimate Companions*, I interviewed numerous individuals whose memories and insights were extremely helpful in reconstructing the lives and times of the principal figures. I thank the following for their time and energy:

Don Bachardy, James Hunt Barker, Richard Beard, the late Otis Bigelow, Robert F. Bishop, Robert W. Bishop, Bill Blizzard, Robert Chapman, the late Mrs. Lew Christensen (Gisella Caccialanza), Laurie Douglas, Mel Fillini, Jack Fontan, Charles Henri Ford, the late Mrs. Jared French, Gene Gaddis, Terry Gallowhur, Gary Garrett, Mrs. Dwight Godwin (Marie Jeanne), Gordon Hanson, Peter Hanson, Francis Burton Harrison Jr., John Hohnsbeen, Charles "Chuck" Howard, Gilbert Ireland, Randy Jack, Brooks Jackson, David Langfitt, Michael Leonard, Davie Lerner, the late José Martinez, Robert "Buddy" McCarthy, Carlos McLendon, the late William Christian Miller, Elaine Brown Mischke, the late Francisco Moncion, James Ogle, Wilbur Pippin, Ralph Pomeroy, James Radich, Jerry Rosco, Thomas Royal, Joe Santoro, Thomas Schoff, Richard Sisson, Charles "Tex" Smutny, Harold Stevenson, Dick Sweet, the late Russell Thompson, Ed Torgeson, Ray Unger, Umberto Visbal, William Weslow, John Wisner, Jack Woody, and Anthony Ynocencio.

For the final quotation about history's "delightful undermining of certainty," I wish to thank the noted English historian Dame Veronica (C. V.) Wedgwood.

I also drew upon the following publications:

Bérubé, Allan, *Coming Out Under Fire*. New York: The Free Press, 1990.
Buckle, Richard, and John Taras. *George Balanchine: Ballet Master*. New York: Random House, 1988.

Cadmus, Paul. "Art: Paul Cadmus," interview by Donnell Stoneman (1976). *Long Road to Freedom*. Edited by Mark Thompson. New York: St. Martin's Press, 1999, p. 142.

Collaboration: The Photographs of Paul Cadmus, Margaret French, and Jared French. Santa Fe, N.M.: Twelvetrees Press, 1992.

Easton, Carol. *No Intermissions: The Life of Agnes de Mille*. Boston: Little, Brown, 1996.

Gaithorne-Hardy, Jonathan. *Sex and the Measure of All Things*. London: Pimlico, 1998.

George Platt Lynes: Photographs from the Kinsey Institute. Edited by James Crump. Introduction by Bruce Weber. Boston: Bulfinch Press, 1993.

George Platt Lynes: Photographs 1931–1955. Introduction by Jack Woody. Pasadena, Calif.: Twelvetrees Press, 1980.

George Platt Lynes: Portraits 1927–1955. Edited by Jack Woody. Santa Fe, N.M.: Twin Palms, 1994.

Givner, Joan. *Katherine Anne Porter: A Life*. New York: Simon & Schuster, 1982.

Grimes, Nancy. *Jared French's Myths*. San Francisco: Pomegranate Artbooks, 1993.

Isherwood, Christopher. *Diaries: Volume One, 1939–1960*. Edited and introduced by Katherine Bucknell. New York: HarperCollins, 1996.

Jenkins, Nicholas. "Reflections: The Great Impresario," *The New Yorker*, Vol. LXXIV, No. 8 (13 April 1998), pp. 48-61.

Jones, James H. *Alfred C. Kinsey: A Public/Private Life*. New York: W. W. Norton, 1997.

Kent, Allegra. *Once a Dancer . . .* New York: St. Martin's Press, 1997.

Kesten, Joanne, and Maggie Fogel. *The Portraits Speak: Chuck Close in Conversation with Twenty-seven of His Subjects*. New York: A.R.T. Press, 1998.

Kirstein, Lincoln. "The American Ballet in Brazil, Argentina, Chile, and the West Coast," reprinted in *Ballet: Bias and Belief: Three Pamphlets Collected and Other Dance Writings of Lincoln Kirstein*, pp. 77–95. With an Introduction and Comments by Nancy Reynolds. New York: Dance Horizons, 1983.

———. *By With To & From: A Lincoln Kirstein Reader*. Edited by Nicholas Jenkins. New York: Farrar, Straus & Giroux, 1991.

———. *Flesh Is Heir: An Historical Romance*. New York: Brewer, Warren, & Putnam, 1932.

———. *Mosaic: Memoirs*. New York: Farrar, Straus, & Giroux, 1994.

———. *Paul Cadmus*. San Francisco: Pomegranate Artbooks, 1992.

———. *Pavel Feodorovitch Tchelitchev, 1898–1957*. Santa Fe, N.M.: Twelvetrees Press, 1994.

———. *Quarry: A Collection in Lieu of Memoirs*. Pasadena, Calif.: Twelvetrees Press, 1986.

———. *Rhymes of a PFC*. New York: New Directions, 1964.

———. *Rhymes and More Rhymes of a PFC*. Revised and enlarged edition. New York: New Directions, 1966.

———. *Thirty Years: The New York City Ballet*. New York: Alfred A. Knopf, 1978.

Leddick, David. *Naked Men: Pioneering Male Nudes, 1935–1955*. New York: Universe Publishing, 1997.

Letters of Katherine Anne Porter. Selected and edited and with an introduction by Isabel Bayley. New York: Atlantic Monthly Press, 1990.

Livingston, Lili Cockerille. *American Indian Ballerinas*. Norman: University of Oklahoma Press, 1997.

Lynes, Russell. The daring eye of George Platt Lynes (unpublished manuscript in the possession of George Platt Lynes II).

Paul Cadmus: Enfant Terrible at Eighty. Produced and directed by David Sutherland. 60 minutes. Videocassette.

Pohorilenko, Anatole. *When We Were Three: The Travel Albums of George Platt Lynes, Monroe Wheeler, and Glenway Wescott, 1925–1935.* Santa Fe, N.M.: Arena Editions, 1998.

Pomeroy, Wardell B. *Dr. Kinsey and the Institute for Sex Research.* New York: Harper & Row, 1972.

Rathbone, Belinda. *Walker Evans: A Biography.* Boston: Houghton Mifflin, 1995.

Reynolds, Nancy. *Repertory in Review: Forty Years of the New York City Ballet.* New York: Dial Press, 1977.

Rorem, Ned. *Knowing When to Stop: A Memoir.* New York: Simon & Schuster, 1994.

Simmonds, Harvey, Louis H. Silverstein, and Nancy Lassalle. *Lincoln Kirstein: The Published Writings, 1922–1977, A First Bibliography.* New Haven: Yale University Press, 1978.

Stout, Janice P. *Katherine Anne Porter: A Sense of the Times.* Charlottesville: University of Virginia, 1995.

Stravinsky, Igor, and Robert Craft. *Dialogues and a Diary.* Garden City, N.Y.: Doubleday, 1963.

———. *Themes and Episodes.* New York: Knopf, 1966.

Taper, Bernard. *Balanchine: A Biography.* New York: Times Books, 1984.

Tommasini, Anthony. *Virgil Thomson: Composer on the Aisle.* New York: W.W. Norton, 1997.

Tyler, Parker. *The Divine Comedy of Pavel Tchelitchew.* New York: Fleet Publishing, 1967.

Watson, Steven. *Prepare for Saints.* New York: Random House, 1998.

———. *"Four Saints in Three Acts* Is Born," interview by Roland Suleski. *The Harvard Gay & Lesbian Review,* Vol. VI, No. 2 (Spring 1999), pp. 39–41.

Weber, Nicholas Fox. *Patron Saints: Five Rebels Who Opened America to a New Art, 1928–1943.* New York: Knopf, 1992.

Weiermair, Peter. *George Platt Lynes.* Berlin: Bruno Gmünder Verlag, 1995.

Weinberg, Jonathan. *Speaking for Vice.* New Haven: Yale University Press, 1993.

Wescott, Glenway. *Continual Lessons: The Journals, 1937–1955.* Edited by Robert Phelps and Jerry Rosco. New York: Farrar, Straus & Giroux, 1990.

Wilson, Edmund. "Katherine Anne Porter," pp. 219–223, and "Glenway Wescott's War Work," pp. 275–279, reprinted in *Classics and Commercials: A Literary Chronicle of the Forties.* New York: Farrar, Straus and Company, 1950.

———. *The Fifties: From Notebooks and Diaries of the Period.* Edited by Leon Edel. New York: Farrar, Straus and Giroux, 1986.

———. *The Sixties: The Last Journal, 1960–1972.* Edited with an Introduction by Lewis M. Dabney. New York: Farrar Straus Giroux, 1993.

Windham, Donald. *Tanaquil.* New York: Holt, Rinehart & Winston, 1977.

Index

Page references to illustrations are in boldface.